Nineteenth-Century Fictions of Childhood and the Politics of Play

Drawing evidence from transatlantic literary texts of childhood as well as from nineteenth and early twentieth century children's and family card, board, and parlor games and games manuals, *Nineteenth-Century Fictions of Childhood and the Politics of Play* aims to reveal what might be thought of as "playful literary citizenship," or some of the motivations inherent in later nineteenth and early twentieth century Anglo-American play pursuits as they relate to interest in shaping citizens through investment in "good" literature. Tracing the societal and historical construct of play as it surfaces time and again in children's literary texts and exploring children's literary texts as they surface time and again in situations and environments of children's play, this book underscores how play and literature are consistently deployed in tandem in attempts to create ideal citizens—even as those ideals varied greatly and were dependent on factors such as gender, ethnicity, colonial status, and class.

Michelle Beissel Heath is an Associate Professor of English at the University of Nebraska, Kearney, USA, where she specializes in children's literature and in nineteenth-century British literature. She has published articles on children's citizenship, play, gender, and literary texts of the long nineteenth century.

T0347209

Studies in Childhood, 1700 to the Present

For a full list of titles in this series, please visit www.routledge.com.

This series recognizes and supports innovative work on the child and on literature for children and adolescents that informs teaching and engages with current and emerging debates in the field. Proposals are welcome for interdisciplinary and comparative studies by humanities scholars working in a variety of fields, including literature; book history, periodicals history, and print culture and the sociology of texts; theater, film, musicology, and performance studies; history, including the history of education; gender studies; art history and visual culture; cultural studies; and religion.

Recent titles in this series:

Space and Place in Children's Literature, 1789 to the Present
Maria Sachiko Cecire, Hannah Field, Malini Roy

Ethics and Children's Literature
Claudia Mills

The Child Savage, 1890–2010
From Comics to Games
Edited by Elisabeth Wesseling

British Hymn Books for Children, 1800–1900
Alisa Clapp-Itnyre

Nordic Childhoods 1700–1960
From Folk Beliefs to Pippi Longstocking
Edited by Reidar Aasgaard, Marcia Bunge, and Merethe Roos

Nineteenth-Century Fictions of Childhood and the Politics of Play
Michelle Beissel Heath

Nineteenth-Century Fictions of Childhood and the Politics of Play

Michelle Beissel Heath

LONDON AND NEW YORK

First published 2018 by Routledge

2 Park Square, Milton Park, Abingdon, Oxfordshire OX14 4RN
52 Vanderbilt Avenue, New York, NY 10017

Routledge is an imprint of the Taylor & Francis Group, an informa business

First issued in paperback 2019

British Library Cataloguing-in-Publication Data
A catalogue record for this book is available from the British
Library

Library of Congress Cataloging-in-Publication Data
CIP data has been applied for.

ISBN: 978-1-4724-8733-9 (hbk)
ISBN: 978-0-367-88507-6 (pbk)

Typeset in Sabon
by codeMantra

To Scott, Sonnet, and River, who keep me playful

Contents

List of figures

Acknowledgments

My heart holds deep gratitude for all of those—and there are many—who have helped to make this book possible. I could not have written this without the tremendous support of my family, particularly those who have lived with its writing on nearly as daily a basis as I have. I am thankful, too, for the early guidance and continued encouragement of the indomitable Judith Plotz. The support of my university, college, department, and colleagues—particularly Susan Honeyman, Megan Hartman, and Marguerite Tassi, who have been willing not only to offer cups of tea but periodically to poke at sections of drafts—has also been invaluable. I am thankful for a faculty development fellowship (sabbatical) and departmental faculty development support (including the aid of student extraordinaire, Ashley Shaffer), as well as several university Research Services Council grants, which have provided me with writing time as well as opportunities for archival research. I was honored and thankful to receive—and immensely assisted by—a Children's Literature Association (ChLA) Faculty Research Grant, an Everett Helm Visiting Fellowship from the Lilly Library at Indiana University, a Mary Valentine and Andrew Cosman Research Fellowship from The Strong National Museum of Play, and a Cosmos Club Foundation Grant. Without these grants and fellowships, the archival work represented in these pages would not have been possible. The Lilly Library and The Strong have also been gracious in allowing me permissions to publish photographs of nineteenth century games and related play images. My thanks to the staff of the V&A Museum of Childhood, the Lilly Library, and The Strong National Museum of Play for their help in locating late nineteenth and early twentieth century board and card games, as well as to the staff at the British Library, the Bodleian Library, and the Library of Congress. Any acknowledgments I make would be amiss without offering gratitude to Claudia Nelson, who along with Ann Donahue (formerly of Ashgate), pursued this project with enthusiasm and offered much-needed advice as it was taking shape. I am grateful as well for the helpful insights of my anonymous reader. Thanks, too, to the editors and assistant editors at Routledge (Taylor and Francis), for all of their help in seeing this project come to print. The bulk of what appears here is previously unpublished and new to this book, though I do at times make reference to work on play and on the late nineteenth century playground movement I have published earlier, particularly in *The Journal of the History of Childhood and Youth* (volume 7, number 1, Winter 2014). The exceptions to this are a brief analysis of the Uptons' Golliwogg texts I mention in chapter three, which I consider to a greater extent, and alongside the work of Allan Ahlberg and Enid Blyton's Noddy books, in *Jeunesse: Young People, Texts, Cultures* (volume 5, number 1, Summer 2013) and the section on croquet I offer in chapter two, which appears in an earlier incarnation as "Not 'All Ridges and Furrows' and 'Uncroquetable Lawns': Croquet, Female Citizenship, and 1860s Domestic Chronicles" in *Critical Survey* (volume 24, number 1, 2012, pp. 43–56).

Introduction
Playful literary citizenship

Literature and citizenship, when intersected by notions of childhood, produce revealing similarities. Both, in incarnations designated as "good" ("good" literature/"good" citizenship), are often viewed, as we will see, as essential to childhood with the promises it suggests and yet as beyond a child's grasp. Both, too, are often inflected by adults with didactic intent not infrequently mitigated by senses of play. They are seen as necessary to remedy deficiency inherent in the state of being a child, but only in altered, abridged, or simplified forms—and in forms that are cast as instances of play (and thereby child-worthy). Consider, for example, the justification offered for Jack and Holman Wang's recent and newly re-issued (2016–2017) "Cozy Classics" series of board book primers for "children aged 0+":

> The concept for Cozy Classics is simple: every classic in the series will be condensed to 12 child-friendly words, and each word will appear alongside a needle-felted illustration. Each word is carefully selected to relate to a child's world. . . . The books work as word primers, even without any reference to the original stories. If you, as a parent, can fill in some of the original tale as part of the reading experience, so much the better!
>
> (www.mycozyclassics.com/about/)

Offering the argument that "the series will invigorate the genre of the infant primer whose usual concept categories . . . have become overly familiar," the justification for the series places responsibility for "creat[ing] a fun 'literary-rich environment' that will pave the way for success with reading" onto parents and their abilities to convey "just that little extra bit of enthusiasm because they are sharing a story or characters they love themselves" and to "model an engaged and affectionate relationship with books" (www.mycozyclassics.com/about/). In other words, adults need to fill in children's educational deficits with "good," literary classics but those classics need to be reduced to twelve-word versions to make them more "friendly" for children in acknowledgment of children's apparently limited or deficient capabilities. Following its sense of the need to convey the texts enthusiastically and as an "affectionate relationship," the justification also points out that "in the minds of many, classics are associated with academics, but no classic was written for the classroom; every one was written to give pleasure" (www.mycozyclassics.com/about/). The goal of the series, supposedly, is "to get away from the classroom and have kids grow up thinking of The Great Books as great fun" (www.mycozyclassics.com/about/). In such a view, "Great Books" become a form of pleasure or even play. Coalescing in the rationale for Cozy Classics, then, are ideas of childhood as a period of pleasure and fun (play) as well as of lack—limited and deficient.

The rationale given for Jennifer Adams' and illustrator Alison Oliver's BabyLit series, which appeared in 2011 around the same time as the Cozy Classics, is more succinct but just as telling. It advocates "BabyLit" as "a fashionable way to introduce your toddler to the world of classic literature," elaborating,

> At BabyLit, we believe in the power of reading. Why? Because books take us places. Good places. And when we read with a child, we go places together. It's more than just reading. It's learning. It's experiencing. It's growing. If a million copies of our books encourage just one parent to read with their child, we will have succeeded. And printed a lot of books.
>
> So while the world wonders why babies need classic literature, we will be reading.
>
> Won't you join us?
>
> (babylit.com/pages/about-us)

Pointedly not answering the question of "why babies need classic literature" in favor of its focus on adults (if "our books encourage just one parent"), the BabyLit series is even more explicit in its adult didactic perspectives and insistence on play paired with "good," classic literature. While Cozy Classics tries to sell reading "the Great Books as great fun," the BabyLit texts transform literature quite literally into play. Presenting playful titles for their origin authors ("Little Miss Austen," "Little Master Dickens") as well as playful text and illustrations,[1] the publishers take the additional step of rendering the books into actual articles of play. Offered alongside, and drawn directly from, the board books are dolls, puzzles, apps, a memory game, and even play-sets for enacting dramatic, imaginative play with paperboard punch-out card figures and stages fashioned from the sets' boxes. BabyLit's didactic intent is even more pronounced as well: while the Cozy Classics series attempts a semblance of narrative, the classic literary texts which provide the foundation for the BabyLit series are reduced to thematic, didactic, and even traditional primer concepts. Of the twenty-six Baby-Lit books published as of spring 2017, four turn classics into counting primers, three into colors primers, two into language primers, and two into sounds primers, with the others taking as their themes a variety of concepts at times loosely related to their origin texts: flowers (2015, *The Secret Garden*), friendship (2017, *A Little Princess*), animals (2014, *The Jungle Book*), camping (2014, *The Adventures of Huckleberry Finn*), shapes (2015, *Treasure Island*), nonsense (2013, *Jabberwocky*), opposites (2013, *Sense and Sensibility*), emotions (2015, *Emma*), weather (2013, *Wuthering Heights*), ocean (2013, *Moby-Dick*), anatomy (2014, *Frankenstein*), fashion (2013, *Anna Karenina*), monsters (2016, *The Odyssey*), fairies (2016, *A Midsummer Night's Dream*), and playtime (2016, *Little Women*). Though they sometimes markedly stray from their origin texts—as with the illustrations for *A Little Princess: A Friendship Primer*, which features a black Becky reminiscent more of the 1995 film directed by Alfonso Cuarón than the likely white, class-bound Becky of Frances Hodgson Burnett's original conceptions—the BabyLit texts do attempt to stay somewhat true to their "inspiration" texts, a fact apparent in the frequent use of quotations from origin text generally dispersed throughout each book and other minor or now obscure details from origin texts that make their way into the BabyLit versions (such as the frog servant from Lewis Carroll's *Alice's Adventures in Wonderland* or the portrayal of silver—not ruby—shoes in L. Frank Baum's *The Wonderful Wizard of Oz*).

As the examples of these board book series indicate, even when their purposes or connections may seem tenuous or contrived ("why babies need classic literature"), adults today do wish to surround children with "good" literature under the impression that it offers inherent didactic benefit. To make such literature appear in line with expectations of childhood, it is reduced or condensed (to be more "friendly" or "appropriate" for children, who in such a view are inherently deficient, unable to grasp such literature in its full, true form) and aligned with play—made "fun" or literally into playthings. This tendency to invest children with literature and play for a larger didactic, moral, and even "civilizing" purpose, however, has a long history, a history that is perhaps most marked in the long nineteenth century—from which the majority of the Cozy Classics and BabyLit board books notably also draw their literary inspirations—when material and social conditions joined together to enable women and girls, particularly of the middle classes, to enter in games and sports even more.[2] Material and social conditions by the end of the nineteenth century also allowed for the mass production of relatively inexpensive card and board games for the middle classes and encouraged play (including playground and play center) movements across the Atlantic to address perceived needs of the working and immigrant classes as well as the middle classes. These movements in turn harnessed ideas of imperialism and aestheticism to foster boy scouts' play and to envision idealized worlds made possible by the beauty of playful children. Embedded in these bouts of play and potential were ideals and representations of what was deemed "good" literature and notions of what appropriately playful and literate children should strive for and could be: great citizens.

The aim of this book is to reveal what might be thought of as this "playful literary citizenship," or some of the motivations inherent in later nineteenth and early twentieth century Anglo-American play pursuits as they relate to interest in shaping citizens through investment in "good" literature. Play, as a societal and historical construct, surfaces time and again in children's literary texts while children's literary texts similarly surface time and again in situations and environments of children's play. In both contexts, this book argues, play and literature are consistently deployed in tandem in attempts to create ideal citizens—though what those ideals were varied greatly and were dependent on factors such as gender, ethnicity, colonial status, and class.

In addition to being remarkably reliant on nineteenth century texts for their inspirations, the Cozy Classics and BabyLit board books also offer a notable blend of classic literature written ostensibly for adult audiences as well as classic literature written primarily for child or youth audiences. With few exceptions, too, the classics they focus on are primarily drawn from British and U.S. literature. This originally mixed audience, transatlantic focus—for texts and ideas aimed at North American if not Anglo-American audiences—is also neither new nor surprising. Texts are more fluid in readership than is sometimes imagined: adults not only read children's texts to their progeny, they sometimes today indulge in reading what has become known as "young adult" literature while children, past and present, make forays into reading what today is generally considered literature for adults. Reflecting in part the global, colonial era in which they found themselves, nineteenth century writers for children in Britain and the U.S. were strikingly transatlantic in their identities and affiliations. Frances Hodgson Burnett read and was influenced by Harriet Beecher Stowe's *Uncle Tom's Cabin* (1852) as a child, moved to the U.S. in her teens, and spent much of her adult life crossing back and forth over the Atlantic Ocean. Her texts—which are filled with hybrid children including, most famously, Mary Lennox, Sara Crewe, and Cedric Errol—also reflect that transatlanticism, as does their "nationality" status, with *The Secret Garden* (1911) and *A Little Princess* (1905) often perceived as British and *Little Lord Fauntleroy* (1886) as American in criticism. Both Robert Louis Stevenson and Rudyard Kipling married Americans and lived for a brief period in the U.S. (as well as in other countries). Kipling, who features an American boy in *Captain Courageous* (1897), wrote *The Jungle Books* (1894) in Vermont and, like Burnett, was fond of hybrid child characters (Mowgli and Kim are prominent examples). Even writers who tended to remain put could not avoid transatlantic ideas and influences. Charlotte Yonge portrays Indiana (though unflatteringly) in *The Trial* (1864) and found her work admired by Louisa May Alcott, with Yonge's *The Heir of Redclyffe* (1853) even featured in Alcott's *Little Women* (1868). Both Lewis Carroll and Edith Nesbit offered, as I observe in chapter one, disparaging analyses of the U.S. and its inhabitants' tastes as gaudy and shoddy, but their very references to such tastes indicate the U.S.' impossible-to-avoid presence and influence and the transatlantic realities of the period's literary, publishing, and other worlds.

Not only did prominent writers of the day make transatlantic tours (Charles Dickens and Oscar Wilde, for example) or become notable expatriates (like Henry James) so of course did ideas, including ideas of leisure, play, and literature, make fashionable tours, spark transatlantic trends, and find new homes. Alcott features both British visitors and croquet on U.S. soil in *Little Women*; the boy scouts, founded in Britain by Sir Robert Baden-Powell, became a global phenomenon with a notable branch in the Boy Scouts of America; and many late nineteenth century family card and board games in the U.S. take as their topics British writers and literary texts. In similar transatlantic fashion, Anne Abbot's U.S. game of *Dr. Busby* may well have inspired the popular British game of *Happy Families* and the U.S. playground movement helped to inspire British writer Mary Ward's play center movement, while Ward served as an honorary member of the Playground Association of America. In recognition of this literary, cultural, and thought environment, this book consistently takes a transatlantic approach in its considerations, analyzing texts, movements, and archival materials from both sides of the Atlantic. U.S. archival collections of late nineteenth and early twentieth century board and card games are particularly rich—however, those collections also emphatically betray a British literary, cultural, and historical influence and legacy.

This book takes as a primary focus notions of play, though in doing so I recognize that such an approach is a bit perilous: play is a fascinatingly fraught term and has been for generations. Both the late nineteenth century child saving movement in the U.S. and play center movement in Britain were concerned with preserving or "restoring" children's play, often by transforming children's play environments (removing children from the city to the country or from the streets to "safer" sites with the idea that play either could not or could not safely occur in urban environments or on streets, ideas still prevalent today in some views of children as out of touch with nature). This has resulted in what John R. Gillis calls the "islanding of children," with children "systematically excluded from the former mainlands of urban and suburban existence" (316). Yet concerns over children's play are at times justified, with debates raging today centering on fears of over-scheduled children and the jeopardizing of children's recess times at school. Implicit if not explicit in these concerns, as the rationales for the literary classics board books themselves suggest, is the fact that play is consistently considered an essential component of childhood and widely understood as necessary for child development—so much so that article 31 of the U.N. Convention on the Rights of the Child (1989) specifically recognizes "that every child has the right to rest and leisure, to engage in play and recreational activities appropriate to the age of the child." The entire world—194 countries—has ratified the Convention treaty or, really, all countries but two: Somalia and, notably, the U.S.

Still, though play is effectively universally recognized as an if not the epitome of childhood, what play *is* is far from certain. Concerns over children's play today also surface in dilemmas over whether or not video games or electronic toys "count" as play, and the breadth of what may be considered play is evident even in the classic literature board books, with the BabyLit take on *Little Women* (rendered "a Playtime Primer") emphasizing extensive variety. The "playtime" activities listed—perhaps in line at times more with nineteenth century views of leisure than those of today—include singing, gardening, sewing, picnicking, writing, dancing, playing (music), skating, drawing, and reading. The card and parlor games the March friends and family indulge in in Alcott's book are not called out in specific, nor is an activity such as rowing or boating, but a croquet mallet and ball do make an appearance in the "picnicking" illustrations. As the board book's lengthy but already non-exhaustive listing suggests, with the broadness of the possibilities it encompasses, play is frequently categorized, with, for example, prominent play advocate Penny Wilson calling attention to Bob Hughes's "taxonomy of play" with sixteen play types (23–24) and Brian Sutton-Smith, in his landmark *The Ambiguity of Play* (1997), including elaborate lists of activities while outlining seven contemporary (and conflicting) rhetorics of play. At the same time, however, Wilson, like many, attempts to define play, putting forth as a professional definition for British playworkers today, "play is a set of behaviors that are freely chosen, personally directed, and intrinsically motivated" (5). Yet, as Sutton-Smith reminds us, play is culturally and historically contingent, a fact which, in his words, leads to inevitable "ambiguity": "because forms of play, like all other cultural forms, cannot be neutrally interpreted, it is impossible to keep ambiguity from creeping into the relationship between how they are perceived and how they are experienced" (216). All of this—notions of ambiguity, the cultural and historical forces that invest meaning, interpretations, and contradictions in ideas of play, as well as the exhaustive scope of what we may include (or contest) as play at any given time, and play's consideration as an inherent right of childhood—bring us back to the early play philosopher Johan Huizinga's attempts to delineate play: in his view, play is "irreducible" and an "irreducible" part of children's nature (7). Play, it seems, is ultimately inscrutable.

Inscrutability or even impossibility of absolute definition, however, do not negate necessity of discussion. Joining Marah Gubar, who argues for returning to "talking about children in children's literature criticism" (450), and several others in providing manifestos for the field of children's literature, Robin Bernstein specifically calls for children's literary scholars to "embrace the historical integration of children's literature, material culture, and play" ("Toys are Good for Us" 458). This book strives to respond to that call even as it recognizes the important scholarship that has already been done or begun on such intersections. This scholarship includes Megan Norcia's notable work on imperial connections in nineteenth century parlor games and puzzles[3] and Bernstein's own work in *Racial Innocence* (2011) on play, performance, and "scriptive things"—"a scriptive thing, like a playscript, broadly structures a performance while allowing for agency and unleashing original, live variations that may not be individually predictable" (58). Bernstein insists that "agency emerges through constant engagement with the stuff of our lives" (58). The "stuff of our lives" includes, of course, the playthings[4] the middle classes in particular consumed as part of their senses of child's play in the nineteenth and early twentieth centuries, when, as Karen Sánchez-Eppler recognizes, "the merchandising of children's toys" made possible by middle-class values of leisure, "epitomized how leisure, not work, would drive the consumption patterns of mature industrial capitalism" (820). Agency, too, erupts in play, an idea also demonstrated in Sánchez-Eppler's discussion of nineteenth century U.S. "street-children," for whom, she concludes,

> play serves not as a measure of leisure but as a mechanism of resistance, a means of claiming autonomy and pleasure on their own, non-productive, terms—of thumbing their noses at the middle-class values that this same play nevertheless helps to install.
>
> (838)

Connected here are play, class, and material culture, but also gender, which Sánchez-Eppler finds to be a stopping-point: "And yet in recognizing this resistance we see well the difference that is gender: how for girls . . . there is no way to figure work as a game" (838). It is these concerns—play, material culture, gender, and class values (particularly as they relate to values of idealized citizenship)—that form the focus and nexus of this book and its long nineteenth century centering. Indeed, as Sánchez-Eppler points out, between 1830 and "by the time Macy's opened the [U.S.'] first toy department in 1875," there were "enormous and extremely swift shifts in cultural understanding of childhood, work, and play" (820). Such shifts were apparent on both sides of the Atlantic, with play entrenched in the very worldview of the Victorians. Extending

Sutton-Smith's ideas, Matthew Kaiser even goes so far as to argue that for the Victorians the world wasn't so much "at play" as "in play," which

> means a world that throws itself headlong into play, inside it, where it constructs a parallel universe, a ludic microcosm of itself, which eventually displaces that world. The membranes of play, its elastic fibers, stretch to the point where they encircle all of existence.
>
> (105–106)

Without doubt, play was pivotal to the Victorians and their approaches to it are revealing not only of the past but of the legacy we experience still.

Citizenship, as scholars such as David Buckingham, Verbjørg Tingstad, and Sarah Banet-Weiser have observed, is also intersected by material culture and attitudes of consumerism. Buckingham and Tingstad note that "the idea of the child as sovereign consumer often slips into the idea of the child as citizen, an autonomous social actor" (3), while Banet-Weiser, analyzing the cable network Nickelodeon, asserts that "commercial media play a pivotal role in creating cultural definitions about what it means to be a citizen—indeed, our sense of ourselves as national citizens emerges *from* (not in spite of) our engagement with popular media" (2). For nineteenth century children it is not a stretch, I think, to consider literary texts and perhaps even the then-new play environments and trends as "popular media." But citizenship emulates play in another notable way: as Ruth Lister phrases it, citizenship is "a contested concept" and as such "there is no one single definition of citizenship" (9). Most considerations of citizenship today begin with T.H. Marshall's "Citizenship and Social Class" (1949), which in Tom Cockburn's words, elucidates "three dimensions" of citizenship: "civil, political, and social rights," wherein

> civil rights are connected with issues such as freedom of speech … and access to the legal system; political rights apply to access to political institutions for the articulation of interests; social rights are the basis to claims for welfare.
>
> (8)

Lister observes that citizenship today encompasses as well ideas of community and "participation rights," acknowledging that today there is "more emphasis on identity and a sense of belonging and on the relationship between individual citizens" and that "rights more generally are today being theorized in terms of practice as well as status" wherein "fulfilling the duties and responsibilities of citizenship constitutes a practice" (10). Underscoring the challenges of defining citizenship, Cockburn suggests that citizenship "assumes a combination of rights, participation, belonging, fulfillment of obligations and responsibilities, and an availability of resources," while "children's citizenship is shaped by a whole concatenation of factors that are too many to list exhaustively" (10–11).

This "concatenation of factors," as with those that influence notions of play, reflect and are weighted by historical and cultural elements, including gender as well as "ideas of place, nation, race, and ethnicity" (12). Lorinda B. Cohoon's study of *Serialized Citizenships* (2006) centers on "nineteenth-century boyhood citizenships" for good reason: only boys could be viewed as potential citizens. Until the passage of universal adult suffrage, which did not happen until well into the twentieth century, women and girls (as well as many non-white men and many lower and working class men) in the U.S. and Britain could not actually be true, full citizens, as Courtney Weikle-Mills emphasizes in *Imaginary Citizens* (2013). Reminding us that children in the U.S. only accidentally—unintentionally—became citizens with the adoption of the fourteenth amendment in 1868, Weikle-Mills argues that throughout the nineteenth century children as well as "women, slaves, and sometimes even animals" "came to be understood as 'imaginary citizens': individuals who could not exercise civic rights but who figured heavily in literary depictions of citizenship and were often invited to view themselves as citizens despite their limited political franchise" (4). Her views align with Cockburn's sense that

> the history of modern citizenship is characterized by the expanding struggle and conflict for equal inclusion into society. All forms of citizenship in their historical realities are established out of conflicts, and, despite the lofty ideals of equality and fraternity, are deeply hierarchical and stratified.
>
> (7)

For children, the effects of the lack of "full" citizen status and participation are apparent yet today. As Cockburn phrases it,

> perhaps, 'children's citizenship' is a misnomer, as children are in some respects 'not citizens': they have not 'come of age' and consequently do not have many of the privileges (such as full voting rights) or the obligations (such as full financial responsibility) that adults hold.
>
> (1)

Or, as Elizabeth F. Cohen illuminates, "children in democratic politics inhabit an uncertain space between alienage and full citizenship" (221). They

> are simultaneously assumed to be citizens—they hold passports and except in the rarest of cases receive at least one nationality

at birth—and judged to be incapable of citizenship in that they cannot make the rational and informed decisions that characterize self-governance.

(221)

They are, as the literary classics board book series also imply, perceived as deficient, limited, and lacking or, in the most optimistic sense, "in-between." Yet, as Cockburn points out in making his case for "rethinking children's citizenship," noting that "the age at which citizenship is possible changes radically over time and place, and is rarely agreed upon by commentators," concepts of child citizenship "reflect the social construction of childhood" (1–2). As he asserts, "times change, and evaluation of competencies can change also," as they have with regards to women and others (3). In his historical reckoning, Cockburn points out, too, that "in the United Kingdom the concept of citizenship has changed from one of subjects to citizens in almost a seamless manner" (7). As we will see, slippages and distinctions between visions of U.S. citizenship and British subject-hood nevertheless manifest themselves in Baden-Powell's boy scouts' U.S. encounters.

Considerations of children's citizenship have gathered renewed attention since the U.N. Convention on the Rights of the Child but, as Weikle-Mills' and Cohoon's studies affirm, the nineteenth century was a crucial period for developments in attitudes towards children's citizenship and many of those developments, this book suggests, arose or were reinforced through considerations and conceptions of children's play and through literary portrayals. Indeed, as Allison James and Adrian L. James acknowledge, "the apparent benevolence of . . . nineteenth century reforms and the establishment of children's rights to welfare and educational provision can be shown to have worked, ironically, to disable and disenfranchise children as citizens," particularly as they "were designed to remove children from areas of adult and public life under the guise of protection" (36). The various play movements of the period—including the playground and play center movements as well as play movements like the boy scouts—were aspects of these, borrowing Gillis' term, "islanding" reforms. Ultimately, this book explores how nineteenth century portrayals of play, literature, and citizenship call forth ideas of children as, at best, "in-between," "citizens-in-training," ideas reflected as well in Sana Nakata's observations that children have "come to be positioned as future-adult subjects" (129) and in Cockburn's own assessment that "conceptions of children's citizenship are shaped, and largely limited, by the belief that it is *as children* that people are defined, trained, prepared, protected, and categorized for their *future* roles as citizens" (8). The ambiguous, contradictory nature of child citizenship is embedded as well in Lauren Berlant's telling analysis of what she labels "infantile citizenship" and "the paradoxes, limits, and dreams encoded in this ideal citizen form" (28).

In its considerations of child citizenship, this book hinges itself on these strains of contradiction, on child citizenship imagined almost exclusively as future citizenship, with children as "in-between," and, in idealized forms, perpetual "citizens-in-training." Such views, as Chapters 2 and 3 in particular show, are limited, time and again, by gender—with ideals of girl "citizenship" predicated on the reality that nineteenth century girls could never actually be "citizens" in ways that boys (or white, middle and upper-class boys) could. For both boys and girls, though, such "in-between" or "citizen-in-training" conceptualizations accentuate schisms and fractures in depictions of childhood. For girls, in fiction dedicated to them, such conceptualizations bring to the fore an impossible dual nature: never able to develop into full citizens, girls are already as "womanly" as they can be in their citizenship positions and yet, as girls, they are still envisioned as "in-between" or lacking, still in need of being taught to adhere to and internalize societal expectations of childhood coded as girlhood. Ironically, in other words, they are at times presented as already-women who must be taught to be children. For boys, such conceptualizations foster hybridity and de-humanization in texts depicting boyhood, including in boy scout portrayals. As "in-between" beings, boys in these imaginings are simultaneously superhuman and un-human, or de-humanized. They are deficient, lacking, and yet, as boys who are envisioned as one day able to become actual citizens, full of potential. This idea of potential, coupled with beauty and national and imperial connections, is also influenced at the end of the nineteenth century by aesthetic comprehensions of childhood and evident at times in the physical components of nineteenth century board and card games.

Throughout the book I employ a predominantly literary-historical, material culture approach, drawing in my arguments evidence from children's literary texts as well as from nineteenth and early twentieth century children's and family card, board, and parlor games. I also draw evidence from nineteenth and early twentieth century children's games manuals, boy scout materials, and croquet manuals as well as from articles from play, sport, and children's and literary periodicals, such as *The Playground*, *The Field*, and Yonge's *The Monthly Packet*. In Chapter 1 I examine artifacts from the nineteenth and early twentieth centuries, a period often designated a "golden age" of children's literature and of children's and family play in Britain and the U.S. Considering U.S. and British family and children's board, card, and parlor games in particular, I note how such games emphasize didacticism, morality, femininity, and the home to promote ideals of citizenship and enhance respectability and draw from literary foundations and sentiments of patriotic allegiance to reinforce these goals. More pointedly, I document how those literary groundings and patriotic ideals simultaneously acknowledge an imperial worldview and colonial inheritance and betray anxieties of a young nation (and occasionally an older one). These betrayals suggest some of the ways in which children were steeped in a sense of nationalistic, "good citizenship" allegiance through material culture and "playful" social practices. In Chapter 2 I trace the contradictory nature of girls in nineteenth century girls' fiction—not ever to be fully citizens, girls are portrayed both as in need of rearing to ensure their value as adult nurturing caretakers and as fully adult as they ever will be, with regards to citizenship expectations. To become more "appropriately" childlike, girls are depicted as in need of becoming more or differently "playful" or as in need of directing their "playfulness" to nurturing, caring responsibilities for the benefits of male, actual or able-to-be-citizen relatives. This channeling of playfulness is especially prominent in the discourse surrounding croquet and is featured in the texts of Yonge, Alcott, and Carroll, whose works point to the larger cultural unease incited by croquet (and girls' play) and seek to critique and rehabilitate the sport just as girls' fiction sought to rehabilitate girls, fictional and otherwise, for their allowable form of good "citizenship," "womanly duty."

In Chapter 3 I turn attention to boys and examine in particular the U.S. reproduction of Baden-Powell's *The Wolf Cub's Handbook* (1916 Britain; 1918 U.S.) alongside Kipling's *The Jungle Books* and *Kim* (1901). As with notions of girls' citizenship evident in attitudes towards croquet, boys' citizenship was described in terms of duty and obedience, with games harnessed to these ideas. Unlike croquet-playing girls, however, who were confined in literary and other imaginings to the domestic family circle, games-playing and sporting boys were given the world, or at least empire, as playing-field. Aligned with views of children as "citizens-in-training" still today, and consistently offering gender and citizenship (if not storytelling and play) as performance, Kipling's and Baden-Powell's representations of boys, I argue, are simultaneously de-humanized (made animal, object, machine, pawn) and full of human potential (for cross-cultural communication, good deeds), at the same time extraordinary and incomplete. In Chapter 4 I underscore ways senses of aestheticism and child citizenship surface in the works—literary, philanthropic, and political—of Burnett and Nesbit. For both authors, I argue, notions of child citizenship were intricately bound up in matters of class, beauty, and play even as their portrayals of games and play display tensions between the potential of children's citizenship for "beautiful" change and conservative notions of knowing and keeping to one's place (and class). In my conclusion, I consider the mid twentieth century adventure playground movement and its parallels to the work of Enid Blyton. In particular, I argue, Blyton and her *Famous Five* books can be seen as heirs to the nineteenth century ideas of playful and literary citizenship I trace throughout this book, ideas that, of course, influence children and expectations of childhood still today.

Notes

1 For example, depictions of the "5 Sisters" in *Pride and Prejudice: A Counting Primer* (2011) include Lydia and Kitty as mirror images and each holding a sign pointing to the other that says "I'm with Lydia" or "I'm with Kitty."

2 For analyses of the rise of girls' and women's sports/athletics in the period, see (for example) Sally Mitchell's *The New Girl: Girls' Culture in England, 1880–1915* and *The Girl's Own: Cultural Histories of the Anglo-American Girl, 1830–1915* (edited by Claudia Nelson and Lynne Vallone).

3 See, for example, Norcia's "Puzzling Empire: Early Puzzles and Dissected Maps as Imperial Heuristics" and "Playing Empire: Children's Parlor Games, Home Theatricals, and Improvisational Play." Ira Bruce Nadel earlier offered criticism on Victorian play as well and, though not directed at concerns of childhood or children's literature in particular, David Guerra also offers notable analysis of parallels in avatar use and perceptions of agency in Milton Bradley's *The Game of Checkered Life* (1860) and Walt Whitman's *Leaves of Grass* (1855), suggesting, for instance, that "Bradley's game participated in an emerging discourse, one that insisted that the relationship between selfhood and society or selfhood and history was not passive" (15).

4 For additional analysis of playthings and agency, particularly regarding toy narratives and consumer culture, see, for example, Susan Honeyman's work, such as "Manufactured Agency."

1 Cultivating citizenship in the parlor

Transatlantic rivalries and respectability in nineteenth century board, card, and parlor games

Near the center of the R. Bliss Manufacturing Company's *Robinson Crusoe* game board (1898) is a hill adorned with a flag. Given standard popular associations with islands and colonialism, at first glance the flag makes perfect sense—the Western explorer/colonizer, upon setting foot on the island has, as popular images and ideas go, stuck the flag in the hill to claim the territory as his, and more particularly, as part of his nation's empire. This association is so common that Terry Pratchett critiques it (and imperialism, to a degree) in his Robinsonade, *Nation* (2008), by having an island inhabitant ask another, "How about if I take a canoe and sail it to the trouserman island [England] and stick my flag in the sand. ... Will that make it our place?" (337). The answer, of course, is "No ... They would laugh. Flags are like guns that flap. If you have a flag, you need a gun" (337). A second glance, however, renders the flag on the *Robinson Crusoe* game board a bit of a puzzle: in all of its wind-blown splendor, the flag is clearly a U.S. flag (Figure 1.1).

Despite its subtitle referencing the "un-inhabited Island on the Coast of America," *Robinson Crusoe* is primarily the story of the English-born

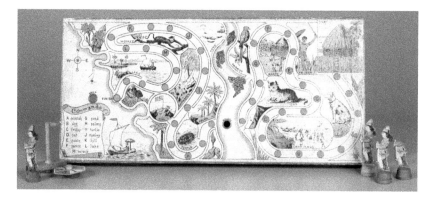

Figure 1.1 R. Bliss Manufacturing Company's Robinson Crusoe Game (1898). Courtesy, The Strong, Rochester, New York.

(though with German father) Robinson Crusoe who, if he were to plant a flag upon the island on which he finds himself stranded, would most likely choose either the flag of Great Britain or the English flag.[1] That Crusoe wouldn't choose a U.S. flag is even more certain due to the fact that the U.S. flag—or even the U.S. itself—didn't exist when the book was published (1719) and when Crusoe arrived at the island (30 September 1659, as Crusoe indicates in his journal and as a Parker Brothers 1895 *Robinson Crusoe* game card helpfully elucidates with a "Record Post" illustration). Potentially similarly strange appearances of U.S. flags occur with The R. Bliss Manufacturing Company's *Stanley Africa Game* of 1891. The game, which portrays racial stereotypes, takes as its subject matter Henry Morton Stanley's 1887–1889 "Emin Pasha Relief Expedition." Though Stanley, more famous for his earlier expedition to find Dr. David Livingstone, spent time in New Orleans and gained his adopted name through that time, served in both sides during the U.S. Civil War, and worked for a New York paper, he ultimately was born, knighted, and died in Britain, and the expedition the game depicts was organized by British businessmen. A player of the game would be excused for believing Stanley's now-infamous exploits to be decidedly U.S. accomplishments, however, given the prominence of (though unconventional) U.S. flags on the game board and the flag as one of its game pieces.

The presence, at times anachronistic, of the U.S. flags indicates, I would argue, not only the games' U.S. manufacture and creation by a U.S. company (Bliss Manufacturing was founded in Rhode Island) but attempts to align the U.S. with Britain's imperial legacy—appropriating Britain's literary legacy along the way. A year after the publication of the Bliss *Robinson Crusoe* game, following the Spanish-American war, Rudyard Kipling observed the U.S.' imperial "maturity" ("have done with childish days" and "search your manhood") through the poem "The White Man's Burden," which linked the U.S.' acquisition of the Philippines with older, European imperialism (line 50; 53). Defoe's novel has long been associated with British colonialism (from its references in Wilkie Collins' imperialism-inflected *The Moonstone* [1868] to comments by James Joyce and postcolonial critical considerations today). It has, moreover, also long been associated with childhood, children's education, and fostering imperial ideology for children. It is the one book Jean-Jacques Rousseau allows his fictional child Emile to read, it spawned an entire generally imperialism-oriented literary genre (the Robinsonade) which, particularly at the end of the nineteenth century, inspired many works of children's literature including R.M. Ballantyne's *The Coral Island* (1858) if not Robert Louis Stevenson's *Treasure Island* (1883), and it is sometimes even viewed as children's literature itself.[2] As L.J. Swingle condescendingly suggests, comparing Defoe's eighteenth century novel to Lewis Carroll's *Alice's*

Adventures in Wonderland (1865), "people who have never actually read Daniel Defoe's *Robinson Crusoe* often think of it as a children's book. It is a tale, so they suppose, that belongs on the shelf of the playroom" (xiii). In his view, "we adults" should "rescue *Robinson Crusoe* from the playroom and begin thinking about its significance for ourselves" as it "belong[s] in the library downstairs, where adults retreat to contemplate the shadowy mysteries of their own minds and experience" (xiv). Late nineteenth century game creators and parents seemingly disagreed: not only were multiple versions of the *Robinson Crusoe* game produced by leading manufacturers at the time—one each at least by Bliss, McLoughlin Brothers, and Parker Brothers, all circa 1890—those games were cast as decidedly for children. The Parker Brothers version (1893) indicates in its "Rules for Playing" that "the popular story of 'Robinson Crusoe' forms the basis of this little game for children" while the cover of the R. Bliss version suggests its being for children through the juxtaposition of its advertising, clustering around the title "The Favorite Games" not only the title of the *Robinson Crusoe* game but of other Bliss games based on child lore and childhood activities: *The House that Jack Built, Visit to the Farm, Ride-A-Cock-Horse, Old Woman in a Shoe*, and *Babes in the Woods*.

As such examples indicate, late nineteenth and early twentieth century board and card games mark revealing intersections between games and play, empire and nation building, and perceptions of children, literature, and "good" citizenship.[3] As I aim to show in this chapter, U.S. and British board, card, and parlor games of the period—recognized by collectors and curators such as Margaret K. Hofer and Brian Love as a "golden age" of such games—promote games as respectable for children and families (freeing them from the, for example, moral blemishes of gambling and other addictions) by emphasizing didacticism and morality—or, really, what good citizenship should be—along with femininity and the home; they also drew upon literary foundations for inspiration and strove to bolster patriotic allegiance for a presumed audience of families and children considered primarily, in Sana Nakata's terms, as "future-adult subjects" with regards to citizenship potential (129). Both literary foundations and patriotic allegiance were used to enhance respectability further and to promote citizenship ideals even more. A focus on respectability is especially notable in the U.S., where creators found themselves forced to acknowledge a literary heritage with Britain even as they strove to establish an independent literary and civic legacy. Time and again, political-literary motivations inherent in U.S. family and children's board games and card and parlor play in the late nineteenth and early twentieth centuries demonstrate both attitudes of child citizens as primarily "citizens-in-training" and a fierce exchange over literary, cultural, and national respectability.

"Persons of literary taste and culture are always delighted" and "children are always entertained": Redeeming games for child "citizens-in-training"

Games feature prominently in literature throughout the last few centuries and particularly in the nineteenth century. Jane Austen, who frequently played cards with family members, portrays similar playing in her novels while William Wordsworth hints at the commonplace presence of cards in childhood in the first book of *The Prelude* (1850). Lewis Carroll's Alice books, which I consider further in the next chapter, essentially revolve around games: races, croquet, and cards in *Alice's Adventures in Wonderland* (1865) and children's games ("I love my love with a …" alphabet game) and chess in *Through the Looking Glass* (1871). Yet many of these depictions of card and games-playing hint strongly at the darker sides of cards and gambling, as with the card play and gender battle in Alexander Pope's *The Rape of the Lock* (1717) and the dice game (with the stakes being the Mariner and crew) between "Death" and "The Night-mare Life-in-Death" (lines 187–198) in Samuel Taylor Coleridge's *The Rime of the Ancient Mariner* (1798, revised 1817). The association of cards with gambling is also apparent in William Makepeace Thackeray's depiction of Rawdon Crawley in *Vanity Fair* (1848), a portrayal which seems to have inspired George Frederick Pardon, who adopted the pseudonym "Captain R. Crawley" for many of his game and card manuals published in the latter half of the nineteenth century (the manuals often also contain information on betting for the games he describes). Potential darker sides are also on display in the various children's and adult games played in Charles Dickens' *Great Expectations* (1861) by characters such as Estella and Magwitch (tellingly for Pip, his very name is the word which designates the markings on playing cards)[4] while Dante Gabriel Rossetti even wrote a poem detailing the deleterious, seductive nature of cards entitled "The Card-Dealer" (1852). The U.S. writer Francis Bret Harte secured fame through his own poem describing disreputable card play (within the context of anti-Chinese immigration sentiment in the U.S.) in "Plain Language from Truthful James" (1870).

As these examples help illustrate, in the eighteenth and nineteenth centuries cards and games playing was fraught with social and cultural contradictions. In 1876, C.LB.'s game of *Tyche: The Fireside Oracle* still observed in its "Publisher's Announcement" that "many object to games of chance in which something is won or lost, as calculated to stimulate a taste for gambling" (2–3). Yet, while playing cards have long been negatively associated with gambling, the nineteenth century polite society custom of leaving a calling card while paying a visit actually stems, Roger Tilley suggests, from playing cards—the blank backs of original playing cards were recycled into spaces on which visitors left messages when the person to whom they were paying a visit was absent (130–131). Notably, too, as Janet E. Mullin discerns in her exploration of the nascent eighteenth-century beginnings of the rise of the middle classes in England, games were important in helping men and women of the "middling sort" "to construct and project their own self-image" and aided them in fostering social connections and in promoting business (990). Mullin argues that the middling sort "adapt[ed] card play to their own use" (992), an adaptation likely only continued and strengthened throughout the nineteenth century as the middle class came into its own. Simultaneously, then, games represented commonplace social practices of the sort that helped to create the middle classes and the development of middle class and national respectability and were indicators of dangerous characters, morals, habits, and risk. Children and youth, as Wordsworth's and Carroll's texts also indicate, were not exempt from the social, moral, and economic expectations and risks of such play. As Mullin notes, in the eighteenth century

> simple games such as commerce helped to introduce young children to the rituals of both cards and company, often at a table of their own with parents or indulgent family friends. As the young ones grew and began to stretch their social wings, they joined more advanced adult players at more involved games, absorbing lessons in risk management as they dropped their pocket money into the pool.
> (994)

Hofer observes that, by the 1880s, "materialism rather than morality became the focus of games, with players achieving success through competitive, capitalist behavior" (78), yet, as Mullin's analysis of eighteenth century card play hints, "materialism" and "competitive, capitalist behavior" were long latent (or not so latent) aspects of such play, features also emphasized by the use of games for purposes of monetary gain in their contributions to tax income (playing cards were heavily taxed) and accumulation of profits (the goal of which likely in part explains the profusion of commemorative games celebrating such things as the centenary of the U.S.' Revolutionary War that surfaced at the end of the nineteenth century). Still, as Mullin's references to "rituals," "social wings," and "lessons" imply, attempts to soften or mitigate the negative, material associations of card and games play were also at work, and such attempts are on full display in later games, which emphasize didacticism and morality, femininity and the home, and literary and patriotic connections to broadcast their appeal to child and family players (and parental pocketbooks). Indeed, later games tend to reflect, sometimes even through competitive and capitalist impulses, perpetual didacticism and moralism when it comes to the young, attempts that can be understood as aligning with a purpose of helping to foster notions of good citizenship in youth. In other words, as part of an attempt to broaden the appeal of games by diminishing their unpleasant connotations, family and children's card and board games contributed to views and ideals of middle class identities, which were adopted as notions of what constitutes "good" citizenship presented to child "citizens-in-training."

McLoughlin Brothers' *The Game of City Life* (1889), for example, offers an explicit defense that overtly highlights didactic moral intent and civic (connected with "civilizing" and "good citizenship") purpose in the form of privileging "the virtues of life" over "wickedness or crime" (3) (Figure 1.2).

The game's instructions explain that *The Game of City Life*

> is not intended simply to present to the eye a series of pictures of city life, neither is it intended only as a pleasant pastime; but while it does accomplish both these objects, it goes still farther, and its highest value lies in the fact, that while it furnishes an unusually interesting game, it at the same time imparts a strongly pointed lesson in morality; showing the value of good qualities, kind actions,

Figure 1.2 McLoughlin Brothers' The Game of City Life (1889). Courtesy, The Lilly Library, Indiana University, Bloomington, Indiana.

honesty and faithfulness, as against wickedness of every form. In short, whoever wins a game at "City Life," does so because he or she strives for the cards representing the virtues of life, and to avoid those representing wickedness or crime.

(2–3)

The "good citizen" (and capitalist) underpinnings are especially apparent in the cards that make up the game. *City Life* is played by collecting tricks of cards that dictate the number of game counters gained from or placed back into a center pool of counters. The player with the most counters, which are representative of "virtues," at the end of the game wins. The cards that cost a player counters depict figures associated with sloth, addiction, and fraud (the impoverished are generally viewed through such lenses in the game) or people or acts that, of perhaps of particular importance in a capitalist society, threaten or damage property or business rights (and occasionally life). These examples of "bad citizens" include "Corner Loafer," "Drunkard," "Beggar—Imposter," "Gambler," "Burglar," "Sneak Thief," "Rum Seller," "Wife Beater," "Reckless Driver," "Dishonest Clerk," "Defaulting Bank Cashier," and "Hand Cart—No License." Woman and children—and their moral lapses that threaten "virtue" and good citizenship—are given prominent places in these cards, with counters also taken for "Street Gamin," "Truant School-Boy," "Boys' Fighting," "Child Lost" and "Cruel Woman," while the fraudulent beggar is also depicted as a woman. By contrast, cards that allow a player to gain counters privilege respectability primarily through industry, and offer examples of "good citizens": "Laborer," "Washerwoman," "Working Girl" (a female worker, not the slang version of prostitute), "Soldier," "Sailor," "Mechanic," "Merchant," "Priest," "Alderman," and of course "Capitalist." Civic authority figures—and their roles in disciplining delinquent citizens/residents or in preventing property and other damage—are revealingly prominent. When taken in combination with ("catches") certain "wicked" or "criminal" cards, these symbols of civic authority and seemingly aspirational citizenship also garner counters: "Judge" (if "catches" "Wife Beater" or "any other evil doer"), "Mayor" (with "Rum Seller"), "Chief of Police" (with "Defaulting Bank Cashier,"), "Police Captain" (with "Truant School-Boy"), "Inspector of Police" (with "Child Lost"), "Policeman" (with "Reckless Driver"), "Detective" (with "Dishonest Clerk), "Night Watchman" (with "Burglar"), and "Fireman" (with "a Fire").

As the prominence of women and children in *City Life* also indicates, another strategy employed to heighten the didactic morality and senses of good citizenship and to diminish the potential negative associations of games was to link games overtly to femininity and the parlor, to take advantage of the idea of the nurturing, maternal domestic sphere epitomized by figures such as Coventry Patmore in *The Angel in the House* (1854–1862) and John Ruskin in "Of Queens' Gardens" in *Sesame and Lilies* (1865). The gambling often associated with gaming was typically perceived of as a masculine vice, as evidenced by, for example, Pardon's *The Handy Book of Games for Gentlemen* (1860), tellingly dedicated to "His Royal Highness Albert Edward, Prince of Wales, The First Gentleman in England." To distinguish themselves from unsavory reputations, games and game manuals for children and families emphasized women and the home. A circa 1876 manual of pastimes including "new out-of-door sports" (ix) not only bears the elucidative title *The Home Book for Young Ladies* but features as its frontispiece "The Home Circle," a female-dominated image which includes children building a house of cards on the floor. Girls and women similarly outnumber boys and men in the frontispiece for *Cassell's Book of In-Door Amusements* (circa 1882), where "Fireside Fun" takes up the central image, surrounded by depictions of "Blind Man's Bluff," "Nine Pins," "Whist," and "Parlour Magic." The "Publishers' Preface" for *Protean Cards* (1879) by the "Editor of *St. Nicholas*" (Mary Mapes Dodge) takes similar pains to emphasize "innocent and profitable enjoyment for the home circle," labeling it "the greatest good of all" (5), a sentiment concurred by W.C. Smith's game of *Centennial, Seventy-Six* (1876), which listed a facet of its purpose the "furnishing of an innocent and instructive home amusement, thereby enhancing the attractions of the home circle" (box cover). To solidify "home circle" connections, games also made a point of highlighting female creative origins. *Tyche*, for example, asserts that it is "superior to all other domestic games" as it "is the work of a Literary Lady of Chicago" ("Publisher's Announcement" 3). In its 1897 "new edition" of the game of *Authors*, Parker Brothers similarly emphasizes feminine origin while tying *Authors* to the game of *Dr. Busby*, a well-established game also invented by a woman (Anne Abbot) and then acquired by the company:

> The Game of "Authors" was invented in Salem, many years ago by a number of young ladies, and was first published in Salem. It was elaborated from the old game of "Dr. Busby," which was invented and published in Salem in 1840.
>
> (instruction booklet 1)[5]

Like *Dr. Busby*, *Authors* was a tremendously successful game with respect to popularity and profits, but it highlights the successes not only of didactic morality and feminine "influence" in easing undesirable connotations of games but of the use of literary connections—at times with feminine influence—to do so. Premised on literary knowledge, particularly authors and some of their notable works, *Authors* throughout the years tended to feature male writers; however, women did make notable appearances. Louisa May Alcott may have featured in the game from its inception and certainly was not infrequently included but other female writers were given prominence at times, too. McLoughlin Brothers' *Improved Star Authors* (1887) highlights, for example, Alcott as well as Harriet Beecher Stowe, Felicia Hemans, Charlotte Brontë, Elizabeth Barrett Browning, Jean Ingelow, and George Eliot, while a few versions of the game, including McLoughlin Brothers' *Queens of Literature* (1886), even exclusively featured women writers.

Tellingly, too, *Authors* was frequently advertised to young people and parents in morally-approving terms. A.B. Carroll's *The New Game of Authors* (1885), for instance, declares that "persons of literary taste and culture are always delighted with the cards" (7) and in its revised form (1889) insists that "children are always highly entertained with these games" (11). The game's instructions further direct the "Young Man" to use the game as an excuse to call on his admired young lady for "if she possesses the least particle of literary culture she can't refuse" while informing the "Young Lady" that her playing of the game "in preference to so much small talk" will result in her "friend" "respect[ing]" her "more, to say nothing of the benefit you will both receive" (7). "Parents," meanwhile, are assured in the revised 1889 version that

> if you have a set of the New Author Cards on your center table, the boys and girls will perhaps not desire to use those cards which are at least disreputable from their associations if not absolutely harmful in their influence.
>
> (12)

As A.B. Carroll's *Authors* game's assurances to "parents" regarding "disreputable" "associations" and "harmful" "influence" imply, the game's literary theme was perceived as bolstering both its moral and didactic effects and as evidence of its players' cultural—and presumably "civilizing"—inclinations.

The success of *Authors'* literary theme in helping to secure games from the taint otherwise associated with games and playing cards is further obvious from the degree to which other games adopted *Authors'* strategy for play. Many later card games were designed to emulate *Authors*, with games repeatedly focusing on paragons of good citizenship with, for example, games of "Great Men" (politicians, statesmen, artists, and musicians as well as writers) abounding by the end of the century, and with many games based on the same patterns for play, with players trying to acquire a full set ("book") of generally four cards. The "Directions for Playing" *Centennial Seventy-Six*, for example, simply indicate "it may be played in the same manner as the popular game of Authors." George S. Parker's *The Dickens Game* (1886) and E.G. Selchow and Company's *Carnival of Characters from Dickens* game (1876) both adapt *Authors*, with the games being versions of *Authors* drawing from Dickens texts and characters (Figure 1.3).

Figure 1.3 George S. Parker's The Dickens Game (1886). Courtesy, The Lilly Library, Indiana University, Bloomington, Indiana.

Carnival of Characters from Dickens goes even further, however, as it is devised not only as a version of *Authors* centered on Dickens' texts but as a means of playing "all games (without exception) that can be played with common playing cards." In the process, the game's explanatory card clarifies, "this game supplies a want long felt in society. It is a high toned, literary game, combining all of the attraction, fascination, and skill required in the various games that can be played with the common playing cards" (Figure 1.4).

Despite, or really because of, their Dickens and *Authors* literary focus, the cards can be satisfyingly used as standard playing cards for games such as Cribbage, Euchre, and Whist, for, according to the explanatory card, "the unpleasant associations that attach to playing cards are, in this game, entirely dispensed with."

The use of literary themes to "dispense with" "unpleasant associations" seems to have been a tried and true strategy by the end of the century, as literature—and often renowned British literature—was a remarkably popular theme for family and children's board and card games on both sides of the Atlantic. As early as 1852 a card game based on *Uncle Tom's Cabin*, published that same year, was devised (V.S.W Parkhurst's famous

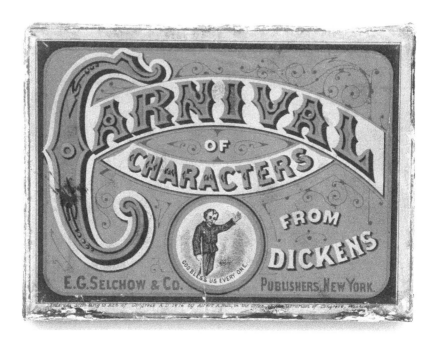

Figure 1.4 E.G. Selchow and Company's Carnival of Characters from Dickens Game (1876). Courtesy, The Lilly Library, Indiana University, Bloomington, Indiana.

Uncle Tom and Little Eva) and other literary-inspired games soon proliferated. These include the already-mentioned *Robinson Crusoe* games, Shakespeare games, games based on John Bunyan's 1678 *Pilgrim's Progress* (such as McLoughlin Brothers' *Game of Pilgrim's Progress*, circa 1875), Dickens games (including not only *Carnival of Characters from Dickens* and *The Dickens Game* but George S. Parker & Co.'s *The Good Old Game of Oliver Twist*, circa 1880), and *Sherlock Holmes* games (1904, Parker Brothers, multiple editions). These games appeared alongside an 1886 George S. Parker & Co. game based on Sir Walter Scott's *Ivanhoe* (1820), a circa 1900 J.H. Singer *Game of Ali Baba or the Forty Thieves*, and games likely alluding to Mark Twain's *The Innocents Abroad* (1869), such as Parker Brothers' *The Amusing Game of Innocence Abroad* (1888) and McLoughlin Brothers' *Game of the Bewildered Travelers* (circa 1875), among others.

Indeed, games, cards, and books, as these examples indicate, share a history. As Hofer points out, "the earliest game known to have been produced in America, *Traveller's Tour through the United States*, was made by a New York City bookseller in 1822" (16) and games were sometimes even designed to resemble books while stored (19). Moreover, "improvements in printing and paper making enabled the large-scale commercial production of board games" at the end of the nineteenth century, especially "advances in chromolithography, a color printing process perfected in the 1870s that created bold, richly colored images at affordable prices" for the middle classes (Hofer 14). Certainly, the late nineteenth century was a prolific one for books and novels and also games—it saw the rise of many notable game manufacturers like Bliss, McLoughlin Brothers, Parker Brothers, Milton Bradley, and Selchow and Righter in the U.S. and J.W. Spear, John Jaques, and Chad Valley in Britain (though the British tradition began at least a century before). Overall, the parallels between games and literature are so strong that Tilley's waxing nostalgic gushing at the end of his history of playing cards could, except for its reference to gambling, nearly completely apply to books:

> over the centuries they have patiently comforted man when bored, entertained him when sociable, afforded excitement when in the gambling mood, instructed him when he needed to learn, and provided space for propaganda when he wanted to state a case.
>
> (180)

Cards and games, like books and literature, have also gathered enough enmity at times to warrant, according to Joyce Goggin, "bans" that "often took the form of public burnings accompanied by sermons on the[ir] immorality" (15).

The fact that, like the publisher of *Traveller's Tour through the United States*, many early game manufacturers were also book publishers, many of which advertised in their catalogues not only games and toys but picture and toy books, may help to explain why the proliferation of children's games also paralleled the explosion of children's literature (and increased attention to children's culture) in the nineteenth century in England and the U.S. Indeed, Tilley goes so far as to suggest that "perhaps the main feature of [the "last quarter" of the nineteenth century] in England was the great output of children's games" (168), while David Parlett suggests that "the development of board games and card games for children [as opposed to adults] is historically recent and particularly characteristic of western culture, dating back not much further than the late eighteenth century" (x). Without doubt, by the end of the nineteenth century, board and card games, as Frances Hodgson Burnett's parlor baseball board game playing Cedric Errol (Little Lord Fauntleroy) and Edith Nesbit's *Magic City* (1910) *Halma* figures signify, were viewed as common and shared childhood experiences, though their novelty was also indicated by Nesbit's disdain over "bought at a shop, games in boxes" (*Wings and the Child* 118) and by references in other texts. In Henry James' *What Maisie Knew* (1897), Sir Claude buys the child Maisie "ever so many games, in boxes, with printed directions ... to while away the evening hour" but "the evening hour indeed often passed in futile attempts on [the adult governess] Mrs. Wix's part to master what 'it said' on the papers," the games' directions (91).

This novelty and shared history point to the other literary means used to render games suitable for children and families: association not only with literature but with children's literature. To take advantage of illustrations and materials ready-made for toy and picture books, a striking number of games at the end of the nineteenth century centered on nursery rhymes and fairy tales, genres frequently depicted as passed down by women and especially fitting for the nursery, which was an additional potential boon in marketing to parents and families. McLoughlin Brothers in particular created many games based on child lore, with *The Merry Christmas Games* set (1890) offering a compendium of such games, including *Old King Cole, Baa Baa Black Sheep, Puss in the Corner, Jack Spratt, Little Jack Horner,* and *Just Like Me* (a game which offers many nursery rhymes). These joined with other McLoughlin Brothers' nursery rhyme and fairy tale games, such as *Mother Goose and Her Friends* (1892) and *Cinderella, or Hunt the Slipper* (1887),[6] as well as similar games by other companies, such as Parker Brothers' circa 1895 *Jack and the Beanstalk* and circa 1890 *Little Mother Goose* (Figure 1.5).

Figure 1.5 McLoughlin Brothers' Mother Goose and Her Friends Game (1892). Courtesy, The Lilly Library, Indiana University, Bloomington, Indiana.

Many game creators were also authors of or associated with children's literature. As already observed, *St. Nicholas Magazine* joined the game-creating fray in 1880 with a collection of *Protean Cards* which could be used to play over fifty "amusing and instructive" games, including a "Game of the Poets" featuring "English poetry, blank verse, or rhyme, ranging from Shakespeare to Mother Goose" (Dodge 5; 15). Anne Abbot followed the publication of her *Dr. Busby* game with that of a book a year later, *Doctor Busby and His Neighbors* (1844); she was also a children's writer and editor, briefly, of the periodical *The Children's Friend*. Famous children's authors such as Charles Lutwidge Dodgson (Lewis Carroll) and Samuel Clemens (Mark Twain) turned their hands to game-inventing as well, with limited success: Dodgson, a consummate inventor, created many games, including an "arithmetical croquet" game, and Clemens devised *Mark Twain's Memory-Builder* (1891, patented 1885), "a game for acquiring and retaining all sorts of facts and dates."

And, of course, children's literature of the period, including that by Twain and Carroll, formed a popular subject for games meant to be more appropriate (and good citizen-producing) for families and children. Stoll and Edwards created an *Adventures of Tom Sawyer and Huck Finn* game (1928) while Alice, who dispels cards at the end of her adventures in Wonderland, was transformed into cards herself on both sides of the Atlantic. In the U.S. Selchow and Righter produced a trick-taking game in 1882 while in England Thomas de La Rue & Co. created a "Go Fish" Alice game around 1899. Both versions adapt John Tenniel's original illustrations. In the first few decades of the twentieth century, H.P. Gibson & Sons offered a card game based on J.M. Barrie's Peter Pan works, Thomas de La Rue & Co. offered a game centered on Bertha and Kate Upton's Dutch Dolls/Golliwogg books, and Parker Brothers produced *The Wonderful Game of Oz* (1921), while a card game based on Joel Chandler Harris' Brer Rabbit tellings was also created around this time and around 1890 Burnett's *Little Lord Fauntleroy* (1886) was turned into playing cards by The Russell and Morgan Printing Company. Unlike the other games, the *Fauntleroy Playing Cards* are standard playing cards; they simply borrow images from a few of Reginald Birch's illustrations for Burnett's text in a likely attempt to elevate the cards from otherwise problematic associations. Tellingly, the cards feature three notable scenes from Birch's illustrations, with one scene displayed on the card backs, one depicted on a special "Ace" title card, and one used as the advertising image on the cards' box container. The cards came in at least two decks (black and red) with the same illustration of the head and face of Cecil Errol (Fauntleroy) used for each deck's box cover and with the same image of Fauntleroy riding a horse (showing off his "mastery" through sporting capability) on the Ace card image in each deck. The image on the card backs, however, differs between decks.

It suggests what game designers and the general public at the time may have considered some of the most appealing aspects of the text, with the black card deck showcasing an image of Fauntleroy and his grandfather exchanging caresses (the "shall I be your boy" image labeled "The Earl" on the cards) and the red card deck presenting an image of the bootblack Dick giving the gift of the red silk handkerchief to Fauntleroy. In both cases, the chosen image reflects likely "good citizen" attributes of loyalty and affection, as well as the raising of class status (while actually, of course, maintaining or restoring the status quo with respect to class status).

Class and fantasies of class mobility were in fact popular subjects for literature for youth and games at century's end, and often overtly center on ideas of good citizenship (industry and employment) and the rewards of such citizenship. As Hofer observes, Horatio Alger-esque figures and ideas took shape in the form of games such as McLoughlin Brothers' the *Game of District Messenger Boy* (1886) and *Game of the Telegraph Boy* (1888) (86). Similar circa 1890s games include Edgar O. Clark's *Postal Delivery Boys*, J.H. Singer's *The Shop Boy*, Parker Brothers' *The News Boy Game* as well as its game of *The Office Boy*, while J. Ottmann Lithography Co.'s *The Game of Success* appeared around 1910. The good citizenship aspirations of these games are frequently explicit: McLoughlin Brothers' *The Errand Boy* (1891), for example, asks its players—prominently illustrated as male youths—to navigate moral and capitalist waters (framed in terms of enterprise, diligent labor, and prosperous employment), avoiding such things as "drunkenness," "laziness," and "embezzlement" (literal spots of trouble which put one back or lead to "prison" in the game) and striving towards spots depicting "honesty," "attain[ing] wealth," and "retir[ing[from mercantile business" with significant personal riches. The ultimate goal, prominently illuminated at the center of the board, and making clear the supposed connections between industry, employment, and ideal citizenship, is to be "an honorable & respected banker, and a good citizen."

Ultimately, as Robin Bernstein observes, "the history of children's literature exists not in opposition to, but in integration with, the histories of children's material culture and children's play" (459). Bernstein argues that we need to "stop erecting arbitrary barriers between children's literature and play with material culture" as "such boundaries make sense for most other genres of literature, but [for children's literature] they are counterfactual and counterhistorical" (459–460). As the *Robinson Crusoe, Pilgrim's Progress*, Shakespeare, and nursery rhyme games, among many others, remind us, however, those boundaries may be "arbitrary" and "counterfactual and counterhistorical" for other genres as well. Instead, it may be fruitful to think of the nineteenth century in Caroline Levine's terms of network rather than nation, to remember that authors, literary texts, folklore, and child lore cross and defy national boundaries and periods of time. Fairy and folk tales were popular and popularized in England in the nineteenth century, for example, but certainly originated earlier and often outside England, just as nursery rhymes did. *Robinson Crusoe* is not typically considered a nineteenth century text, having been published nearly a century before; however, it experienced a surge in popularity in the mid and latter nineteenth century, as nineteenth century texts such as *The Moonstone*, Robinsonades like *The Coral Island*, and the U.S. games well document. Games in games manuals of the time likewise resist easy periodization and global placement: many games encouraged in nineteenth century games manuals (and now) originated much earlier than the nineteenth century, such as hide-and-seek and hopscotch. Games manual authors also frequently borrowed freely from one another and across national divides. John D. Champlin and Arthur E. Bostwick, in their *The Young Folks' Cyclopaedia of Games and Sports* (1890), for instance, call attention to the fact that "many other works on sports and games published in [the U.S.] are merely reprints of English books" (iii) and even a cursory glance at games and manuals of the period confirms much borrowing from book to book and game to game, as indicated, for example, by the A.J. Fisher *The Game of a Fashionable Boarding House* U.S. game of 1874, which merely recycles the characters from John Jaques' circa 1850 British *Happy Families* game, itself possibly a spinoff of Abbot's U.S. *Dr. Busby* game.[7] In other words, games cross from nation to nation, culture to culture, and can span centuries, if not millennia. Still, by the end of the nineteenth century, it was clear that games had acquired negative connotations which women, children, families, and "good" literature—and their "civilizing" if not "good citizenship" associations—were deployed to cleanse.

But another strategy was forcefully employed to purge negative possibilities from games, one that relied on nineteenth century networks but sought hard to re-frame networking into notions of nation, to overlay the realities of the U.S. and British transatlantic network into a patriotic rivalry dependent on conceptions of national identity. In the U.S. in particular, to salvage games for families, game designers also turned to patriotism and politics, nation-based versions of (future) citizenship. Indeed, despite the general timelessness of games and games' tendencies to defy national borders, late nineteenth and early twentieth century games also insistently offer a particular sense of the circumstances of their origins or interpretations. This sense is often grounded remarkably in space and time, as when J.K. Benson, with strong nineteenth and early twentieth century flair, describes the tag game of "Prisoner's Base" through sides of British and Boers in the 1907 *The Book of Sports and Pastimes* (87). In other words, even as they defy periodization and national borders, at times ironically, games of the period demonstrate notable tendencies towards patriotic nationalism, adhering to Hofer's observation that "games manufacturers produced enormous numbers of educational games between the 1870s and 1900s, catering to an audience sold on the notion that well-educated children provide the foundation of a moral, democratic, and prosperous nation" (54). At the same time, games for children and families point to political critiques, conversations, and disagreements and underscore inequality and cruelty embedded even within democratic and fun-games-playing sentiments.

In Britain, educational patriotic games included games detailing the Kings and Queens of England and games describing British counties and their products while the numerous U.S. patriotic card games of the period include many games documenting events and dates in U.S. history, particularly the colonial period and wars such as the U.S.' civil war. There are, for example, James S. Schoonover's *Battles of the Civil War* game (1888), Richards & Kibbe's *Signers of American Independence Game* (1877), L.A. Tuttle's *The National Game of '76* (1881), E.H. Snow's game of *The Lion and the Eagle, or the Days of '76* (1883), and Chester Metcalf's game of *One Hundred Events of U.S. Colonial History* (1876). There are also Emile Pingauklt's *Patriotic Game* (1887) and S.B. Goodspeed's *The Game of American Patriots* (1892) and multiple games describing U.S. presidents or the path to the presidency, even incorporating the electoral college, such as Frank G. Thomson's *National Game of Presidents* (1881), Milton Bradley Company's *The Game of American Politics* (1888), John R. Van Wormer's *Political Bluff* (1892), S.W. Carr's *Presidential Electoral Game* (1892), and E.B. Treat's *Races to the White House* (1881). Like *The Carnival of Characters from Dickens* game and The Russell and Morgan Printing Company's *Fauntleroy Playing Cards*, many of these games strove to remove playing cards' negative stereotypes by providing alternate cards by which standard playing card games could be played for, according to *Tyche's* "Publisher's Announcement," "many people refuse to keep the common playing cards, because they think the associations to which such cards tend are below the proper standard" (3). *The Lion and the Eagle*, for example, consists of patriotic suits of lions, eagles, crowns, and bells and offers "American" and "British" "sides." Similarly, around the time of the U.S.' Civil War, the American Card Company, "confident that the introduction of national emblems in the place of foreign in playing cards ... would be hailed with delight by the people of the American Republic, introduced the Union Playing Cards" (box cover). The images depicted on these cards were "Goddess of Liberty in place of Queen, Colonel for King, Major for Jack" and suits of "Eagles, Shields, Stars and Flags" (box cover). To promote the *Union Playing Cards*, the American Card Company boasted that they were "the first and only genuine American cards ever produced. The success of these cards bearing national emblems ... is unprecedented in the card trade. They have already become the leading cards in the American market" (box cover). Explicit patriotism and didactic, "civilizing" and good citizen-producing intentions are apparent, too, in *Centennial, Seventy-Six*, which asserted,

> In presenting this game to the American public, if one or both of two things are attained,—first, the furnishing of an innocent and instructive home amusement, thereby enhancing the attractions of the home circle; secondly, but not least, introducing the subject of American History in an attractive manner, thus inspiring the minds of the young to the further study of the history of their country, to emulate the example and revere the memory of their patriot ancestors, for the precious dowry of freedom bequeathed them, to be preserved and handed down to posterity, the object of the author will have been accomplished.
>
> (box cover)

The U.S.' "precious dowry of freedom" was explored further by other games of the period which demonstrate national interest as well as political critique. These notably include J.W. Burdette's *The Anarchist* (1886), "a game devised and intended to illustrate in an interesting and amusing manner the destructive and subversive influence of the anarchist in the community," and W.T. Buckner's *Game of National Finance* (1895), which presents players with various options for a national currency: the gold standard, a silver basis, a copper bottom, greenback, bimetalism, or trimetalism (Figure 1.6).

In these games, revealing political stances at times surface: the words "A Radical" appear on the bottom of a greenback card in the *Game of National Finance*, for example, while the silver basis is described as being advocated by "the masses" and gold is indicated as "sound money," "more valuable since [its introduction] in 1873," but not popular because "the people don't know what they want." In *Political Bluff*, political party stances are described as such: the Democratic Party is for "Free Trade" and "Free Whisky," Republican Party issues are "A Protective Tariff," "an Honest Dollar," and "A Free and Honest ballot for All," the

Figure 1.6 Cards from W.T. Buckner's Game of National Finance (1895). Courtesy, The Lilly Library, Indiana University, Bloomington, Indiana.

Alliance Party is for the "Abolition of National Banks" and "Demands Government Pawn Shops," and the Prohibition Party is for "Universal Suffrage" but "Opposes Everything Practical" (Figure 1.7).

Political commentary, at times satiric, embedded in late nineteenth century games is an inheritance from what Tilley describes as "the age of cardboard ridicule" wherein seventeenth century card makers "started a new fashion by producing cards which satirized contemporary affairs, made political and religious propaganda, and illustrated current events" (118). Yet it is also a reminder that unquestioning patriotic loyalty was not the only possibility for "good citizenship" on display at the time—and that sentiments of liberty and democracy can sometimes obscure problems.

Embedded in their times, nineteenth and early twentieth century games and recreations were not infrequently imbued with prejudiced and racist perspectives and, as will be more evident in arguments in later chapters, also existed with the reality of girls' inability to ever be full citizens (since they lacked suffrage rights) and tended to de-humanize even those boys who could—eventually—be full citizens but were not yet so. Consistently, then, even within seeming contexts of democracy and liberty, tensions abounded, often through unremitting reminders of inequality and occasional overt bouts of cruelty. This is sometimes even recognized by games and games manual authors, who tended to try blithely to explain it away, as *Cassell's Complete Book of Sports and Pastimes* (1892) does in its description of the game of "The Farmyard," where one player is tricked into braying like a donkey:

> if it were not understood that joking of all kinds is considered lawful in most game playing, we might be inclined to think that in this game of the Farmyard a little unfairness existed.... Still, as "in war

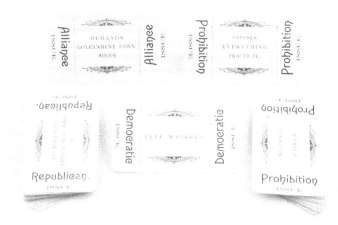

Figure 1.7 John R. Van Wormer's Political Bluff Game (1892). Courtesy, The Lilly Library, Indiana University, Bloomington, Indiana.

all things are fair," so it seems to be in amusements, most hearty players evidently being quite willing to be either the laughers or the laughed at.

(766)

The manual concludes, "it is needless to remark that this game is seldom called for a second time in one evening" (766). An acknowledgment of unfairness is also admitted for the game of "Hunt the Whistle" (essentially a "joke" version of the parlor form of "Cinderella, or Hunt the Slipper"), where the whistle is hidden on the person looking for it without that person knowing: as Alfred Elliott states in *The Playground and the Parlour* (1868), "this is really a capital game—except for the whistle hunter!" (224). The dual sense of (ironically) "democratic" possibility limited by inequality offered in children's games and their descriptions in the period is perhaps best conveyed by the well-known throw-down game of "King of the Castle." While children playing "King of the Castle" can try to be king, those who succeed must immediately strive against being deposed and literally violently overthrown. Ultimately, being able to be and remain king rests solely on physical might. Those not up to the task through physical strength and endurance will never be king. Worldly inequalities, including class distinctions and subjecthood, remain despite the game's seeming egalitarian potential. The violence and inequality inherent in the game are on broad display in *The Boy's Modern Playmate* (1891), which pairs its description of the game with that of another game named "Cock-Fighting." Like "King of the Castle," "Cock-Fighting" relies on physical strength, agility, or dexterity and violence if not dependence on individual personal popularity: two child (presumed boy in both description and illustration) "combatants" are "trussed like a couple of fowls," "placed face to face, their toes touching, and are left to fight it out," "striving to knock each other down, each to overbalance the other without losing his own equilibrium" (Wood 147). If a child falls over while "trussed," he is reliant on "his friends" to help him up (147). The de-humanizing/animalizing element of the games also appears in the explanation for "King of the Castle," which concludes,

> the writer once saw a lot of lambs play this game in splendid style ... just like a parcel of boys, showing a wonderful individuality of character amongst them—some very plucky and not to be denied, some making a great parade of charging, but doing next to nothing, and others merely prancing and frisking about.

(147)

Similar contradictions despite promises of equality persist in other games, particularly those that play with gender and courtship conventions. An example is the use of "forfeits," which are generally actions that have to be completed as a result of having made a mistake in or having been un-successful in a game: many forfeits are tricks that are meant to provide laughs for the other players; however, deviant potential is sometimes present, as with the forfeit that requires one to kiss the person you like best without others knowing it.[8] To do so, one can kiss the admired person when no one is watching, kiss everyone of the opposite sex, or kiss everyone, a possibility that allows both homosocial and heteroso-cial potential. A similar potential is offered in the version of "Postman's Knock" detailed in *The Games Book for Boys and Girls* (1897), where the person playing the postman "names some member of the company, generally of the opposite sex," as recipient of a letter and determines upon a number for payment whereupon "the person for whom the letter is supposed to be must then pay for it with kisses instead of pennies; af-ter which he or she must take a turn as postman" (55). The "generally of the opposite sex" is of course noteworthy, intimating as it does that the kisses need not always be bestowed on those of the opposite sex. Still, as with other children's games, the open, freeing, and equalizing ten-dencies of the game are juxtaposed with other attributes of unfairness and inequality: throughout the game, the "postman" holds a privileged position, determining both who gives kisses and how many kisses are to be given. As a result, those who are admired in this game will know it, and those who aren't will know it, too. *The Games Book for Boys and Girls* version of "Hiss and Clap" allows for comparable gender devi-ance and unfairness, indicating but not insisting that "it will make more amusement if when a boy is sent outside the room a girl be chosen as the person to whom he has to kneel; and the opposite if a girl be outside the room" (51). Despite its freeing potential, the game is quite cruel. Like "Postman's Knock," its outcomes are likely linked to popularity: as Benson's *The Book of Indoor Games for Young People of All Ages* (1904) explains for its version of the game, if a player guesses incorrectly which player has "chosen" him or her, instead of being applauded, she or he "is hissed so vehemently that he is only too glad to escape from the room" (81). One can imagine a similar desire to escape from the game of "The Stool of Repentance": based on a former Presbyterian practice, the game involves players "say[ing] all sorts of things about" another player, "the culprit," who has left the room; when that player returns, she or he sits on "the stool of repentance" and has to guess who has made what "charges" against him or her (*Games Book for Boys and Girls* 47).[9] As an example, *The Games Book for Boys and Girls* proposes the follow-ing: "someone said you were vain; can you guess who it was?" (47). The cruelty is made supposedly more equal by the fact that "if the culprit guesses correctly … the person who made the accusation becomes the 'culprit' in his stead" (47–48). Of course, if "the 'culprit' is unable to guess correctly, he must go out of the room again whilst fresh charges are made against him" (48).

In their tensions and contradictions of democracy and freedom, inequality and cruelty, nineteenth century games for children bear witness to Nesbit's admission in *Wings and the Child* (1913), her nonfictional exploration of education and children's play, that "such are the needs for sympathy and justice, leisure and liberty. These things are admitted by all but the driest economists to be the rights of adults, but not, alas! always admitted as the rights of children" (190). Perhaps the strangest tension manifest in nineteenth century games for children and families, however, is that between national patriotism and colonial debt, between literary homage and national rivalry. The various methods games employed to redeem themselves at the end of the nineteenth century (connections with women, families, the home, childhood, good literature, and national patriotism) fostered some strange bedfellows—most notably, fascinating intersections between morally "good" (and frequently if not primarily British) literature and nation-building patriotic, pro-U.S. perspectives. To encourage ideal citizenship in U.S. families and youth, U.S.-based games of the time, as the Bliss Manufacturing Company's *Robinson Crusoe* game testifies, appropriated British literature. Just as frequently, however, they turned that appropriation into transformation and deployed sleights-of-hand to confront the reality of a two-hundred-year-old or so national history compared with that of centuries (if not a millennium) older.

"I am here; America's ahead!," or "author of the leading manual on parliamentary rules": Dueling with literary legacies and national pride in nineteenth century games

In her famed novel for the young, *Little Women* (1868), Louisa May Alcott, as I suggest further in the next chapter, presents a revealing episode of croquet-playing, describing it as a combative bout in which "the Englishers played well; but the Americans played better, and contested every inch of the ground as strongly as if the spirit of '76 inspired them" (156). After the U.S. Americans beat the English players at what was at that time essentially the British national pastime, the youngsters in the novel have a telling bout of "Truth" (game and concept) and then settle down to "a sensible game of Authors, to refresh our minds" (163). The transition is illuminating: the youth turn from a presumably non-sensible British diversion to a "sensible" U.S. one, a card game developed only a few years earlier. *Authors* was, moreover, a game which Alcott highly approved: she wrote a testimonial for A. B. Carroll's 1889 version of the game indicating that she had "examined your Authors and think them both useful and instructive to the young players" (14). In her testimonial as well as novel, Alcott suggests the game is a perfectly suitable middle-class pastime for children and families in the U.S., a view reinforced through other games' emulation of it, but the game had other significant effects: as Lara Langer Cohen and Meredith L. McGill reflect,

> the game condensed the field of authorship by equating "Authors" writ large with the particular writers it assembled. The selective elevation of these authors to "Authors" helped reinforce what we have come to know as a national literary canon, while demonstrating how canons can be formed through mass cultural phenomena as well as through more familiar, top-down, critical or institutional fiat.
>
> (210)

In other words, *Authors* helped create and cement the U.S.' national literary foundation and reputation. In so doing, however, it embodied the national and cultural skirmishes evident in Alcott's text as well as throughout games of the period.

Notably, in fact, not only did Alcott provide a testimonial in support of the game, so did eminent British authors, particularly Tennyson, who wrote that he "begs to thank Mr. Carroll for his sets of English and American Authors, which he has no doubt will be very useful for children" (A.B. Carroll, Revised edition 14). Like the mixed nationality of players in Alcott's own text and despite its U.S. origins, the game of *Authors* was divided between a U.S. and British literary legacy. Of the eleven or twelve authors originally depicted in the cards, which tended to include both Alcott and Tennyson, generally half were British. The version to which Alcott and Tennyson provide testimonials was expanded to 200 cards, but it maintained this essentially equal division: 100 cards featured British authors and 100 featured U.S. authors. In this way, the game, like Alcott's text, tried to present the U.S cultural and literary landscape as on an equal (if not superior) footing with Britain's. To do so, though, the game had to resort to some broad definitions of authorship, particularly when it came to U.S. authors. Among the U.S. "authors" appearing in the game are George Washington, Patrick Henry, Henry Clay, Abraham Lincoln, and Caleb Cushing, whose card cites his literary credentials consisting of his being "author of the leading manual on parliamentary rules" (Figure 1.8).

A similar scenario unfolds with other U.S. literary-oriented games: most, if not all, combine U.S. and British authors, acknowledging a shared literary past or inevitably being forced to look to Britain for supplementary support even while trying to suggest a great U.S. literary tradition of its own. C.J. Daggett's *Chi Rho* game (1892), "rejoic[ing] in literature," places, for example, Edgar Allen Poe alongside Elizabeth Barrett Browning and Shakespeare, and the *Queens of Literature* game acknowledges among its queens Barrett Browning, Charlotte Bronte, George Eliot, and Jean Ingelow along with Alcott. An 1889 version of the game (McLoughlin Brothers' *Improved Authors: The Queens of Literature*) offers a similar British/U.S. mix, including Burnett and Isabella M. Alden (Figure 1.9).

Figure 1.8 Cards from A.B. Carroll's A New Game of Authors, Revised Edition (1889). Courtesy, The Lilly Library, Indiana University, Bloomington, Indiana.

Figure 1.9 McLoughlin Brothers' Queens of Literature Game (1886). Courtesy, The Lilly Library, Indiana University, Bloomington, Indiana.

An authors list provided by *Tyche: The Fireside Oracle*, which involves "your character and destiny as told by seventy-seven poets," mixes minor and major poets from a variety of nations, but particularly the U.S. and Britain. Games such as Welcome L. Beckley's *Game of Quotations* (1889), where the goal is to recognize notable quotations, generally from literary texts, similarly show such mixes, with

U.S. theological writers like Hosea Ballou appearing alongside references to Pope, Scott, Shakespeare, and Thomas Moore. A key to an earlier *Game of Quotations* (1878) by Clay Herrick makes clear just how overwhelming the British literary presence was: despite a few allusions to U.S figures such as Benjamin Franklin, Patrick Henry, and Washington Irving, the vast majority of the cited authors are British. Seemingly to avoid the problem of dubious "authorship" (as well as to capitalize further on the popularity of versions of *Authors*), games creators at times explicitly acknowledged their literary broadening, simply calling themselves things like *A Game of Characters* (F.G. Decker and O.F. Decker, 1889) or, as with the game of *Literary Whist* (1887) by N.O. Wilhelm, offering subtitles such as "Or, Games of Great Men" and (for one game to be played with the *Literary Whist* cards) "Children's Great People." Wilhelm overtly included in *Literary Whist*'s game materials cards representing "poets, prose writers, statesmen, warriors, [and] scientists," so that, for instance, Jefferson Davis appears alongside John Stuart Mill. *Literary Whist* even goes so far as to weigh in on the relative literary prestige of British versus U.S. authors. One of the games its materials make possible, "Great Men's Casino," stipulates the giving of additional points at the conclusion of the game to players who hold cards depicting writers (13). The cards for "each great American Poet" earn holders an additional point, while two "great men" are specially named: Charles Dickens and Benjamin Franklin. The holder of the Dickens card, however, only receives one additional point while the holder of the Benjamin Franklin card is allotted two extra points (9).

Similar devaluings and even transformations are on display in other games of the period. Although the card representing Sherlock Holmes in Parker Brothers' *Sherlock Holmes* game retains value at the end of the game, being worth five points to criminal cards' one point, the complexity of the character is obscured as Holmes is transformed into a figure who merely takes other players' cards through "sweeps." Cards indicative of detective work and deduction—hallmarks of Arthur Conan Doyle's portrayal of the character—such as "clue" cards are ultimately worthless. Parker Brothers' *The Game of Robin Hood* (1893) reduces Robin Hood and his "merry men," particularly Little John and Friar Tuck, by transforming them into mere "robbers" and by centering the game, notwithstanding its title, around the Sheriff of Nottingham: "the game represents the attempt of the Sheriff to pass from the town of Nottingham to one of the King's Castles" (box cover interior). Players take charge of pawns representing either the robbers or the sheriff and, according to the game's instructions, "it cannot be easily stated who stands a better show of winning the game, one of the robbers or the Sheriff" (box cover interior).[10] As with the privileging of Benjamin Franklin over Dickens, shifts in focus from Holmes' formidable deductive brilliance to mere luck of the draw and from a British hero of legend to an often-rendered villainous character hint at possible desires to "Americanize" the texts and games by, for example, siding at times almost implausibly with seeming upstarts and underdogs.

Other games of the era received potentially "Americanized" treatment as well. George S. Parker and Company's *The Good Old Game of Oliver Twist* uses as its cover image a reproduction of George Cruikshank's "Oliver Asking for More" illustration ("Please, Sir, I want some more"), an image reminiscent of a David and Goliath underdog perspective as it forcefully contrasts the seemingly feeble Oliver with a formidable image of the workhouse master. The game follows an underdog approach as well, providing its own "twist" of rendering the rascal Artful Dodger almost as valuable as Oliver Twist. In the game, players take turns blindly choosing a card from each other and making matches, with the objective being to be the last to hold the Oliver Twist card. Whichever player has the Oliver Twist card has the further advantage of being able to keep all cards received and not having to make any matches (so as to increase the chances of retaining the card longer). Whoever draws the Oliver Twist card also gets to call out "more" and receive an additional card from each player (direction booklet). The Artful Dodger card, however, offers a similar advantage, enabling its holder, if that holder doesn't also have the Oliver Twist card, to take two cards from other players. Even child lore did not escape a transformative, "Americanizing" bent: Albert A. Hill's game *Right and Wrong, or the Princess Belinda* (1876), "promises," according to its directions card, "to become as popular as the famous story of '*Cinderella; or, the Glass Slipper*.'" The game consists of a narrative meant to be interrupted at designated times by players holding certain cards. The narrative describes Belinda conducting a tour of the world and universe, ultimately leaving England to cross "the Atlantic in a cockle-shell, the sails of which were the wings of THE AMERICAN EAGLE. Strange as had been the adventures of Belinda, she was glad to reach once more her HOME IN WONDERLAND" (capitalization in the original). In other words, in its re-conception of fairyland, *Right and Wrong* re-casts its Wonderland as the U.S., a placement likely unrecognizable to, for example, Lewis Carroll's Alice and certainly different from her experiences.

In fact, Carroll's own Wonderland dealings emphasize how little he likely sympathized with pro-U.S. sentiments or seemingly U.S. tastes. Martin Gardner, citing Charles Morgan in *The House of Macmillan: 1843–1943*, observes that Carroll "took one look" at the first edition of *The Nursery Alice* (ultimately published in 1890), a version of *Alice's Adventures in Wonderland* aimed at "children aged from Nought to Five" (*Nursery Alice* "Preface"), "and decided that the pictures were too gaudy" (Gardner vi). According to Morgan, "No copy, [Carroll] said … was to be sold in England; all were to be offered to America. They were offered, and declined as not being gaudy enough" (qtd. in Gardner vi). As

Carroll's quoted comments hint, the nation-based rivalry evident in late nineteenth century U.S. games was both echoed and rebuffed by Britons. Nesbit, for example, has her sleep-inclining, work-avoiding Great Sloth in *The Magic City* disparagingly speak "like an American" (141) and rails against the U.S. "cinematograph" in *Wings and the Child*:

> we have now for fun the elaborate hurting of one American person by another American person; for scenery, American flat-iron buildings; for romance the incredibly unimportant emotions of fleshy American actresses and actors … and when the good young man marries the good young woman in a parlour grossly furnished according to American ideals, you feel that both of them are well punished for their unpardonable existence.
>
> (46)[11]

The transatlantic Burnett, however, was much more nuanced in her views. In her autobiography *The One I Knew Best of All* (1893), Burnett describes her and her sister's childhood as respectful but lacking in the "enterprise" essential to a young, developing nation:

> The two were English children, brought up in a simple English nursery in the most primitively conventional way. Such a life is not conducive to a spirit of boldness and enterprise. In matters of point of view they would have seemed to the American mind incredibly young for their years. If they had been American children they would have been immensely cooler and far less inclined to ultra-respectful attitudes toward authority.
>
> (296)

That Burnett saw advantages and disadvantages to both the U.S. and Britain is also evident in *Little Lord Fauntleroy* when, at the end of the text, the older U.S. grocer stays in England out of admiration for its traditions and older ways while the younger, "bolder," more "enterprising" bootblack, the bootblack's brother, and the brother's young son return to the "younger," more adventurous and "enterprising" U.S. Fauntleroy himself, of course, serves to blend older traditions and newer enterprises, reinvigorating and ironically reinforcing the English aristocracy with democratic ideals, just as the bootblack's and his relations' successes in the U.S. are made possible through the aristocrat's monetary investment in them.

Games, even those broadly available in the U.S., too, were not always uncritical or universally privileging of the U.S. over Britain, as the many versions of the *Game of Nations* from about 1890–1910 attest. Depicting national or cultural stereotypes, many editions of the game were produced by McLoughlin Brothers at the turn of the nineteenth and twentieth centuries, with Milton Bradley chiming in with a version or two at times. With the exception of *The Philosopher's Travels, or the Game of Nations* (circa 1900), which stereotypes many individual nationalities in generally unflattering ways (including both "The Yankee" and "The Englishman"), the various editions tend to feature four broad geographic regions outlined in maps given on cards: Europe, Asia, America (North and South combined), and Africa (with, at least in a circa 1900 Milton Bradley edition, British and other European acquisitions well labelled, the carving up of and "scramble for" Africa well detailed). Awareness and knowledge of these regions are further conveyed through accompanying cards for the game which feature portrayals of family units (mother, father, child) and then either supposedly representative animals or dwelling places. Depictions of Africans in the game frequently veer between scantily clad "native" and minstrel stereotypes, while stereotyped depictions of Native Americans (generally North American) are given for America. Overall, editions of the game consistently demonstrate Eurocentric senses of "progress," with Africans and Americans depicted as inhabiting huts and teepees while Asians and Europeans (in stereotyped Asian and European style clothing) reside in pagodas and manors.

Eurocentric portrayals correspond with similar—though more aligning the U.S. with Europe—sentiments expressed in other games: in his *Gaskell's Popular Historical Game* (1884), for example, Charles A. Gaskell emphasizes the game's focus on "the progress of thought and social life" and points to "men like Kepler, Newton, Galileo, da Vinci, etc." as "the true heroes and demigods of history" for

> to such as these we owe almost everything we possess—the clothes we wear, the houses we live in, the books we read, the songs we sing, the railroads and telegraphs we use—indeed, even much of the food we eat, and in short, everything which distinguishes us from the savages of Africa or of the South Sea Islands.
>
> (2–3)

Unlike with the *Game of Nations*, Gaskell is anxious to and strives hard to present the U.S. as a land of "progress" "distinguish[ed]" "from the savages": included among his catalog of "true heroes and demigods of history" are U.S. statesmen and two U.S. authors. In *The Game of United States History* (1903), Richard G. Boone similarly prioritizes ideas of progress, offering a "General Statement to Teachers" arguing that history is represented by "abiding forms of human conduct" and "various social institutions" but "the theme of them all is human life as it progresses, together with the machinery of government and home and school and church and social codes, as the means of its advance" (1–2). Solidifying Western and Eurocentric viewpoints, too, are games advertised by Elmer E. Johnson in 1895. These games are especially notable for their titles and those titles' omissions: *A Trip Through the United States*, *A Trip Through Europe*, and *The World Visited*. For U.S. games players and creators, if not for British ones, there was Europe, the U.S., and then the rest of the world, seemingly undistinguishable and undistinguished.

A fascinating combination of Western, Eurocentric ideas of "progress" and "advancement" as well as literary and patriotic, nationalist traditions and rivalries mark the various race for the North Pole games marketed at the turn of the nineteenth and twentieth centuries. Attempts to reach the Pole captured headlines (and children's texts, including one of Florence and Bertha Upton's Golliwogg books) throughout the world and were aimed at bestowing national glory through new avenues for exploration, if not colonization. *The North Pole Game* (1907) addresses attempts by individuals from different nations—and notably, of course, explorers from Britain and the U.S.—to make the trek to the pole while the *Game of the Mariner's Compass* (circa 1890) has players begin their imagined journey to the pole from two revealing "centers": London and New York. F.A. Colwell's *The Race for the Pole* (1896) game explicitly connects patriotic, national-glory seeking exploration with national literary heritage and hints at the notion of "passing the torch" from Britain to the U.S. evident in Kipling's "The White Man's Burden" a few years later. The game's explanatory booklet opens with an unattributed quotation from the British (Scottish) poet Robert Burns' "To a Mouse" (1785), the well-known lines "The best laid schemes o' mice an' men/ Gang aft a-gley" (lines 39–40), and closes with lines from the U.S. author Harte's poem "An Arctic Vision" (1867): "all ye icebergs make salaam/ You belong to Uncle Sam" (lines 38–39). In the lines quoted from Harte's poem, the presence of the word choice "salaam" brings forth resonances of the British empire but replaces the imperial authority, offering the U.S.' Uncle Sam in place of John Bull. Tellingly, literary as well as imperial and conquest might are transferred (if not transformed) in the game booklet's pages with the transition from Burns at the booklet's opening to Harte at its closing. The game's view on such matters is certainly without doubt: the booklet observes that "the reader will watch with interest for the one who shall proclaim to the world 'I have reached the pole,'" ultimately questioning, "shall it be Scandinavia or Great Britain? Or shall it be the American eagle which shall swoop down upon that object and screech: 'I am here; America's ahead!'" The answer, it would seem, lies with the hyperbolic figuration of the American Eagle, emphatic use of exclamation, and concluding lines borrowed from the U.S.' Harte.

Ultimately, the seeming rivalry demonstrated in U.S. and British games and at times literary texts in the nineteenth century and at the beginning of the twentieth resound with anxieties of a young nation (and occasionally an older one worried about the potential might of a younger upstart) and its desires to see itself and its citizens as equal in every way to the country of its colonial origins—even if that sometimes meant using broad criteria to arrive at a seemingly rich, lengthy literary tradition. Considered together, the nineteenth and early twentieth century games' emphasis on respectability through didactic, citizen-inspiring morality, femininity and the home, a great literary tradition, and homage to overtly patriotic and civic-minded themes and figures suggest some of the ways in which citizens and particularly young citizens viewed as "citizens-in-training" were steeped in a sense of nationalistic allegiance through material culture and social practices. Grand literary and civic heritages were so often blurred together—so that notable statesmen could stand in for great authors—that U.S. games of the period in particular can be seen as representing contests for visions of national culture, with political respectability in the form of literary greatness and pride of national character and noble citizens at stake. In these contests, U.S. games make clear, the U.S. intended to prevail. Britons, of course, often were determined otherwise. In both cases, children, literature, games, and citizenship were cast in complex alliances, alliances further complicated, as we will see, by gender, art and aesthetics, and ever-shifting attitudes towards what was and could be the proper realm of play.

Notes

1 The present-day Union Jack was not adopted until 1801, with the union of Great Britain and Ireland.
2 For analysis of *Robinson Crusoe*'s shifting place as adult and children's literature, see Teresa Michals' "Rewriting *Robinson Crusoe*: Age and the Island."
3 Megan A. Norcia offers related analysis of nineteenth century play pursuits such as parlor games and home theatricals in "Playing Empire," concluding "domestic games had an equally persuasive effect in shaping an imperial ideology" while

> party games and home theatricals, played by girls and boys of a range of ages, maintained an important role in initiating children into their imperial responsibilities, gaining such a hold over their imaginations that these children rehearsed and reproduced the Great Game in their own improvisational games and, in varying degrees, in their adult lives.
>
> (309)

4 My thanks to Leona Fisher for pointing out to me the definition of the word "pip."
5 Abbot is also often, though most likely falsely, attributed with inventing *Authors*.
6 "Cinderella, or Hunt the Slipper" was also a popular parlor game depicted in many games manuals of the period. For the parlor game, children would sit in a circle with the "hunter" in the middle, passing a slipper secretly about until, according to William Clarke's *The Boy's Own Book* (1861 edition), "the slipper is found in the possession of any one in the circle, by the player

who is hunting it"; at that point, "the party on whom it is so found takes the latter player's place" (51).

7 The game of *Happy Families*, still played today, produced many nineteenth century knockoffs, including J.W. Spear & Sons' *Merry Families* (circa 1905) and Thomas De La Rue & Co.'s *Cheery Families* (circa 1893). It even inspired a late twentieth century children's picture book series by Allan Ahlberg. For more discussion of the game and later picture book series, see my "Oh, Golly, What a Happy Family!"

8 See, for example, A.C. Maxfield's *Popular Games for Evening Parties* (30–31) and *The Games Book for Boys and Girls* (91). Certain forfeits and games like "Postman's Knock" also, of course, raise concerns regarding consent.

9 The idea of the "Stool of Repentance" was popular in games of the period: an image of such a stool is centrally located on *The Game of Success* as well.

10 Robin Hood-themed games abounded at the end of the nineteenth century and also include George S. Parker's *Ivanhoe* (1886), based on Sir Walter Scott's 1820 novel, and McLoughlin Brothers' *The Bugle Horn, or Robin Hood and His Merry Men* (circa 1890).

11 An irony is that the *Halma* figures defended by the book's child protagonists against the sloth, and the *Halma* game Nesbit in general defends in *Wings and the Child*, are probably actually products of U.S. invention. Though often thought of as British, *Halma* seems to have been created around 1883 by two U.S. men, George Howard Monks and Thomas Hill, though it is likely based on an earlier British game, the circa 1854 *Hoppity*.

2 Never and always a woman

Citizenship, croquet, and the nineteenth century growing girl

In March 1898, as the Spanish-American war was beginning to unfold and in the midst of a craze for national, patriotic, and rivalry games explored in the previous chapter, *The World* newspaper published its own patriotic games for subscribers to cut out, paste onto pasteboard, and play. For the Sunday, 6 March edition this game was the "Historic Game of the Life of Washington," titled "Patriotic—Game of Washington—Entertaining" in the adjoining article which doubled as game instructions (16). The following week, Sunday, 13 March, saw the printing of the "Historical Game of the Life of Abraham Lincoln," where players, its accompanying article/instructions title and subtitle indicate, "Follow the Fortunes of 'Uncle Abe'" as "Here's a Game for Americans, Young or Old, That Will Amuse and Educate" (16). The games certainly stay true to their didactic intent as each outlines biographical events for its respective former president. Each game has notable differences in play: the George Washington game involves using a spinner and moving game pieces along a path marked by circles while the Abraham Lincoln game is propelled by the tossing of improvised "dice" (marked and unmarked sides of buttons tossed in a cup), in response to which game pieces are moved in a weaving pattern to the right and left. Yet a shared feature of the games is a divided board, with each player having a symmetrical "side" on which to play/move. Since each side is the same, whichever player makes it from "birth" to "death" (Mount Vernon Tomb or Ford's Theatre attendance) on his or her side first "wins." The result is a game limited to two players where the very idea of equality and rivalry are exaggeratedly illustrated.

Notions of rivalry and equality also spill over to the topic that takes up a fascinatingly equal amount of article space on the page offering the Abraham Lincoln game: "America Will Soon Lead the Styles," subtitled "We Copy from the Foreigners Now, but They'll Copy from Us Before Long" (16). The article begins with the pronouncement, "the time is not far distant when American dress will be as distinctive and worthy of imitation as the French fashions are today" (16). As a rationale for this pronouncement, "gradually," the article suggests, "we are finding out that many of our own countrywomen have original ideas in regard to personal adornment equal in beauty and chic to those which come to us from across the water" and that "it only remains for us to install a leader of fashion" (16). Here lies the rub, however, for "in this democratic country such an institution"—a fashion leader, apparently— "is well nigh impossible. We must look to a class, not to an individual, for inspiration" (16). In its commentary on the mass—designated a bit peculiarly as "class"—nature of democracy, the article turns to the "theatrical" for the U.S.' fashion glory, to the actresses who now "must be attired faultlessly" (16). To give weight to its topic, the article insists that "the choice of dress is not a thing to be lightly considered and relegated to the chance of odd moments" for "what we accomplish in the world is due greatly to personal influence, and this is gained in large degree by the impression made by personal appearance" (16). Quickly, then, an article on style juxtaposed with a national, patriotic game of "Great Men" turns to considerations of democracy, rivalry, and "good citizenship" for women.

An irony, of course, is that women of the period in the U.S. and Britain could not actually be citizens. They were, in Courtney Weikle-Mills' phrase, "imaginary citizens" until accorded full suffrage later in the twentieth century. As such, in representations they were at times imbued with seeming traits of "good citizenship" even as the limits of that citizenship also break forth in those representations, as when the article on style makes nods to democracy but recognizes that for women citizenship (and/or "what we accomplish in this world") is confined to "personal influence," supposedly including, of course, influence over those male relatives and friends who could vote. Beginning with an exploration of girls' fiction from the last quarter of the nineteenth century and the first few decades of the twentieth century, followed by an analysis of croquet and its rendering by some of the era's most prominent authors for youth, this chapter notes the contradictory portrayals of girls as problematic players and impossible creatures. In line with Claudia Nelson's extended study of the nineteenth century phenomenon of, as her book title elucidates, *Precocious Children and Childish Adults*, girls in the texts I explore are typically and paradoxically "old girls," characters who experience "age inversion," which Nelson discerns, "even in the works of a single author . . . may have radically different valances inflected by factors that include gender, social class, and the larger themes of the surrounding text" (180). Seeking "to illuminate" "how and to what extent the idea of age as a construct . . . was accepted by writers from the mid-nineteenth century up to the Great War," Nelson concludes that "the idea that childhood as a psychological condition could be ended, prolonged, or restored, deliberately or inadvertently, via outside human agency is clearly one that circulated widely in the nineteenth century" (179). Not ever to be fully citizens—unlike the hybrid boys persistently marked as incomplete citizens-in-training suggested in my next chapter—girls in texts of the time are both in need of rearing to ensure their value as adult nurturing caretakers and as fully adult as they ever will be, with regards to citizenship expectations. In other words, as an outgrowth of such conflicting sentiments, girls' fiction frequently presents female child protagonists who, like many of the children in texts Nelson examines, are preternaturally old, but who are taught throughout the pages of the text to be more "childlike"—or more "appropriately" childlike, generally within the prescriptions of gender—and therefore have their childhood "restored" by being more or differently "playful" or channeling their "playfulness" into nurturing, caring responsibilities for the benefits of male relatives (aka, actual or able to become actual citizens). Such channeling is especially prominent in the discourse surrounding croquet, which captured controversial attention in the 1860s and thereby secured the attention of notable writers—particularly Charlotte Yonge, Louisa May Alcott, and Lewis Carroll—whose works, even as they point to the larger cultural unease incited by croquet's (and girls') appearance, play, and ultimate potential, seek to critique and rehabilitate the sport just as girls' fiction sought to rehabilitate girls, fictional and otherwise, for "womanly duty." As this chapter will strive to trace, considerations of female responsibilities for good citizenship at the end of the nineteenth and beginning of the twentieth centuries echo and re-frame fraught discussions regarding playful girls and women from the 1860s. In both later and earlier (and in-between) accounts, at stake were women's/girls' places—roles, influences, duty—and potentials as family members, players, and "citizens."

"A real child instead of a sharp old woman": Becoming a woman by becoming a girl

Following its consideration of "across the water" rivalry, democracy, and senses of women's good "citizenship" as "what we accomplish in this world is due greatly to personal influence," the Sunday, 13 March 1898 article paired with the Abraham Lincoln game in *The World* naturally glances to Britain and imperial "family" legacy:

> A few years ago it was said that the American women were given to extreme ornateness in dress. Our English cousins were wont to laugh at the overdressed American. The tables now seemed to be turned.
>
> The American girl walks the streets in severely simple tailor-made gown, while the English woman seems to have turned her thoughts to feathers, furbelows and flounces. This is especially notable in travelling. Last summer in an English first-class railway carriage there were two Americans and four Englishwomen. Our countrywomen were attired in neat, severely plain but exceedingly well-made gowns, with plain travelling hats. The English women wore gowns of silk and satin, trimmed with lace, while their hats were

gorgeous with artificial flowers and drooping features. It was morning and the ride was a long one.

(16)

In this description, which seems to heap praise as well as criticism on
both English and American "cousins," the idea of the "tables" being
"turned" and the length of the morning ride (taken in tandem with the
title and subtitle of the article) seem to sway fashion in favor of the U.S.,
despite the "severe" plainness of the U.S. outfits. The perhaps frivolity
evident in the alliterative English thoughts of "feathers, furbelows, and
flounces" may indicate this as well. Strikingly, however, while the English
are consistently labelled women, there is a slippage in the description of
the Americans, who at one point crystallize into "the American girl."
Compared to Britain, the U.S. is still young.

This slippage suggests other revelations, too. On the page prior to that of
the game of a "Great Man," Lincoln, and fitting in with the article on U.S.
versus French and British styles on its back, is an intriguing advertisement-
article that, like the game on its opposite side, essentially takes up the entire page. Its competing primary headlines read "Newest Golf and Bicycle
Costumes from Photographs Made Especially for the Sunday World" and
"Styles for the Athletic Girl." Despite titular emphasis on "the athletic
girl" and statements such as "the '98 bicycle girl is a creature of brilliant
colors," the article-advertisement's description of the clothing items shown
primarily emphasize "women": "No woman on earth has the strength
to ride in a heavy skirt," "the mooted question with women is whether
a circular or divided skirt looks the best," and "the new bicycle hat is
quite the prettiest that has yet fallen to the wheel-women" (15). In these
descriptions—as in fiction of the time—female figures are simultaneously
girl and woman, hybrid and yet *not* hybrid figures in ways that were expected for boys at the time, as I explore in the next chapter with Rudyard
Kipling and Robert Baden-Powell's boy scouts. Indeed, despite the sense
of critics like Don Randall that for G. Stanley Hall in his ground-breaking
Adolescence (1904) females were "perpetual adolescents," it is notable
how rarely female adolescence was allowed to permeate the pages of girls'
literature of the period (10). As scholars like Anne Scott MacLeod have
noted, "the characteristic girls' novel centered on heroines of about twelve
to sixteen years old, girls who stood just at the end of childhood and on
the verge of young womanhood," yet female adolescence is often curtailed
in nineteenth century girls' fiction, with protagonists suddenly becoming
disabled—bedridden with back paralysis or leg injuries in many novels
or be-spelled into deep sleep in fairy tales—just as they reach the cusp of
adulthood, or, really, upon adolescence (14). As MacLeod expresses it,
"how guilelessly and yet how plainly these authors drew the analogy between physical crippling and the limitations a girl faced as she approached
womanhood!" (21). Girls in fiction of the time are generally fortuitously

healed or magically awakened once they learn the often hard lesson of "womanly" propriety, leaving off "girlish" headlong behaviors to adopt nurturing and self-sacrificing tasks of supporting the men (fathers, brothers, uncles, etc.) in their lives, or once they can be safely married. They "discover," as Rose Campbell, the protagonist in Louisa May Alcott's *Eight Cousins* (1875), emphasizes to her uncle guardian in the book's concluding chapter, "what girls are made for. ... To take care of boys" (260). In other words, adolescence itself is thwarted even in texts with seemingly adolescent girl characters, as those characters are portrayed initially as girls and then, in response to sudden tragedy, as women learning and living after surviving abrupt, life-altering challenge(s). Even in texts where such a stark transition isn't offered—in texts, for example, that follow their protagonists for a shorter period of time, say a year or two—a competitive girl/woman discourse and slippage is pronounced. Indeed, time and again in nineteenth and early twentieth century girls' fiction on both sides of the Atlantic, girls/women are portrayed as incredibly childlike or as mini adults, and contradictorily often both at the same time.[1] Apparently without sensing the irony, often too the thrust of the tales is to foster girls' advent into womanhood by teaching them to be children, "restoring" their childhood, generally through play.

The introduction of Rose Campbell in *Eight Cousins*, for instance, focuses on Rose's depression after the loss of her father and her resulting un-childlike ways, with her great aunts despairing that "she was unlike any child they had ever seen, and they felt very much as if they had the care of a low-spirited butterfly" (2). Their attempts to cheer her fail miserably as the "odd child" (3) is simply not taken with childish (and at times decidedly gendered "girlish") allures: sweets, dolls, playmates, and even boarding school independence all fail. Presented with "a spicy retreat, rich in all the 'goodies' that children love," "Rose seemed to care little for these toothsome temptations" and when one great-aunt "planned a doll's wardrobe that would have won the heart of even an older child," "Rose took little interest" and was "caught" "wiping tears away," while the attempt at a playmate was "the worst failure of all" and the aunts earlier gave in to her "pathetic petition" to delay a return to school (2; 38). Despite her unchildlike behaviors, however, the text persistently labels her a "little girl" (8) or "little daughter" (7) and even has her appearance in the opening chapter highlight her smallness as she enters and leaves the kitchen by way of the "china-closet" (4) slide, which was "cut for the admission of bouncing Christmas turkeys and puddings" and therefore "plenty large enough for a slender girl" (9). Solidifying this view of her as a small child/girl, upon meeting her, one of her cousins refers to her as a "little thing" (12). The cousin's remark, however, produces some revealing results: an emphatic cry of "I'm thirteen and a half, though I *do* look small," a cry put forth on behalf of "indignation at this insult to her newly acquired teens" (12). The "little girl" is actually an adolescent, a teenager, barely still "a child" at all.

In fact, despite the text's emphasis on Rose's status as "little girl," the problem she poses is one of being too adult—and so, throughout the pages of the book, to be a successful woman, Rose must learn to be child-like. This lesson her guardian begins immediately by, for example, pooh-poohing her notion that she is "too old to play with boys" (24) and that she is "too old for running" despite her boarding-school teacher's assertion that "it was not ladylike for girls in their teens" (47). Through her uncle's guidance, Rose finds herself delighting in such things as playing with her boy cousins and taking a daily run or playing "a lively game of battledore and shuttle-cock" when prevented from running by bad weather (260), and excited at the prospect of skating and sledding (215). She, in other words, recovers her (mental as well as physical) health by "recovering" her childishness, a fact emphasized when her guardian, a doctor, presents his evidence to her aunts at the end of his year's experiment at child-rearing. Rose is described as "happy now, being out nearly all day" in child-worthy exploits and her improving success is marked by two photographs provided by her uncle (264). The first, taken a year earlier and before her uncle's intervention, is acknowledged to be "very like her when she came," with, tellingly, "quite her sad, unchildlike expression and thin little face" (264). The photograph of her at the present moment is noted to be "a 'charming likeness'" "and a striking contrast to the first one, for it was a blooming, smiling face, full of girlish spirit and health, with no sign of melancholy" despite "thoughtful" "soft eyes" and "lines about the lips" that "betrayed a sensitive nature" (264–265). Within the space of a year, assisted by play in particular, Rose changes from "unchildlike" to "full of girlish spirit and health."

Notably, in other words, joining with her return to childishness is a reinforcement of her gender, the "girlishness" of her "girlish spirit and health" (265). Just as she must learn to be more child-like, Rose must learn her gendered duties, which primarily surround taking care of her male relations and learning to exercise her feminine "influence." She must take what MacLeod explains was "the bargain offered nineteenth-century women: influence in exchange for freedom; a role as 'inspiration' in place of real power; gratitude and affection from family rather than worldly reward or renown" as "woman's sphere was moral rather than intellectual, domestic rather than worldly; her power was indirect; her contribution to the world was through husband and children, her reward their love and respect" (4). Agreeing that she should "have a trade," Rose's guardian sees gendered responsibilities "a necessary part of" Rose's "training," once she is "well and strong" (171). In particular, he transforms the concept of trade she proposes into an "accomplishment" that is

one of the most beautiful as well as useful of all the arts a woman can learn. Not so romantic, perhaps, as singing, painting, writing, or teaching, even, but one that makes many people happy and comfortable, and home the sweetest place in the world.

(170–171)

In short, he turns masculine-inflected notions of "trade" into the more acceptable and conventional idea of feminine "accomplishment" and exhorts her to learn "housekeeping" (172). To encourage her in the womanly endeavor, he sends her to her great-aunt to learn the craft, with the understanding that the great-aunt "is not elegant, but genuinely good, and so beloved and respected that there will be universal mourning for her when her place is empty" as "no one can fill it" (172). In this way, Rose is indentured to one who will safeguard her way on the path to womanly "citizenship" through personal influence for her Great-Aunt Peace, heart-broken in love upon the death of her would-be husband on their wedding day, is a model of womanly personal influence:

> for thirty years she had lived on, fading slowly, but cheerful, busy, and full of interest in all that went on in the family, especially the joys and sorrows of the young girls growing up about her. To them she was adviser, confidante, and friend in all their tender trials and delights. A truly beautiful woman, with her silvery hair, tranquil face, and an atmosphere of repose about her that soothed whoever came to her!
>
> (37)[2]

To acquire her good womanly "citizenship" of personal influence, Rose must retrieve her health with her childhood while also learning to serve and influence those around her, especially her male relatives.[3] Much of the text shows her service to her seven, all boy, cousins, and her growing awareness and use of her "influence" over them to help them undertake such things as bravely and "manfully" enduring the challenges of illness to keep from becoming blind (121) and abstaining from cigar-smoking (182–184). The advantages of this service are clearly conveyed in the text: agreeing with the healthy orphan serving-girl, Phebe, that "girls had better learn to take care of themselves first," Rose's uncle also accedes to Rose's counterargument, "that's because *she* hasn't got seven boy cousins," by clarifying, "she is right nevertheless, Rosy, and so are you, for the two things go together, and in helping seven lads you are unconsciously doing much to improve one lass" (260).[4] Importantly, too, the advantages of her service and influence with regard to citizenship are confidently asserted: when Rose's role in the cigar-smoking abstinence campaign comes to light,

> the elders were well pleased, and Rose received a vote of thanks, which made her feel as if she had done a service to her country, as

she had, for every boy who grows up free from bad habits bids fair to make a good citizen.

(184)

By becoming more appropriately "childish," primarily through play, and learning and adhering to her prescribed gendered position, the never-to-be-full-citizen Rose is lauded as instrumental in creating ideal to-be-full-citizens out of her boy cousins.

Writing even closer to the end of the century, and at the entry of the twentieth, Frances Hodgson Burnett offers similarly too-old girl protagonists redeemed through recognition of womanly nurturing and childish play, figures who often also have to learn to be more childlike, if not to be actual children. *A Little Princess* (1905) opens with its description of Sara Crewe as possessing "a queer old-fashioned thoughtfulness in her big eyes" and her being "such a little girl that one did not expect to see such a look on her small face. It was an odd look for a child of twelve, and Sara Crewe was only seven" (5). Sara, moreover,

> was always dreaming and thinking odd things and could not herself remember any time when she had not been thinking things about grown-up people and the world they belonged to. She felt as if she had lived a long, long time.
>
> (5)[5]

Her saving graces—from the vantage points of childhood, girlishness, and femininity—are her love of dolls and her nurturing, "motherly young person" (29) tendencies, which lead her to be an "adopted mother" for Lottie and to provide emotional and other support for Ermengarde and Becky and eventually for her male guardian just as she provided nurturing and bolstering companionship for her "boyish" father (12). In Burnett's *The Secret Garden* (1911), Mary Lennox is consistently described as an "old woman": she is proclaimed to be like one early on by Mrs. Medlock (14), whose pronouncement is soon echoed by Ben Weatherstaff (32) and Martha Sowerby, who calls her a "queer, old-womanish thing" (54). Weatherstaff even goes so far as to suggest, when Mary deigns to do something coaxing (befriending a robin) or playful (skipping rope) that "tha' said that as nice an' human as if tha' was a real child instead of a sharp old woman" (32) and "p'rhaps tha' art a young 'un, after all, an p'raps tha's got child's blood in thy veins instead of sour buttermilk" (55). A good portion of the book seems aimed at teaching Mary to be—and transforming her into—a good girl child, one who can make actual gardens grow and nurture her cousin Colin. She needs to learn to transfer her attention—and incipient but inherent nurturing skills—to the domestic realm and her family life, to England and her cousin and uncle-guardian rather than to India and the imperial realm of boys (hinted at more in the next chapter). As such, her gardens fail to grow in India but flourish in England; she transfers, as Jerry Phillips suggests with the idea of "a rajah in Yorkshire" (180), her "imperious Indian voice" (*The Secret Garden* 32) to her male cousin; and the girl who "wonder[s] if" her uncle "had sent a doll, and also wonder[s] what she should do with it if he had" (122) learns to play with a skipping rope and to run races (with Colin winning, of course) rather than to lose herself in the great manor's portrait gallery of dead ancestors or secrete herself in the English manor's "Indian room," playing with its ivory elephants and native mice (189). Indeed, by text's end, she offers these imperial and exploratory entertainments to Colin and with him "they saw more rooms and made more discoveries than Mary had made on her first pilgrimage" (189).

Juxtaposition of adult-like tendencies and child-producing play appear again and again in children's literature of the era. In his own playful if at times flippant analysis of play and the works of J.M. Barrie and Lewis Carroll, James Kincaid observes this tendency in two of the age's most famous girl characters, Alice of Wonderland and Wendy in Neverland: "Alice, just like Wendy, wants so badly to grow up, she more or less is grown-up now, probably was born grown-up" (288). Tellingly, he suggests, "as a consequence, she is a great menace to the child" (288). Detecting the alignment in these texts of childlike behaviors and play with adult gendered prescriptions, Kincaid hints at the texts' "skillful channeling of resentment and danger into the feminine and maternal" (286) and darkly argues that "Wendy comes into the play [*Peter Pan* (1904)] as an intruder, a disturber of the peace and play, sets up a school, and is last seen on a broomstick, where she should have been all along" (285). I will turn to Alice more shortly with a consideration of croquet, but J.M. Barrie is certainly clear about Wendy's maturity, domesticity, and motherliness in *Peter and Wendy* (1911): not only does she delight in being "just a nice motherly person" despite being "only a little girl" with "no real experience" (65) who rather literally sets up house and housekeeping in Neverland and later engages herself and her female descendants for spring cleaning (152–153), but "she was one of the kind that likes to grow up" and "in the end she grew up of her own free will a day quicker than other girls" (146).

The "resentment and danger" Kincaid notes "channeled" "into the feminine and maternal" can also be read as anxiety regarding women's potential power, a consistent response to which in children's texts is to direct that potential to—or, more positively, give it free reign in—realms of domesticity, interiority, and imagination. Texts of the period typically circumscribe girls/women to the domestic sphere, dismissing play and the freedoms and power it might otherwise intimate as "merely" childlike and childish—and therefore both non-threatening and somehow more womanly. Or they insist that girls leave off boyish play (ultimately the realm of men and full citizens) to come into their own as women, as might be argued at times for Alcott's Jo March in *Little Women*

(1868), is the lesson Katy Carr must learn after her accident in Susan M. Coolidge's *What Katy Did* (1872), and is what Nelson even cites as a flaw of Dora in Charles Dickens' *David Copperfield* (1849–1850), noting that "Dora Copperfield, for instance, cannot move beyond the pleasures of play to take up her responsibilities of housekeeping and wifehood, an incapacity that directs attention to the costs of homemaking for the woman" (102). Just as frequently, texts of the period strive to mitigate—or more "appropriately" "allow"—girls' playful potential by giving it the space of the imagination. Time and again girl characters of the period—Anne Shirley of L.M. Montgomery's *Anne of Green Gables* (1908), Rebecca Randall of Kate Douglas Wiggin's *Rebecca of Sunnybrook Farm* (1903), Sara Crewe, Rose Campbell, and even Mary Lennox, Alice, and Wendy Darling—are depicted as dreamers, storytellers, writers, book-lovers, generally as highly imaginative creatures with vivid internal lives and worlds. As Alcott describes it, Rose loves

> the library where her father's books were stored. Here she read a good deal, cried a little, and dreamed many of the innocent, bright dreams in which imaginative children find such comfort and delight. This suited her better than anything else, but it was not good for her.
> (3)

Rose, like many of her female literary peers, must even learn to tame the play of her imagination. Notably, however, while their boy counterparts are given the physical world in which to play and explore, girls are given their own minds.[6] The power of their play—their power—may be cast as imaginary but it is implicitly acknowledged, as Rebecca's is in the opening pages of Wiggin's text, where readers discover that Rebecca's

> face [is] illuminated by a pair of eyes carrying such messages, such suggestions, such hints of sleeping power and insight, that one never tired of looking into their shining depths, nor of fancying that what one saw there was the reflection of one's own thought.
> (7)

That the girl child does in fact "reflect" "one's own thought" is conceded to be but a "fancy" even as the girl child's own "sleeping power" is admitted.[7]

Strategies of addressing girl power to mitigate and/or re-direct it and of conflating girlhood and womanhood often at the cost of adolescence are also on full display in nineteenth and early twentieth century gamesspace.[8] In *Pollyanna* (1913), Eleanor H. Porter created another imaginative girl-child who suffers a temporarily disabling accident (this time to bring about the too-prolonged heterosexual marriage of her aunt). Pollyanna Whittier is notorious for "the glad game," a playful activity in which she uses the powers of her invention and imagination—her mind—to transform disappointments, disadvantages, and even misfortunes into happier perspectives, something about which to be glad. In its own re-imagining of the Indian game of Pachisi (adapted as Parcheesi in the U.S. and Ludo in the U.K., with many other variants) to take advantage of the popularity of Porter's tale, Parker Brothers' *Pollyanna: The Glad Game* ("New edition" 1916) intriguingly offers its players a glimpse of the slippage and conflation of girlhood and womanhood. Illustrated in the game's "Rules for Playing" instruction booklet is a "diagram" of the game board based on an earlier edition of the game (Figure 2.1).

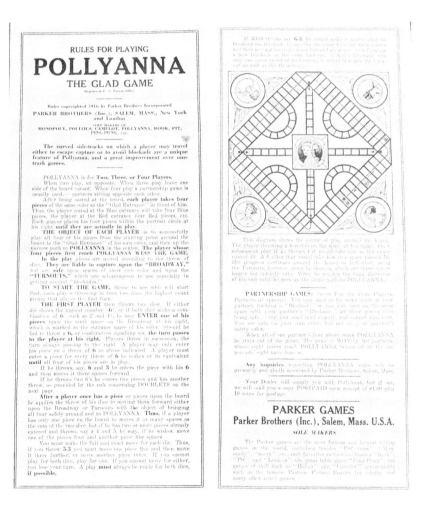

Figure 2.1 "Rules for Playing" Parker Brothers' Pollyanna: The Glad Game (1916). Courtesy, The Strong, Rochester, New York.

Featured on this diagram and the earlier edition are Aunt Polly, the servant Nancy, the homeless boy Jimmy Bean who Pollyanna befriends, and the wealthy John Pendleton (Dr. Chilton, Aunt Polly's eventual husband, is conspicuously absent). In the black and white depiction Pollyanna looks over her shoulder directly out at the game players with her long braided hair decorated with a large, childish bow. She looks, in other words, a decent approximation of an eleven-year-old, which is what she is when the text, which takes place over the course of about a year, begins (2). Jimmy in his tidy hat and hair looks like a boy, Nancy looks like a young woman (or late adolescent; she, too, looks directly out at her audience), and John Pendleton and Aunt Polly look clearly like adults, if a bit severe and foreboding with their turned or in-profile faces. The actual included full color "new edition" game board, however, uses remarkably different illustrations for its portrayals of these characters (Figure 2.2).

Figure 2.2 Parker Brothers' Pollyanna: The Glad Game (1916). Courtesy, The Strong, Rochester, New York.

In the actual game board's illustrations, John Pendleton and Aunt Polly look younger, though still adult, Nancy looks older (perhaps even the same age as Aunt Polly), and while Aunt Polly and John Pendleton maintain their turned or in-profile faces, Nancy and Jimmy have essentially switched positions, with Nancy portrayed in profile like the other "adults" and Jimmy looking directly at the players like the other "child," Pollyanna. Suddenly sporting a worn, falling apart straw hat, unkempt hair, and suspenders, the down-on-his-luck Jimmy in this depiction might well be mistaken for an earlier boy in classic U.S. children's fiction, Mark Twain's Huck Finn. Even more startlingly, clad in sleeveless pink and exchanging her bow and braid for a headband, pearls, and seemingly bob haircut, Pollyanna at the board's center seems closer in age to her Aunt Polly than to the eleven- or twelve-year-old she supposedly is in the text—indeed, in the game board depiction she seems a promising young woman or adolescent. The shift in board illustrations is puzzling but points to the ability of those in the era to see, especially in contexts of play, adolescents and young women as mere "little girls" and girl children as women—their moral, "civilizing" duties (supporting men and boys, making the best out of their lives and helping others to make the best out of theirs, being "glad" in the process, as examples) being of course ultimately the same.

Yet the insistent portrayal of Pollyanna directly gazing at players in both illustrations also serves as a reminder of incipient feminine power (rendered "childish" on the actual game board with its inclusion of a directly-gazing Jimmy), a power that is strikingly exhibited in *The World*'s 13 March 1898 advertising of bicycle and golf clothing. In addition to the article-advertisement describing the women's/girl's clothing already discussed, and the photographs of young women or adolescents wearing such clothing, the full-page spread includes a drawn illustration of bicycle and golf equipment in use (Figure 2.3).

Contrasted with the fully clothed women/girls of the photographs is an ocean shore scene of artfully rendered bare-chested and bottomed mermaids playing on a beach: one mermaid frolics surrounded by golf paraphernalia and a discarded bicycle while another manages to ride a bicycle with fins. Their long, luxuriously free hair waving in the wind, the mermaids keep their chins up and either look directly at the viewer with haunting, dark-outlined eyes or seem to revel in the pleasures attendant on bicycling. Either way their message seems clear: games- and sports-playing females are exotic spectacles, strange yet alluring specimens, teeming with sexuality and capable of siren seduction. Their appeal is manifest, women/girls as well as men/boys may be drawn to them (or to play), and they are powerful and dangerous, if not transgressive and rare (or even mythical and nonexistent), problematic and paradoxical, impossible. In this way, girls' and women's play at the turn of nineteenth and twentieth centuries echoed that of the 1860s when

Figure 2.3 "Newest Golf and Bicycle Costumes," *The World, Sunday, 13 March 1898.* Courtesy, The Strong, Rochester, New York.

croquet erupted in the quiet gardens of British houses and secured its place in literary texts. As girls' domestic fiction throughout the latter half of the nineteenth century and beginning of the twentieth sought to direct girlish power to acceptable domestic and interior realms in part by rendering play childish and thereby innocuous and by eliding at times distinctions between girlhood and womanhood even as games, play, and literature were caught up in senses of national (if not gender) rivalry, so croquet, broadcasting strongly through its very popularity the allure and promising power of women's play, found itself caught up in a similar discourse of sexuality and rivalry and muted by strongly-felt needs to de-threaten it, render its revolutionary potential equally innocuous.

"A bowl of claret-cup on one side and a girl on the other": The rise and fall of croquet

In 1897, Mrs. Mary Whitley, in her *Every Girl's Book of Sport, Occupation, and Pastime*, observed this about croquet:

> The girls of the present day are rather inclined to look down on the game, as it requires neither strength nor agility, the two most coveted qualities of the present generation. But it has its advantages, it is easy to learn: men, women, and children can play on equal terms: "grandpapa" can play, as he has neither to stoop nor run: the curate can play without being called to account. . . . It does not make you hot, and you can take care of your complexion. It is not dangerous: did any one ever hear of a fatal accident at croquet? [sic].
>
> (266)

Ironically enough, the answer to Mrs. Whitley's supposed rhetorical query is "yes." The question itself shows a rather surprising ignorance of a text by a then well-known author of books for children and adults, and certainly for girls, Charlotte Mary Yonge's *The Clever Women of the Family* (1865). In that novel, a prominent female character does just what Whitley finds ludicrous: she trips over a croquet hoop and dies. The result, according to Georgina Battiscombe, is that when "Bessie Keith falls over a croquet hoop . . . and immediately produces a baby," Yonge betrays an "ignorance of the connection between birth and sex" (qtd. in Simmons 12). But the potential danger wasn't confined to fiction: in 1871, over twenty-five years before Mrs. Whitley's own summary of the sport, a games manual observed that

> croquêt is so fascinating a game, that the players can seldom cease their play with a failing light, and will persist even after dusk. ... In consequence, the players cannot direct their stroke with any certainty, and moreover they are always tripping over the hoops. We have seen ladies suffer really severe falls from these dark-coloured hoops, and always advise our friends to have their own painted white.
>
> (*Modern Out-Door Amusements* 144)

Jon Sterngass corroborates such concern in his discussion of croquet and cheating at the game in the U.S., observing that "manufacturers even produced [croquet] sets with candle-sockets attached to wickets to facilitate night games" (400).

Overall, the tone of Mrs. Whitley's late-in-the-century defense of croquet, in contrast to the anxiety over it displayed by the 1871 manual and Yonge's earlier novel, showcases a bemused acceptance. This acceptance was perhaps indicative of the era, but not necessarily of the sport. Spurred on by enthusiasts like the editors of *The Field*, who in 1867 admitted that they "personally devoted considerable time and trouble, as well as occupied space which could ill be spared in the columns of this journal, with the view of encouraging the progress of the game of croquet" ("The Game of Croquet and Its Rules" 349), croquet first surfaced in England in the 1850s and 1860s. It took fashionable circles by storm in the 1860s and 1870s, and then suddenly disappeared, replaced in large part by the new sport of lawn tennis. When interest in croquet rekindled in the 1890s, in an era of New Women bicyclists and lawn tennis fanatics, croquet found itself made into a grandmother sport. It found itself, in other words, almost immediately antiquated, transformed into a "safe" old-fashioned game, one that didn't—unlike New Women free-roaming bicyclists, with fins or not—threaten domesticity or women's supposedly established positions. Having in part given birth to young women's appetite for and acceptance of sports, and thereby helping to make possible the rise in women's sports, including the very lawn tennis and bicycling that usurped it, croquet found itself in a position where its former power, pull, and potential were curtailed, where the accomplishments it enabled weren't (and still aren't) always recognized. Mocked by later commentators, croquet was rendered primarily suitable in accounts like Mrs. Whitley's for children, the elderly, and the clergy. Considered gentle, conservative, and non-controversial, croquet within a few short decades of its arrival had already been given the "mere pastime" status generally accorded to it still today, over a century later. All in all, a detractor of the sport writing as late as 1902 sums up well its critics' position throughout the nineteenth century: "a bowl of claret-cup on one side and a girl on the other may have their attractions, but they do not constitute a game" (Gordon 146).

Recent studies on Victorian and Edwardian sport have done little to disrupt such views of croquet as a quaint pastime or silly vehicle for courtship. Sterngass' article is an exception and even it focuses primarily on refuting the perception that women players focused more on good etiquette than competition. For the most part, when croquet receives a passing nod in critical discussions, its recognition is often undermined. Like Sterngass, for example, Kathleen E. McCrone accords croquet its revolutionary status, noting, for instance, that

> while necessitating neither strenuous exertion nor an immediate reform of female dress or images, croquet was more than a charming leisure activity. Played well the game required a good deal of skill;

and it was of considerable importance to the physical emancipation of women, for it effected a major change in the relationship of women to sport.

(*Playing the Game* 156)

Despite this admission of "considerable importance to the physical emancipation of women" in a book titled *Playing the Game: Sport and the Physical Emancipation of English Women, 1870–1914*, however, McCrone only devotes a couple of pages to croquet. More typical is analysis akin to that of Jennifer A. Hargreaves, who suggests that in addition to "adopting a spectator role as members of an admiring female audience watching the physical antics of men," "women were absorbed into the leisure sphere by the provision for them of 'gentle, respectable games,' eminently suited to the 'weaker sex,' and exemplified by croquet and its indoor derivatives like 'Parlour Croquet,' 'Carpet Croquet,' or 'Table Croquet'" (133). McCrone herself suggests that 1860s women's sports such as croquet suffered from "severe constraints," and—with reference to article titles from the period that consistently combine and conflate women and girls—that girls of the 1880s on were the truly revolutionary ones:

> Whereas a little walking, croquet and gentle calisthenics were thought sufficient exercise for the young lady of the 1860s, her grand-daughter could run, bicycle, climb mountains, play tennis at Wimbledon, golf at St. Andrews, hockey for England, and any number of team and individual games at college and school, and then she could read about so doing in features on "The Sportswoman" or "The Outdoor Girl" in respectable periodicals and newspapers. Despite prejudice, discrimination and restrictions, the lure of sport was obviously irresistible to some Victorian girls.
>
> ("Play up!" 119–120)

It is in the 1880s, rather than the 1860s, when this "lure of sport" "despite prejudice, discrimination, and restrictions" supposedly manifests itself, a belief that effectively undermines the strides against prejudices and other difficulties faced by those croquet-playing daughters of the 1860s who paved the way for their 1880s granddaughters.

These critical views and omissions today belie the revolutionary potential of croquet McCrone in *Playing the Game* and Sterngass rightly point towards, and debates over women's duties for good citizenship and as wives, mothers, daughters, and sisters that surfaced in periodicals, novels, and other writings of the 1860s that grappled with the idea of croquet mallet-wielding women and girls. As one of the first and few Victorian sports that allowed women and men to mix on seemingly equal terms, and in an often private, domestic space that at the same time was a place of acceptable public encounter (the garden), croquet became a complicated nexus, fraught with often contradictory cultural meanings. Such contradictions were obvious to critics, commentators, and writers in the 1860s, and are on display prominently in the works of three notable writers of the period, Yonge's texts, including *The Clever Woman of the Family*, Lewis Carroll's *Alice* books, and Louisa May Alcott's *Little Women*, as well as in larger public and societal discussions. Taken together, these books and their larger discourse use croquet to advocate for national notions of female (almost) citizenship dependent on "womanly" duty even as they offer critiques of manners, morals, and social order frequently dependent on "womanly" ideals.

"Try to make a good hit": Croquet as womanly duty in the works of Charlotte Yonge

In September 1862, "Henrietta," responding to articles and series such as "A Letter to My Grown-Up Granddaughters" and "Women's Work in London," wrote a letter to the editor of *The Monthly Packet*, an Anglican periodical begun and edited by Charlotte Yonge. In the letter, she not only entreats parents to allow young women like her to visit the poor but also pleads with those of her generation not to give district visiting a bad name (332–335). The letter provoked a flurry of replies, with related correspondence appearing in the periodical for nearly two years, at least until March 1864. In those responses many charges against older adults, young women, and society appear. Among the most notable is a charge of "too much of everything" put forth by "Mary," an "elder sister," in May 1863. Mary's letter documents the "perpetual motion" of the lives of young people and comments tellingly that "even our favourite amusement consists in knocking an unfortunate ball from one resting place to another; an unwitting sarcasm on the restless spirit of the age" (555–557). Continuing the charge, Mary complains, girls

> needlessly idle one afternoon after another in never-ending croquet; then, according as they have time or not, for half an hour drop in to evening service. Surely one's greatest earthly friend would little value a chance of half an hour's visit as a rest from croquet.
>
> (558)

Altogether, the discussion of young women's work that appears in the correspondence pages reflects similar discussions on display in articles and stories throughout the periodical: a generational divide between what "Henrietta" in January 1863 refers to as "Young England" (110) and older England and a pervading sense that middle and upper class women must be trained to succeed as wives and mothers by first accepting submission as sisters and daughters. Women's work and play must come second to that submission, second to obedience to parents, elders, and home obligations.[9]

In this context, it is startling at first to read an October 1863 letter by "Velocipede," a self-proclaimed "fast young lady" (444). Her letter directly targets "any Mary or Mona [another respondent], or any other elderly female" in its defense of such pursuits as croquet. Despite believing that it is "really and intrinsically rather a slow game, and only tolerable when the party is a very large and pleasant one which plays it," she insists that her elders would do the same, "if they had a large party of stupid people to amuse" (445). In her excitement over the sport, Velocipede escalates her comments to italicized prose: "What a relief it is, one must experience to appreciate, to produce the hoops and the mallets" and give "at such small expense occupation for everybody for a whole afternoon. So I say, *long live croquet, and may those who object to it never feel the want of it*" (445). After rejoicing gleefully in the merits of croquet, however, Velocipede pauses to give consideration to the idea of feminine duty and echoes much of the other discourse and correspondence of *The Monthly Packet*: "I know how much more moral I should be, if, instead of walking eight miles a day round and round on a croquet lawn, I went four miles there and back to teach in a village school" (446). This is something she cannot do, she insists, for even if she were interested in doing so, it would not fit in with her relatives' views (446). Rather than playing a "dowdy bonnet"-wearing "Lady Bountiful," her first duty is to please her family, which includes helping her mother entertain visitors and entering into her brothers' pursuits (446). Furthermore, she argues, a young lady of her generation must be "fast" and know things, or she "shall have nothing to answer to [her] neighbour's conversation at dinner, should he happen to be a country squire who reads the Times [sic]" (447). To cap all, Velocipede points out at her letter's close that she is still quite marriageable and in fact is engaged to be married. Croquet has not, in other words, ruined her status as an ideal woman: she is still a dutiful daughter and devoted soon-to-be wife and may even be those things because of such pursuits as croquet. The promotion of leisure, and even croquet, Yonge allows to be suggested in her periodical, is part of women's familial and societal obligations. Far from dampening the spirits away from fun, games, and laughter, Yonge encourages them, reinforcing through the letters she publishes Mona's desire for girls not to "forswear" such things as croquet but to have a "mind" that "is well-balanced" so that they "never get into the noisy reckless ways of talking and acting" (219–220).

Attempts to render Yonge's views of pleasure, and most notably croquet, as indicating mere moral danger—as the few critical considerations of *The Clever Woman of the Family* tend to do and as even Velocipede does[10]—actually offer a great disservice to Yonge and her works, which are steeped in the period's discussion of women's duty and its anxiety about women's play, and prominently croquet. Although *The Clever Woman of the Family* presents a detailed and frequently dismissive treatment of croquet, using it as the symbolic sin and deathly punishment of the flirtatious and frivolous Bessie Keith, Yonge in fact encourages the pleasures of games-playing and entertainment by not only allowing promotion of croquet to mark passages of *The Monthly Packet*,[11] but by offering many favorable examples of sports- and games-playing throughout her works and even in *The Clever Woman of the Family* itself. In her depictions of croquet and other amusing pastimes, Yonge defies modern readers by refusing consistency, by refusing to be just the serious, conservative, homely, and presumably anti-pleasure writer of stereotype she is often considered to be. In such a refusal, she may produce bouts of laughter such as with croquet-hoop-death, but laughter, like games and other amusements, is not something she necessarily discouraged—in moderation. In this way, she strives to reconcile the reality of her readership—girls and young women attracted to pursuits such as croquet—with cultural concern about that readership's role in society and especially the home.

Yonge's encouragement of games-playing, and her insistence on moderation, are most evident in a chapter on "Amusement" she offers in her treatise *Womankind* (1877). In that chapter, Yonge gives the following anecdote to illustrate her views on playful pastimes: "We all know the story of St. Carlo Borromeo when he was asked what he would do if the last trumpet should sound when he was playing at billiards: 'Try to make a good hit,' he replied" (122). "If the thing be innocent recreation," Yonge elaborates, "do it as well as possible, and enjoy it without shame or fear" (122). Moreover, she contends, "play or pleasure of some kind is wholesome for the average human being" and "there are pleasures enhanced by numbers" and "duties of friendship and neighbourhood that ought to bring people together" (120). As long as play combines with neighborly sorts of "duties" and does not become an obsession, it is to be encouraged, and especially so, she suggests, if those with greater means—such as "large rooms" and "gardens"—are able to use those means to "set the example as to style, time, and manner" (120). She concedes that "some people there will be always reckless of anything but pleasure and excitement; and if the whole management be left to these, evil will be sure to accrue to the more undecided characters," but these "may be kept straight by the example and good management of those who can carry a sense of duty into the providing and partaking of amusement" (120).

In line with such views, the pages of Yonge's novels are filled with characters having fun, and prominent among all of the examples of fun is croquet. Indeed, when a girl's or young woman's duty is the entertaining of visitors and the obligations of maintaining family and social status, Yonge describes croquet in her novels in accepting terms. In *The Trial* (1864), a sequel to *The Daisy Chain* (1856) which continues the May family story and documents the struggles faced by a young man falsely convicted of murder before and after his innocence is known, the May family finds itself early on confronted with the two new sisters-in-law of one of its members and nothing to do with them. The sisters-in-law propose croquet, but there are no croquet sets available at the Mays' home. Distraught at what to do with her guests and with "dread of the afternoon" upon her, Ethel May is relieved when her brother Tom appears and proposes taking the guests off to play croquet in the public gardens (123). Ethel herself does not play croquet as Tom insists their father needs her, but Tom does not spare their younger sister, Gertrude, from the duty of playing. When Gertrude tries to avoid her social obligations by disappearing into the drawing-room, Tom follows her and orders her out to play croquet, telling her quite bluntly that "it is time to have done being a spoilt baby" (123). Rather than let her elder sister be fatigued by entertaining the guests and the exhaustions of playing the game given the physical dexterity it requires, Tom insists that Gertrude must step up and relieve Ethel of this "duty" (123).[12] To undertake her responsibilities as a woman, and like so many in girls' fiction to follow over the course of the next several decades, Gertrude must play. This same sense of duty in croquet-playing marks the portrayal of Lady Kate Caergwent, originally of *Countess Kate* (1862), in *The Pillars of the House* (1873). Described in terms reminiscent of later imaginative girls, as "an odd girl . . . very clever at headwork, but curiously childish about anything real," Lady Caergwent is also shy, and prone to "shrivel up as if a stranger was a blight" (364–365). All of this makes worse the additional "unlucky thing" from which she suffers: "no dexterity of hand," which makes her "hate" "all games that turn on it, like croquet" (366). Since social gatherings are the countess' duty, there is no way to avoid croquet, "for there is a garden-party to all the neighbours every Tuesday in the summer, and there would be quite a fuss among the natives if Lady Caergwent did not show herself" (366). The outcome is similar to Tom's stepping in to talk with Gertrude and Rose Campbell's uncle-guardian insisting that she run and play, even with the boy cousins she, also a "bashful child" (*Eight Cousins* 11) fears, "for having lived alone with her invalid father, she knew nothing of boys and considered them a species of wild animal" (8). Lady Caergwent's uncle makes her promise not to hide away at social events. So play croquet Lady Caergwent does— badly, and obliged to have others help her. While Gertrude, like Rose and other girls in later children's/girls' fiction, needs to develop such things as the "softness" of femininity (*The Trial* 161), Lady Caergwent's lesson, also prominent in such fictions, is to handle social situations less awkwardly. In both cases, croquet is a more positive moral force than a negative one and in all such contexts play is perceived as girls'/women's familial and "civilizing" duty. Pleasure and amusement, moderated by senses of duty, are expected to produce admirable—and frequently more appropriately feminine—results and better family and societal members and therefore citizens.

Yonge's serialization of *The Trial* (January 1862 to April 1864) appears alongside the flurry of correspondence initiated by "Henrietta" in her periodical, and both seem to rehearse the presentation of croquet as indicator of social status and duty Yonge later draws out in *The Clever Woman of the Family*. While croquet delivers Bessie Keith's downfall, it is also the primary means by which the novel's main character, Rachel Curtis, referred to by her to-be husband as "the uncroquetable lawn" (414), recovers true womanly behavior. The very croquet-lawn that kills Bessie is the site of the croquet-party at which Rachel—after being successfully governed by her husband and his uncle—triumphs by operating in the social sphere without causing undue discomfort through intense "clever," unfeminine behavior and attempts to bring "womanly duty" beyond its socially acceptable sphere. Like Alcott's Rose Campbell, Rachel begins her novel proclaiming her grown status, objecting to her mother's birthday gift of a white rose hair wreath as "one does cease to be a girl" (35) and insisting she is "done with white muslin" as "it is an affectation of girlish simplicity not becoming at our age" (37). Just as Rose must "recover" her childishness through play, Rachel, despite celebrating her twenty-fifth birthday at the novel's opening, must accept that she still is—and apparently always will be—a girl. She must learn and adhere to her appropriate "girlish" domestic and playful place and accept that she is less a "clever woman" than she supposes so that by the novel's end, when she has fully submitted to marriage, motherhood, and male authority, she seems to give up both the idea of having any other vocation and the belief that her "twenty-fifth birthday" is "the turning-point when this submissive girlhood ought to close, and the privileges of acting as well as thinking for herself ought to be assumed" (43). Like the later girls' fiction, *The Clever Woman of the Family* consistently and strikingly—at times troublingly—conflates girlhood and womanhood. It, for example, seems to consider seriously the prospect of a seven-year-old child being trained to be the future bride of a thirty-six-year-old man and offers as an example of happy marriage a sixteen-year-old female married to (though then widowed by) a sixty-year-old man in a marriage that resembles at times more a father-daughter relationship. The widow, Rachel's relative Lady Fanny Temple, also twenty-five at the start of the novel and (good) mother to a brood of children, is frequently described as "but a child herself" (39).

The novel also emphasizes, through the approval of Rachel's future husband, Alick Keith, and Lady Temple's own play, that croquet itself is not at fault for Bessie's moral lapses. Alick, Bessie's brother, is one of the guiding moral figures of the novel and strives both to keep his sister in check and to cultivate Rachel's better, more fittingly "womanly," characteristics. After being tricked by Bessie into playing croquet, Fanny is pacified by Alick's reassurances that "it is a capital game for [her] and [her] boys," that "there is no harm in the game itself," and that his blind uncle—another moral light in the text, and a tremendously respectable clergyman to boot—"is specially addicted to listening to croquet and knows by the step and sound how each player is getting on, till he is quite an oracle in disputed hits" (129). As Yonge's chapter on "Amusements" suggests for all forms of pleasure, the only concern with croquet is with lack of moderation, a trap Lady Temple does unwittingly fall into when a lower-class curate makes too much of the game, but which, unlike Bessie, she remedies, with dismay and embarrassment, as soon as she is aware of the problem. For Alick Keith, croquet is simply a matter of "personal distaste" (128) arising from past circumstances, and only dangerous when "abuse[d] as an engine of flirtation," which is what has annoyed him in the past and which is ultimately his sister's undoing (129).

The sense of croquet as "a wicked flirtation trap"—what Lady Temple initially believes it to be—stems, as the novel observes, from societal views on display in places such as *Punch*, which devoted much criticism at the time to mocking the sport with jokes about "husbandry" versus "horticulture" in the garden (201).[13] With a few exceptions for the upper classes and sports like archery, women and girls in the first and mid portions of the nineteenth century didn't tend to play sports. When they began to do so more and more through the croquet rage of the 1860s, and when, as a result, sports and female players began to invade gardens public and private, society certainly took notice and Yonge was no exceptional member of her society in this regard. While she may be skeptical of the recreational pastime of croquet in her writing, she also saw its need and saving graces. Viewed as a social duty tempered by pleasure, croquet could help to maintain status, reputation, peace, and pleasure amongst families, neighbors, and visitors. It may have its dangers if exploited or made into an obsession, but it could also be an appropriate family game. It was, moreover, a game members of Yonge's own family circle were not above playing: in a letter to a friend written while on holiday in France Yonge remarks in passing that her sister-in-law "Frances is out playing at croquet" (Coleridge 249). No moral weight attaches itself to this reference to croquet—it just is. On holiday, Frances plays croquet and does, I suspect, what Yonge attempts to do in her novels: "try to make a good hit." For Yonge this meant balancing societal changes in feminine occupations with notions of womanly duty grounded in family and home pursuits, including leisure and play. For other writers of the time, it meant reconciling new possibilities in women's pastimes with other expectations of female citizenship duties based on nationality as well as gender and realizations of feminine power.

"The Englishers played well; but the Americans played better": Croquet and the cycle of domestic social obligations in the works of Carroll and Alcott

Throughout the 1860s, croquet manuals and periodicals such as *The Field* acknowledge the subtle yet inherent tendency towards chaos and violence in croquet by continually comparing the sport to the more orderly, "scientific" (and masculine) billiards, and through the very rhetoric of the sport itself: croquet is a game of "dead" versus "live" balls, of "rovers," balls that can range about anywhere and "roquet" (strike and propel) other balls anywhere, and of "tight" versus "loose" croquet. In its ideal form, croquet presumes that the "ground is in apple-pie-order, and that the grass turf has been closely cut, swept, and well rolled," and that "each player is armed with a mallet, and ready for the pleasing fray, which is to drive home, with all mathematical precision possible, the balls through the arches, in the direction marked on the diagrams" (*Game of Croquêt* 12–13). Despite these attempts, however, anarchy maintained its hold on the croquet lawn: mathematical calculations, so useful to billiards players and so fascinating for scholars such as Lewis Carroll, can't take into account all the possible angles created from encounters with turned-up turf and lawn slopes, nor can they always take into account other players' riotous and ball-hurtling instincts, as Carroll comically and perhaps disturbingly portrays in his famed *Alice's Adventures in Wonderland* (1865). While billiards could presuppose conditions of control possible indoors, such as perfectly equal boards of slate and well-ironed green felt coverings, croquet had to deal with the impossibility of such order out of doors, a lack of order epitomized by Wonderland's croquet lawn of "all ridges and furrows"; players who "all played at once without waiting for turns, quarrelling all the while, and fighting for the hedgehogs"; Alice's difficulties with her flamingo mallet and hedgehog balls; living cards that have to straddle balls flying at them (and can choose not to do so); and hostess and matron of the sport—the Queen of *Hearts*, of course—who threatens decapitation at every turn for any or no reason (141–143).

The Queen of Hearts is—and queens are—central to Carroll's vision in the *Alice* books, as critics consistently note. Many scholars, like Michael Parrish Lee, see the Queen of Hearts and "her famous cry" of beheading as representative of "sovereign power over life and death" (510), and notably female sovereign power at that, or, as Carina Garland perceives it, "compared to the Queen of Hearts, the King of Hearts is portrayed as a weak, meek creature who is frightened of his own wife" (29).[14] He is "weakened," she contends, like other men in the *Alice* texts, "because they cannot compete with a vicious and frightening female sexuality that threatens them and Carroll's dream child as Alice moves to join their ranks when she grows into a (female) adult" (30). Yet

Carroll's own summation in *The Nursery Alice* (1890), which distills *Alice's Adventures* for a younger audience, suggests a different interpretation, one enabled by the king's "pardon" of all those under sentence of death in *Alice's Adventures* (150): "she was a dreadfully savage queen" but "they didn't *really* cut their heads off, you know: because nobody ever obeyed her: but that was what she always *said* [sic]" (*Nursery Alice* 43).[15] The queen, in other words, is a decidedly impotent figure—"nobody ever obeyed her"—despite her obvious connections to sexuality on display through her very name and the game with which she is notoriously associated. Carroll, an avid croquet player, was certainly aware of croquet's flirtatious reputation as in his original drawing of the croquet match for *Alice's Adventures Under Ground* (1864) he drew two courtiers engaged in an embrace and kiss (329).[16] For Nina Auerbach, this awareness and connection are also obvious, with Alice epitomizing "both the croquet game without rules and its violent arbiter, the Queen of Hearts" (33–34). Alice, in other words, is inextricably linked to croquet, violence, and (impotent) feminine power. This is evident in the very first chapter of *Alice's Adventures* where "once she remembered trying to box her own ears for having cheated herself in a game of croquet she was playing against herself" (86). Alice's violent boxing attempt further links her to the Duchess, who is later imprisoned "under sentence of execution" for having "boxed the Queen's ears" (142) and the Duchess herself foreshadows the Queen and the Queen's violence as the Duchess initially demands Alice's own head: "Talking of axes . . . chop off her head!" (123). The Duchess' request, like the Queen's for others later, is ignored. Alice's connections to queens and impotent feminine power are even more on display in *Through the Looking-Glass* (1871), the plot structure of which follows Alice's desire to be a queen and her path to queendom as dictated by the rules and possibilities of chess. When she finally does become Queen, however, she discovers it is not nearly as pleasant as she imagined as she finds herself cross-examined by both the Red and White Queens (275–279) and presiding over a rather murderous dinner-party (283–287).

The dinner-party in *Through the Looking-Glass* also calls to mind the visit Alice pays to the Duchess at her house in Wonderland. In both cases, Alice, unaided by Frog "inferiors," struggles to find a way inside, either because of no response to her knocking (*Adventures* 121) or not knowing which bell to ring (*Looking-Glass* 281). Class concerns, then, intersect with domesticity in the texts, which time and again revolve around issues of identity. Early on, for instance, Alice fears she might actually be another child, "Mabel," and "have to go and live in that poky little house, and have next to no toys to play with" (*Adventures* 91) and she is later mistaken by the White Rabbit for his servant and sent on to his own house (103). As these examples, with their references to toys and houses, also indicate, just as queens are central to the *Alice* books, so are games, play, and houses. Not only is the play of language prominent, but so are croquet, cards, chess, races, singing, dancing, and other forms of fun. To play, Alice alternates between gardens and houses, spending much time in *Alice's Adventures* trying to get to the garden she first sees peeping through the tiny door upon her arrival in Wonderland (the garden which ultimately hosts the Queen's croquet) and trying to see the garden she enters in Looking-Glass Land "far better" by viewing it from the top of a hill (*Looking-Glass* 199). This she finds initially impossible, for every time she makes a start for the hill she finds herself "always coming back to the house," even running into it at one point and later exclaiming, "I never saw such a house for getting in the way! Never!" (199). The garden in Looking-Glass Land offers a parody of Lord Alfred Tennyson's *Maud* (1855), but as Margaret Homans observes, referencing John Ruskin's renowned "Of Queens' Gardens" in *Sesame and Lilies* (1865), "to read *Through the Looking-Glass* after reading Ruskin's essay is to find in it a hilarious parody and trenchant critique of Ruskin's endeavor . . . to turn girls into queens" (91). As his diary records, Carroll met Ruskin in 1857 (*Diaries of Lewis Carroll* 128–129) and although the first Alice story was told in 1862, with the initial written version of it given to Alice Liddell on 26 November 1864, a few weeks before Ruskin's 14 December 1864 Manchester lecture that became "Of Queens' Gardens," it is not difficult to see even in *Alice's Adventures* implicit critique of the sort of ideas that elevated Coventry Patmore's *Angel in the House* (1854–1862) and led Ruskin to proclaim in "Of Queens' Gardens" that "wherever a true wife comes, the home is always round her" (145). In the White Rabbit's house in *Alice's Adventures*, the growing girl Alice becomes so large that the home *is* always round her—it envelops and contains her so much she quite literally can't escape it (104) just as in Looking-Glass Land she time and again finds herself back at the house, even "actually walking in at the door," when she tries to get elsewhere (199). Indeed, in *Through the Looking-Glass* gardens and homes (if not entire worlds) are inseparable, as the garden actually *is* in the house, as the entire Looking-Glass Land is ensconced in the mirror in Alice's own drawing-room, if not confined to the chess-board in that mirrored room. As Alice phrases it after going through the looking-glass, "if I don't make haste, I shall have to go back through the Looking-glass, before I've seen what the rest of the house is like! Let's have a look at the garden first!" (198). The garden, it seems, is simply in or part of the house. Notably, too, the confining nature of houses is not contained merely to the dream-worlds of the *Alice* books but is present in the English world of Alice herself: the trip to Looking-Glass Land is precipitated by a snowstorm which keeps (traps?) Alice in the house (*Looking-Glass* 188–189) and the adventures of *Alice's Adventures* end with Alice being told to "run in to your tea" (176).

Through the Looking-Glass, overrun with queens and ending with a dinner-party and technically placing the world in the house,[17] is thoroughly steeped in a discourse of feminine power and domesticity, as is Wonderland. Indeed, Wonderland is a surprisingly conventional and domestic world: public trials are domestic concerns about baked goods, caucus races are rewarded with thimbles just as kisses are transformed into that same artifact in the context of Neverland, tunnels look like pantries and studies, and most of the adventures are simple afternoon garden-party activities (a tea party, croquet, singing, dancing, and cards). At the end of the text, Alice returns home by awakening to do it all over again, to scamper on in to her house to get her tea and begin anew the cycle of female domestic social obligations. It is this very cycle that Carroll critiques through such things as the never-ending tea party and the badly played croquet game even as he acknowledges the rudeness and violence—of Mad Hatters making inappropriate remarks, of croquet games turning threateningly lethal—kept at bay by the societal conventions maintained by such a cycle.[18] Indeed, throughout Alice's adventures, Carroll simultaneously critiques aspects of female and societal conventionality and upholds them, for as Kincaid discerns, "genteel disguises are quietly removed in Wonderland," but their removal often emphasizes why they should be maintained in the first place (291). Even as he illustrates the potential traps of houses, domesticity, and conventionality, Carroll insists on their necessity, shaping his characters' interactions persistently around considerations of and conversations regarding manners, where a lack of polite conventions leads to a lack of polite conventions, rudeness begets rudeness. Just as the Queens can comment on Alice's ascent to her own queendom with the question "but I daresay you've not had many lessons in manners yet?" in *Through the Looking-Glass* (276), so the Mad Hatter and March Hare can commit many ill-mannered acts at their tea-party, including offering a guest wine when there isn't any and insulting a guest's hair and appearance (*Alice's Adventures* 130–131). Alice's behavior is little better and throughout Wonderland she consistently and inconsiderately threatens creatures and then believes they too easily take offense, as when she begins talking of cats and their prey to an audience of mouse and birds (94; 102) and when she insults the "exactly three inches high" Caterpillar by informing it that "three inches is such a wretched height to be" (116).

There isn't a symbolic queen of hearts to point to the flirtatious underpinnings of croquet in Alcott's *Little Women*, but Alcott does portray the game in terms just as violent, flirtatious, and upholding of standards. Set against the backdrop of the rivalry for Meg March's heart by Mr. Brooke and Ned Moffat, the croquet match also presages the battle for Jo's and Amy's hearts by figures such as Laurie and Fred Vaughn. Just as tellingly, Alcott's novel describes the game itself as a violent battle, one that re-plays the U.S. Revolutionary War: "The Englishers played well; but the Americans played better, and contested every inch of the ground as strongly as if the spirit of '76 inspired them. Jo and Fred had several skirmishes, and once narrowly escaped high words" (156). In this way, Alcott's text engages not only debates about good womanly behavior and duty—Meg is aloof from flirtation and Jo manages to keep her temper in feminine check—but intersects those debates with nationalistic pride. In this scene, the Americans consistently show up their English counterparts. Meg and Jo demonstrate themselves to be just as proper and womanly as Kate Vaughn and Jo reveals herself to be both more generous and honorable than Fred as she wins the croquet match without unnecessarily and maliciously croqueting his sister's ball and as she both catches and forces him to admit to cheating at the game (here, as with Alice, "Englishers" do cheat). By the end of the croquet excursion, the English Kate admits that "in spite of their demonstrative manners, American girls are very nice when one knows them" and the roguish Ned admits that "there isn't a bit of flirt in that girl" Meg, confessions that display the superiority of the March girls and true U.S. womanhood (168). Womanly duty here takes on a nationalistic dimension that highlights the value of female forays into the realms of citizenship and sport and games—after all, the "Americans" beat the "Englishers" at what are essentially their own sports of croquet and gentle-folk behavior and then ultimately turn, as I suggest in my previous chapter, to an American game, "a sensible game of Authors, to refresh our minds" (163).

In the process, of course, Alcott critiques aspects of Englishness that her English contemporary Yonge simply wouldn't, but Alcott's critique of English domestic manners and "womanly" duties for citizenship pale in comparison to those of Yonge's compatriot, Carroll. For Yonge, the cycle of never-ending domestic family and social obligations, of womanly duty, is what makes women's lives worthwhile and is all that she desires for aspirations for her young female readers. Alcott, known to have drawn on the works of Yonge,[19] agrees, but offers her own spin, highlighting transatlantic rivalry with notions of good behavior and citizenship expectations and aligning gendered duty with national obligations through the medium of croquet.[20] Carroll, by contrast, saw beyond the cycle of duty as life fulfilment, saw and explored its traps and hazards for the women and girls so often conflated as one and the same. Still, all three writers saw the power and potential of croquet and play, as well as the power and potential evident in "womanly" duties, the strength they offer in maintaining order, particularly through the upholding of societal conventions, and the dangers possible if girls and women were to give up that work: not only sexual prowess, but (supposedly) violence, anarchy, the specters of death and disorder hiding in the shadows of the house. In the 1860s, croquet was poised to propel more and more girls and women into these shadows, into the gardens just outside the house. The danger, it seems, was palpable. In response, discourse and domestic chronicles of the period—novels, periodicals, and manuals documenting croquet, among others—emphasize the importance of social order and a compatibility or balance between pleasure and duty. The rendering of croquet into yet another aspect of womanly duty for good citizenship, into another aspect of a never-ending cycle of domestic social obligations, mitigated some of its potential threat and paved the way for its antiquated status just a few decades later. Likely, too, such attempts to contain the revolutionary pull of the pastime hastened its demise, its replacement by activities seemingly more alluringly revolutionary, freer (at least initially) from constraints of womanly duty and citizenship-bolstering expectations. Saturated in the discourse, debates, and anxieties of their time, 1860s domestic chronicles did their jobs—helping to quell croquet even as they advocated it. Yet, as debates over female play that broke forth repeatedly over the next half century in children's and girls' fiction as well as in the larger cultural discourse indicate, they could not entirely quell the power, potential, and allure of such play. So other strategies were also employed, including merging the very status of girls as women and women as girls, requiring female characters to learn to be more "playful" and "childlike" to contain the power of play within the (often perceived as powerless) realm of child-/girlhood, and casting playful females as sexualized, exotic specimens. How well those strategies worked in response to the rise of ever-multiplying playful pursuits open to girls and women, such as lawn tennis, bicycling, and golf, we may still be feeling the effects of today, yet it is certain that, with croquet, those aiming to contain the power offered by female play merely won a battle, not a war. The skirmishes—whether or not still "inspired" by "the spirit of '76"—continued.

Notes

1 Here I diverge slightly from MacLeod, who argues that "to Alcott, as to most Americans of her time, children were adults-in-process, apprentices to the rigors and demands of adult life. It was not a matter of viewing children as "little adults"; that was not a nineteenth-century attitude" (23). The notion of "adults-in-process" is of course fascinatingly reminiscent of the idea of "citizens-in-training."

2 Aunt Jessie, who secures her "small boys" from the dangers of "popular stories" (in a critique of the work of "Oliver Optic," William Taylor Adams, in particular) at the same time that Rose uses her influence to rid the elder boys of the bad habit of cigar smoking, is another paragon of womanly "citizenship" through personal influence in the novel (184–185).

3 In "'A Highly Satisfactory Chinaman': Orientalism and American Girlhood in Louisa May Alcott's *Eight Cousins*," Lorinda B. Cohoon highlights other aspects of Alcott's attempts to establish Rose's female citizenship, particularly in her contrast with the text's Orientalizing depictions of men from China and its treatment of imperial trade and goods (the Campbell family's wealth arises from its shipping, import/export, business). Indeed, as games and play movements as well as Burnett's works and boys' fiction of the

time also show, discussions of child citizenship often went hand-in-hand with considerations of empire and colonization in the nineteenth and early twentieth centuries.

4 As I will discuss a bit more with Frances Hodgson Burnett's texts in chapter four, class fantasies frequently underpin deployments of play to produce good citizens. Phebe, like so many working-class characters depicted in nineteenth century children's texts, is fascinatingly idealized. Summarized by Rose's guardian as "so she doesn't call desertion, poverty, and hard work, troubles? She's a brave little girl, and I shall be proud to know her" (25), the orphaned and abandoned to a poor-house fifteen-year-old "little girl" Phebe is portrayed as seeing Rose's troubles—grieving the loss of her father after a year and overwhelmed by the conflicting attentions of well-meaning relatives—as greater than her own. She quickly shifts from "wondering how life *could* be dull to a girl who wore a silk frock, a daintily frilled apron, a pretty locket, and had her hair tied up with a bright velvet snood" (6) to "fe[eling] more contented with her brown calico gown and blue-check pinafore; envy changed to compassion" (7).

5 For a more extended analysis of Sara's "old-fashionedness" and its connections to her identity, see Nelson, particularly pages 33–37.

6 Awareness of this is evident in *Peter and Wendy* from its opening page, where Barrie writes,

> until Wendy came her mother was the chief one. She was a lovely lady, with a romantic mind and such a sweet mocking mouth. Her romantic mind was like tiny boxes, one within the other, that come from the puzzling East, however many you discover there is always one more; and her sweet mocking mouth had one kiss on it that Wendy could never get.
>
> (5)

Mr. Darling "got all of her, except the innermost box and the kiss. He never knew about the box, and in time he gave up trying for the kiss" (5). Peter, unlike supposedly even Napoleon (5), manages to get the kiss (145) but Mrs. Darling's mind, connected through imperialism and Orientalism to the "puzzling East" (mysterious Others, like women) remains her own.

7 Rebecca, of course, is in particular increasingly viewed as, in Regina Puleo's words, "deviat[ing] from the patterns established" in girls' fiction (353) or, as Kelli M. Sellers suggests in her analysis of New Woman conceptions and Wiggin's text, "Rebecca may be more progressive than others acknowledge" (108).

8 Another strategy hinted at consistently in the examples in this chapter is to focus attention on costume: clothes and fashion feature in *The World* advertisement and articles and are prominently discussed and challenged in *Eight Cousins*. Anne Shirley of the famed Green Gables despairs over puffed sleeves (Montgomery 68), Mary Lennox permits, in racially charged dialogue, a change from black mourning dress to a white outfit (*The Secret Garden* 24), Sara Crewe's class roles and position are consistently tied to descriptions of her clothing and their fit, including what U.C. Knoepflmacher describes as the "optimistic outlook on life" epitomized by the "rose-colored outfit" of her dancing dress (xi), and even Lewis Carroll, according to his nephew Stuart Dodgson Collingwood, exhorted John Tenniel, "don't give Alice so much crinoline" (130).

9 The debate surrounding women's work is central to Yonge's writing. See, for example, Jane Sturrock's "Something to Do: Charlotte Yonge, Tractarianism and the Question of Women's Work."

10 Her reference to the "dowdy-bonnet"-wearing "Lady Bountiful" walking miles to teach at the village school is a potential swipe at Yonge's famous Ethel May from *The Daisy Chain* (1856) and *The Trial* (1864). Mrs. Curtis, Rachel's mother, and Grace, her sister, are also described as being "sufficed" by "the quiet Lady Bountiful duties" in *The Clever Woman of the Family* (42).

11 For another example, see "R.E.J.A." on "Croquet" (May 1864). For further analysis of these and other *Monthly Packet* correspondence, see Kristine Moruzi's *Constructing Girlhood through the Periodical Press, 1850–1915*.

12 Gertrude also acknowledges the social status of croquet by admitting to having played it at Maplewood, the manor house of her wealthier and more socially adept sister Blanche.

13 See, for example, Linley Sambourne's *Mr. Punch's Book of Sports* (1910).

14 Lee's and Garland's work joins a rich and growing body of analysis of food, things, and evolution in the Alice books. See, for example, articles by Katja Jylkka and Rasheed Tazudeen as well.

15 Critics' consistent focus on language over action here is notable, as is Carroll's presentation of the power of kings. Their power over queens—or to-be queens and girls—is particularly evident in Looking-Glass Land when Alice confronts the dilemma of whether or not she is merely an aspect of ("a sort of thing in") the Red King's dream and therefore subject to his dreaming—and waking—whims for her very existence (*Looking-Glass* 226).

16 If any author is aligned inextricably with games, play, and croquet, it is Carroll, who not only played croquet frequently but even invented his own variants of the game.

17 Parallels may be made with E. Nesbit's "Fortunatus Rex & Co.," from *Nine Unlikely Tales for Children* (1901), which mocks such things as the "refining touch of a woman's hand" and also places the world and universe—in the form of terrestrial and celestial globes—in the house (200).

18 For other considerations of domesticity, conventions, gender, and violence in Carroll's work, see Jennifer Geer's "'All sorts of pitfalls and surprises'" and Nancy Armstrong's "The Occidental Alice."

19 See, for example, Karen Sands-O'Connor's "Why Jo Didn't Marry Laurie: Louisa May Alcott and *The Heir of Redclyffe*."

20 This is not to suggest that Yonge does not also align gendered duties with notions of national citizenship obligations. Kate Lawson, for instance, argues that "the central struggle in *The Clever Woman of the Family* ... is between competing versions of English national identity and national governance, one version nurtured at home in England and the other shaped by experiences abroad in the colonies" wherein "the novel's answer to liberalism and feminism—to mutiny and rebellion—is an embrace of a military code that values masculine rule and submission to authority" (440–441).

3 Citizenship on the world's stage

Kipling's novels of boyhood
and the boy scouts

For nearly fifteen years at the turn of the nineteenth and twentieth centuries, from 1895 to 1909, Florence and Bertha Upton published a series of picture books with a cast of toy characters, primarily five Dutch dolls and a Golliwogg. The Golliwgg was a toy that, Florence recollected, "came from an American Fair" but was lost on a childhood trip visiting relatives in London and not discovered again until she was an adult, whereupon it helped inspire the picture books which were ultimately illustrated by the American-born Florence in England while her British-born mother, Bertha, sent accompanying verses from the U.S. (qtd. in Davis 10). With their sense of progress, technology, modern achievement, and world travel and exploration, Westernized sensibilities in the series I have explored elsewhere,[1] the texts, as Marilynn Olson remarks, "embodied the 'spirit of the age'" (73). On display both in their origin story and the texts themselves, however, is that the "spirit of the age" also encompassed a complicated nexus of hybridity. Was the British-residing Florence Upton a "young American" as David Rudd calls her (137) or Anglo-American as Olson suggests (81), or something else completely? How about her U.S.-residing British-born mother? The books themselves are fascinatingly hybrid as well: generally attributed to Florence as her creation and yet "written" by her mother—though Florence provided the "story" initially through the illustrations. The Golliwogg itself provides similar complications: Florence is generally cited as "creating" the figure, yet the doll was bought, already "created," in the U.S., "associate[d]," in Norma S. Davis' words, "undeniably with the minstrel shows so popular earlier in the nineteenth century" and thereby ultimately unredeemable from charges of racism (9).[2] Moreover, the initially "American" doll took on a life of its own: since the Uptons didn't patent the character, others were quick to capitalize on it (generally under the name "golliwog"), so much so that it became an icon of *British* childhood and was even used as the image of Robertson's jam until 2002.

The Dutch dolls' origins and identity affiliations are even more ambiguous. Reflecting the Dutch dolls' own hybridity are tongue-in-cheek remarks in the tales coupling the Netherlands and Germany and allusions to the Dutch—Deutch—dolls' name and origin countries for the type of toy they are (the dolls even visit Holland in one adventure). The opening tale, *The Adventures of Two Dutch Dolls—and a "Golliwogg"* (1895), may be set in the U.S. as the Dutch dolls use a U.S. flag to make dresses for themselves—a deed quite notable, Olson rightly points out, "in an era that could not have been more aware of flag etiquette than America at the time" (82)—but later volumes in the series are set in a generic "Doll-land" which appears, given its proximity to the English Channel for sea-side adventuring and jaunts to France for fox-hunting, likely located in Britain (emphasizing this further is Golliwogg's dream of Theodore Roosevelt in the final book of the series, "that in a newer world / A man well known to fame, / Had started for East Africa / To shoot its biggest game" [*Golliwogg in the African Jungle* 4]). The adventures of the tales, too, tend to reflect Britain's imperial concerns and the U.S.' increasing interest in exploration and colonization: together the dolls manage to visit in one book (and somehow all on bicycle) the Ottoman Empire, Japan, Paris in France, and an "Eastern Land" that seems to merge India and North America (*The Golliwogg's Bicycle Club* 62); in another book they arrive on a desert isle in overt homage and reference to *Robinson Crusoe*; in another they are first to reach the North Pole (capturing in story form competition between the U.S., Britain, and other nations that, like Crusoe, also inspired games of the period, as I observe in Chapter 1); in another they join a battle with likely allusions to the Boer Wars and/or the Spanish-American War; and in the final book they scoop Roosevelt on his safari hunt by convincing the animals to become part of their zoo so "when that other hunter comes / —*There's nothing to be got!!!*" (*Golliwogg in the African Jungle* 64).

Altogether, the texts in the series offer a blurring of boundaries (including national borders) as an epitome of the times, a blurring reinforced by the dolls' sense of affiliation as performance-based. Time and again in the series the dolls use clothes to perform identity: before setting out on the adventure of a given book, the characters tend to locate or make clothes befitting their ideas of the situation, using clothing to distinguish roles such as hunter, soldier, driver, aviator, and seaside vacationer as well as national and/or cultural identity (they delight, for instance, in donning Holland-inspired costumes). Perhaps the most radical instances of this use of clothing to blur boundaries occur in *The Golliwogg's "Auto-Go-Cart"* (1901) and *The Golliwogg's Fox-Hunt* (1905) where gendered identities as performance are prominently displayed. In response to the question "How does one determine the gender of a toy?," Lois Rostow Kuznets suggests "rarely by its genitalia, mostly by its clothing, hairstyle, and the language used to signify it" (6), and it is by a mixing of language and clothing that the Uptons' texts reinforce the dolls' hybrid performances of identity. The Dutch Dolls—Peg, the largest, who generally wears red stripes; Sarah Jane who rivals the Golliwogg for leadership and generally wears blue stars; Midget, the smallest; and the interchangeable (and often "nude" in the illustrations) Meg and Weg—are consistently gendered "she" in the verses of the texts. However, in *The Golliwogg's "Auto-Go-Cart"* Meg sports a masculine ensemble of hat, tie, umbrella, and mustache, while in *The Golliwogg's Fox-Hunt* Meg or Weg (which is unclear) does not ride sidesaddle and has adopted for costume only hat and boots with spurs while Midget, also not riding sidesaddle, seems to copy the male-gendered Golliwogg in costume.

That these performances, blurrings, and hybrid realizations are not oddities of the Uptons and their series but form part of the vision and realities of the era is plain through a consideration of the figures and movements prominent in the closing and opening decades of the nineteenth and twentieth centuries. As Oscar Wilde and the figure of the dandy were carving out ambiguous possibilities for gender (with ultimate backlash) and aestheticism, explored more in my next chapter, was asserting multifaceted influences, famed other writers for children and adults—Frances Hodgson Burnett and Robert Louis Stevenson, among the most notable—were living hybrid lives, divided or alternating through residence (and often through marriage) between Britain and the U.S. (and for Stevenson, ultimately Samoa). To refer to any of these writers as "British" or "American" rather than, say, "transatlantic" or "worldy" insofar as "worldy" indicates enabled by or products of empire may do a disservice to them, their works, and the contexts that formed them. Perhaps the most prominent example of such a figure, however, is Rudyard Kipling, who married an American woman and lived for a short period in the U.S., and who also lived in and visited India and South Africa. Notably, too, Kipling not only created British and American characters (such as Harvey Cheyne, Jr. of *Captain Courageous* [1897]) but wrote some of the most famous hybrid characters in fiction: Mowgli of *The Jungle Books* (1894–1895) and, like the Uptons' doll characters, the frequent costume/identity-changing Kimball O'Hara of *Kim* (1901).[3] Viewed frequently as representative of the era—at least with respect to its imperial commitments and concerns, if not contradictions[4]—Kipling and his hybrid characters further cement their status as embodiments of their times by the roles they played, the performances of citizenship they offered, in the establishment of Robert Baden Powell's boy scout movement and its heirs. Emulating the literary figures—real and fictional—Baden Powell borrowed from as he outlined the movement and its expansions in handbooks for boy scouts, girl guides, and wolf cubs, the movement became hybrid—simultaneously local, national, and worldly—and premised on patriotism and empire but cognizant of both gender and citizenship as performance entwined in that premise.

In this chapter, I aim to trace some of the ways in which the hybridity prominent in Kipling's fictions is reflected in the boy scout movement which borrowed heavily from those fictions and is further reproduced in fictions spurred by the movement. Examining in particular the U.S. reproduction of Robert Baden-Powell's *The Wolf Cub's Handbook* (1916 Britain; 1918 U.S.), a handbook which has been analyzed little, if at all, by other scholars[5] but which may be most closely aligned with Kipling, premised as strongly as it is on *The Jungle Books*, this chapter highlights some of the ways boys' citizenship was imagined from a British, trans-atlantic perspective—distributed to both British and U.S. audiences—during a period when it was felt to be most in need: just prior to and at the dawn of World War I, following the shocks of the Boer Wars, during the "Scramble for Africa," and alongside the rise of the U.S. as potential imperial power (attested to by Kipling's own infamous 1899 poem "The White Man's Burden"). As with notions of girls' "citizenship" on display particularly in attitudes towards croquet in the 1860s and 1870s, ex-plored in the previous chapter, boys' citizenship was described in terms of duty and obedience, with games harnessed to these ideas. Croquet-playing girls, however, were confined in literary and other imaginings to the domestic family circle; games-playing and sporting boys, symbolized most famously in Henry Newbolt's poem "Vitai Lampada" (1897), were given the entire world and particularly the entire empire as playing-field, a "gift" that served to reinforce their contradictory image as national-patriotic and worldly-benevolent as well as their status as subject-citizens, weighted down by obligations of loyalty and maintenance/continuation of empire.[6] Elizabeth Cohen discerns that "in place of democratic citi-zenship, children hold an ill-defined partial membership," which she tries to redeem by advocating for "semi-citizenship" (221–222), ideas not dis-similar from Tom Cockburn's understanding that children are considered as citizens primarily with respect to "their *future* roles" (8). Aligned with such ideas of partial, incomplete, or yet to come citizenship, or "citizens-in-training," children as not fully citizens but being prepared to be so once they come of age and are accorded full citizen rights as well as responsibilities, portrayals of the figure of the boy by Kipling and in *The Wolf Cub's Handbook* emphasize the figure's hybridity amidst striking contradictions: consistently offering gender and citizenship as a perfor-mance, often of and with storytelling and play, Kipling, Baden-Powell, and their heirs offer representations of boys who are simultaneously de-humanized (made animal, object, machine, pawn) and full of human potential (for cross-cultural communication, good deeds, ideal citizen-ship), simultaneously extraordinary and incomplete.

Kipling's extraordinary, incomplete, and forever "not yet" boys

Undoubtedly the theme most common in the last few decades of rich criticism surrounding Kipling's protagonist boy characters from *The*

Jungle Books and *Kim* is hybridity. U.C. Knoepflmacher, for example, explores "Kipling's 'Mixy' Creatures," Sue Walsh references "'Mowgil the Frog's' amphibious identity" (52), and Judith Plotz considers Kim as "happy hybrid" ("Whose is Kim?" 9) and "adolescent inhabitant of the border territory between childhood and manhood . . . a great criss-crosser of boundaries," a figure who "so freely . . . criss-cross[es] the bounds of British and Indian culture that he is hard to place" ("The Empire of Youth" 112–113). Contributing a similar view in his lengthy exploration of Kipling's "imperial boys" (3), Don Randall argues that "within the discourse of imperialism, conceptions of adolescence and hybridity . . . develop interdependently," with "nineteenth-century representations of hybridity necessarily focus[ed] on progeny" so that "the hybrid, to state the case more pointedly, is first and foremost a certain kind of *child*" and "the child becomes a focal representative of the imperial enterprise, a precarious investment in the national and imperial future, an experiment that may go well or ill" (7).

Indeed, drawing necessarily at times from Homi K. Bhabha's perception of "the ambivalence of hybridity" (113), nearly every account of *Kim* and *The Jungle Books* must inevitably address the protagonists' liminality. Randall generally suggests that Kipling's "imperial boys represent sites of contingency, subject positions in between opposed categories, in between formations of the subject encoded as 'European, imperial' and 'non-European, colonial,'" figures who "mediate and sage the relationship between 'colonizer' and 'colonized,' yet intervene in such a way as to unsettle this same binary opposition in the very moment of its articulation" (3). Teresa Hubel interprets Kim's hybridity slightly differently, arguing that "it is precisely Kipling's construction of Kim as a working-class white who is fully alienated from his class community that allows him to represent Kim as not ultimately belonging to any group" (249–250). Satya P. Mohanty, meanwhile, sees Mowgli as "Kim's immediate ancestor" (320), a connection critics highlight again and again in explorations of Mowgli's own hybridity and liminality. Walsh observes that "much of the recent criticism of Kipling's *Jungle Books*" understands Mowgli

> as both initiating a distinction *between* the human and the animal *and* as destabilizing that distinction. In such an analysis, whether Mowgli is to be considered as "man" or "cub," human or animal, he enters the scene as a potential source of trouble to any impulse towards categorization or classification, signaling the disruption of a presumed clarity of division between natural and unnatural, Jungle and village.
>
> (52)

Christopher Powici echoes this position by asserting that "the distinctions between the human and the animal, between nature and culture, and even between the law itself and its outlaw other, are vulnerable to an ontological zigzagging" in *The Jungle Books* (187), while Walsh herself "read[s] the 'Mowgli' stories . . . as calling into question the borders between child and adult, human and animal, 'native' and white'" (63).

The potential and dangers inherent in—the "ambivalence of," to return to Bhabha—the protagonists' obvious hybridity and liminality are unmistakable in these critical discussions, which thereby hint at some of the de-humanization of and contradictions embodied in the characters I aim to consider further. Perhaps most darkly, Jopi Nyman suggests that *The Jungle Books,* "while foregrounding the translatedness of colonial identity and thus constructing a sense of hybridity, is unable to imagine hybrid identities as being equal to uncontaminated ones" (215). Ultimately, Nyman points out, in terms similar to Hubel's claim for "Kim as not ultimately belonging to any group," Mowgli's divided, multiple status indicates not only contradiction but negation: "Mowgli represents both natives (he is a brother to the wolves) and colonizers (he is a human), thus occupying a place in both but also in neither" (213).[7] Tellingly, too, Randall notes, of Kim, "unlike the man, the boy does not betray and abandon a European selfhood; he has yet to acquire one. Just as the wolfish Mowgli is not yet human, so Kim, the boy of the bazaar, is not yet European" (146). The liminality often associated with hybridity (including the hybridity apparent in senses of boy/child citizenship) suggests "transition" and being in a state of "in-between," but the very phrase "not yet" it can embrace—which is sometimes really a "not ever" —hints at something incomplete as well as contradictory (something and nothing simultaneously) if not, as Randall's suggestion of "not yet human" for Mowgli implies and as we will see further, prey to de-humanization. But the "not yet" also presages the promise of "yet," the potential highlighted in seeming opposition to Nyman's sense of being "unable to imagine hybrid identities as being equal to uncontaminated ones"—for rather than being equal to those around them Mowgli and Kim are described at times as notably superior, in other words, at the same time lacking/incomplete and superior/extraordinary.

For Mowgli, this superiority manifests itself most prominently in his (in)famous gaze. This gaze is central to the opening tale of *The Jungle Books*, "Mowgli's Brothers," and emphasized throughout the Mowgli stories. In the opening tale it is his gaze that jeopardizes Mowgli's life and forces him to leave the jungle for the human village. Bagheera the panther explains the situation in response to Mowgli's question, "But why—but why should any wish to kill me?":

> "Look at me" . . . and Mowgli looked at him steadily between the eyes. The big panther turned his head away in half a minute.
> "*That* is why," he said . . . "Not even I can look thee between the eyes, and I was born among men, and I love thee, Little Brother. The

others they hate thee because their eyes cannot meet thine; because thou art wise; because thou hast pulled out thorns from their feet— because thou art a man."

(13)

In Bagheera's description, it is Mowgli's human characteristics that make him superior, if hated: his "wisdom" over that of the Jungle inhabitants, his opposable thumbs and manual dexterity which enable him to pull out thorns in a service to those inhabitants, indebting them to him, and above all his mastery of the gaze, easy ability to look everyone directly in the eye with confidence and without fear. Mowgli even asserts, "yes . . . all the jungle fear Bagheera—all except Mowgli" (12), a comment which Bagheera confirms with the statement, given "very tenderly," "oh, *thou* art a man's cub" (13). By the final tale of the books, "The Spring Running," Mowgli's status as "Master of the Jungle" is well-established and reinforced again by reference to his eyes, which puzzle Bagheera as, even in the midst of fighting and anger, "his eyes were always gentle . . . they only grew more and more interested and excited" (303). Even minor gazes now demonstrate his superiority: as they talk about his "gentle eyes," "Mowgli looked at [the panther] lazily from under long eyelashes, and, as usual, the panther's head dropped. Bagheera knew his master" (303). Though it is clear that Mowgli is superior to Bagheera, particularly by this point in the story, he does acknowledge Bagheera's own status as "Master of the Jungle" (304), a position reinforced by Bagheera's own hybridity, his experiences among men: admitting to Mowgli that he was born in captivity but broke free, Bagheera points out, "because I had learned the ways of men, I became more terrible in the jungle than Shere Khan. Is it not so?" (12). The text demonstrates the answer during the drought in "How Fear Came," when Bagheera responds to the tiger Shere Khan by "looking him steadily between the eyes" (156). Humanity—and proximity to or knowledge of it—accords superiority here.

However, Mowgli's animal features provide him with superiority as well, for as Mary Goodwin notes, Mowgli "develops to superhuman maturity in the jungle" (106). When he first arrives at the human village, "he did not know his own strength in the least. In the jungle he knew he was weak compared with the beasts, but in the village people said that he was as strong as a bull" (51). Before he is seventeen, he looks older than his youth, "for hard exercise, the best of good eating, and baths whenever he felt in the least hot or dusty, had given him strength and growth far beyond his age" (303). Indeed, when he returns to humankind again in "The Spring Running," his adopted human mother Messua barely recognizes him: she "sink[s] to his feet" and calls him "a Godling of the Woods!" (315), later priding herself on being the first to tell him that he is "beautiful beyond all men. . . . Never have I looked upon such a man" (317). Mowgli as "superhuman," supernatural, and/or "godly" is a theme present throughout Kipling's conceptions of the figure. In "In the Rukh" (1893), a non-*Jungle Books* story which tells of Mowgli establishing a family and accepting service as a forest-guard for the British government, Mowgli is described from the perspective of British and Western (German), white, Sahibs as "a miracle" (334 and 344), "older than" even tales of "Adam in der Garden" in his extraordinary origins (344), and ultimately as "Faunus himself" (341). The text even goes so far as to portray him standing "still fronting the blaze of the fire—in the very form and likeness of that Greek god who is so lavishly described in the novels" (343).

In this way, Mowgli is consistently shown as superior to humans, a superiority reinforced by his relationship to play and stories. Essentially a fable or myth himself (he tells his story in "In the Rukh" to his future wife, with full knowledge that her father and the Sahib Gisborne are listening and watching, and is described in "The Spring Running" *Jungle Books* story as able to be "mistaken for some wild god of a jungle legend"), he knows more of the "truth" of tales than any native in *The Jungle Books* or even the British Gisborne, who does not guess at or initially understand his wolf origins (315). Just as his jungle isolation provides him with strength and ignorance of notions of (human) caste, which enables him to best the village priest in "'Tiger! Tiger,'" at least from a white or British standpoint, his knowledge and embodiment of "true" stories of the jungle and its inhabitants allow him to laugh at the "wonderful tales" told by Buldeo, the seemingly respected "village hunter" (52). Since he is also able to make his entire life a pursuit of leisure—punctuated only by bodily needs for survival—his very existence is that of another sort of "Great Game" than the one between Russia and Britain illustrated in *Kim*. As such, though in "In the Rukh" he admits to "playing by night with my brethren [the four wolves] in the crops" (346), he does not "play games or fly kites" like other human children but does indulge in sport, with the text making clear immediately after its admission of his being "made fun of" by children for his seeming lack of games-playing that he restrains himself from "picking them up and breaking them in two" because it is "unsportsmanlike to kill little naked cubs" (*Jungle Books* 51).

Revealingly, too, despite the frequent references to seeming white and/or British superiority throughout the stories in *The Jungle Books* and the seeming deference Mowgli offers the "Sahibs" in "In the Rukh," his superiority to them is also frequently on display. Drawn to Gisborne as essentially an equal as "there is no man to talk to out there in the *rukh*," the Mowgli of "In the Rukh" outright laughs at the Sahib for not knowing what "a child knows" about the jungle and its inhabitants: "Tck! Tck! And thou are in charge—so the men of the huts tell me—in charge of all this *rukh*.' He laughed to himself" (332). Part of the joke for Mowgli is the very idea that the Sahib is "in charge" of the Jungle; Mowgli, *The Jungle Books* stress, is the true master of the jungle and here his own abilities above those of the Sahib call the Sahibs' authority into question. Mowgli reminds Gisborne early on that "if I rose and stepped three paces into the *rukh* there is no one, not even the Sahib, could find me till I chose" (339). Fully knowing that Gisborne is listening, Mowgli also calls him "the foolish young Sahib" and calls Sahib Muller, who is "the head of the Woods and Forests of all India, Head Ranger from Burma to Bombay" (340) "the big fat Sahib" at the same time that he observes they were proven wrong when "they questioned my power" (347). Moreover, he suggests "it were as easy to have driven the men themselves" and he does in fact "drive" his future father-in-law in one of several instances of his remarkable prowess (347). Later he responds to Gisborne "in no submissive tone" (348) and when threatened with loss of employment, replies "I hear. . . . Also, we will obey—for the last time" (349). Though the context relates to his future wife's propriety in returning to her family before her marriage, the statement—uttered just before a section break highlighting it prominently—seems telling. The final section of the tale it precedes also offers an undermining of the Sahibs' authority, or at least claims to knowledge. When Muller first meets Mowgil he correctly surmises his wolf origins, a fact which impresses Mowgli enough that he comments to Gisborne that "this Sahib knows everything" (342). By the end of the story, however, Muller has forgotten who Mowgli's "people" are and nearly shoots the wolf guarding Mowgli's own baby (349).

Both extraordinary wolf and extraordinary human, Mowgli is and exceeds animal and human in Kipling's depictions, a position that facilitates his privileges but also exacerbates his lacks. From his arrival at Father and Mother Wolf's lair as a toddler, "a naked brown baby who could just walk," Mowgli has of course demonstrated his exceptionality from his lack of fear, pushing aside the wolf cubs to nurse himself and, as Father Wolf ponders "I could kill him with a touch of my foot," the wolf is impressed that nevertheless "he looks up and is not afraid" (4). Mowgli's uniqueness is also clear in "In the Rukh," where Muller insists "Dere will never be a forest-guard like him" and refers to him, tellingly, as "an anachronism" (344). Astutely, however, it is a predator experienced in taking advantage of weaknesses and deficiencies, Shere Khan, the figure who offers Mowgli his initial threats—and whose own powerful influence successfully results in the deterioration of the wolf pack and Mowgli's first being cast out of the jungle—who not only detects but bluntly outlines the lack and negation inherent in Mowgli's hybrid identity. When Shere Khan attempts to reassert his authority by demanding of Mowgli, "Look at me, Man-cub!," he is cowed: "Mowgli looked—stared—as insolently as he knew how, and in a minute Shere Khan turned away uneasily" (156). However, even as he looks away he calls attention to Mowgli's privileged but precarious situation, re-marking "the cub is neither man nor cub, or he would have been afraid. Next season I shall have to beg his leave for a drink. *Augrh!*" (156). In Shere Khan's experience—and the words are uttered just after he has killed a man—even humans, or at least "ordinary" ones, are afraid of Shere Khan and, seemingly, cannot look him in the eye the way Mowgli does. Mowgli is, therefore, not human even as he is also not "cub" or wolf (or child or adult); even as he experiences privileges of both, he is ultimately neither, ultimately lacking.

Time and again, as much as he is portrayed as benefitting from be-ing seemingly simultaneously wolf and human, he is portrayed as suf-fering from deficiencies inherent to each condition of being, benefits and deficiencies dependent on performances of citizenship and gender. Mowgli's hybrid position as "anachronism"—a cunning survivor neither and both human and wolf—permits him to be a valuable public servant, a good subject of empire serving the colonial government, rendering the jungle and its inhabitants tame—or at least controlled—for the British empire. Indeed, by the end of "In the Rukh," due to Mowgli's influence (and commands and desires), the wolves now "fawn" "round Gisborne" and listen to Mowgli's wife, who chastises them and "spurn[s] them aside as they brushed against her bare feet" while she "stood nursing her child" (349). However, much of the story serves as an extended audition for whether Mowgli truly does "fit" the requirements for performances of good citizenship (or really colonial subject-hood, as colonial "native" Mowgli would even as an adult never be accorded full British citizen-ship rights) for the British empire, performance auditions which include shepherding nilghai to show off his abilities and for Gisborne's pleasure, herding a pony and foiling a delinquent servant, and demonstrating how absolutely under his control the wolves are by "playing upon a rude bamboo flute, to whose music four huge wolves danced solemnly on their hind legs" (345). Markedly, such performances are dependent on and limited by gender and sexuality: the story makes clear that Mowgli's true motive (or at least one of his true motives) in gaining government employment, befriending Gisborne, demonstrating repeatedly his supe-riority and authority, and simultaneously cowing and serving Gisborne's servant Abdul Gafur is to woo Abdul Gafur's daughter. Indeed, though he acknowledges he "was a wolf among wolves none the less till a time came when Those of the jungle bade me go because I was a man," he knows, as he tells Abdul Gafur's daughter, "that I am human born, be-cause my heart is in thy hold, little one" (346). His humanity here is de-termined by his dependency, a theme picked up on and extended at times in *The Jungle Books*, yet earlier on in both texts it is Mowgli's animal nature that exposes his limits and dangers—his fear in "In the Rukh" of Gisborne's house as a "trap" when a "curtain" noisily falls and his naïve appreciation of the "rich" things on display, which earns Abdul Gafur's scorn as well as the slander that he is "only a thief from the jungle" (331), and in *The Jungle Books*, the animosity of Buldeo, the priest, and others and being ejected from the village for his "beast" sorcery (62). Viewed with suspicion by male human authorities (hunter, priest, Abdul Gafur as potential father-in-law, and even, at times, Gisborne Sahib) for being too animal or, in the context of empire, going too "native," and by the wolves for being too human, Mowgli is cast out of both wolf pack and human village. Being both and neither, in other words, ultimately causes him to lack home and community.

The result is for him to become "Master of the Jungle" and create his own community amongst "The Jungle People" consisting of friends like his four wolf brothers, Baloo the bear, Bagheera, and Kaa the snake. To make that work, however, the text must insist on Mowgli's de-humanization, render him animal, a process on display in the final Mowgli story of the *Jungle Books*, "The Spring Running," even as the fundamental unsustainability of that rendering surfaces. Having returned to the jungle after failed village life, but now independent of pack life, Mowgli enjoys himself thoroughly—and entirely as an animal. Referring to him as being "like all his people," in this case the jungle animals, the text describes Mowgli's pursuit of past spring "flittings" (307) while suggesting he only understands things in reference to physical, bodily—and thereby seemingly animalistic—terms. Yet his not being fully animal makes these references incomplete: overcome by "a feeling of pure unhappiness," Mowgli's initial recourse is to "[look] himself over to be sure that he had not trod on a thorn" (307). He notes that "his stomach is heavy" (308) and is repeatedly convinced that he has "surely eaten poison" (309).[8] His moodiness, however, aligned symbolically with the arrival of spring and mating season, and coupled with the insistence (contrary to its telling in "In the Rukh") that the jungle will not again cast him out but "Man goes to Man at the last" (320), appears clearly to be that of strong emotions connected bodily to human adolescence. Even as he is most de-humanized, most unable to grasp the tumult of human emotions and humanity engulfing him, his very humanity draws him out of the jungle and precludes him from any further performances of his wolfishness.

Tellingly, too, Mowgli's identity and performance as wolf are dependent upon a gendered version of masculinity that keeps him separate from women outside of the (at times fiercely) nurturing mother figures Raksha, the Mother Wolf, and Messua.[9] Pointedly preceding his realization that he must leave the jungle is his sight of a girl outside a village (319). Yet that girl, who both "screamed" and "gave a deep sigh" (319) at the unexpected sight of Mowgli, leaves the pages of the story without further contact and the tales end merely with Mowgli in the midst of the emotionally difficult task of leaving the jungle again. The abruptness of such an ending, as critics rightly observe, hints at the inability to conceive of Mowgli as successful adult straddled between both states of being, or, really, as a fully complete human, for it is a divided, multiple Mowgli who is ascendant in "The Spring Running," admitting in his fright at the tumult of emotions coursing through him, "I was afraid—and yet it was not *I* that was afraid" (312). "In the Rukh," generally viewed critically as either or both inevitable in its depiction of Mowgli as British government servant and unsatisfying, attempts to offer such a glimpse at an "adult" Mowgli, but even there Mowgli is still an adolescent emerging into adulthood.[10] Even in the midst of portrayals of adolescent crisis if not sexual awakening, the Mowgli tales cannot imagine a complete Mowgli, fully adult, fully wolf, or fully human. His entire existence, supernatural prowess as well as naivety and other deficiencies, is predicated on incompleteness, being almost but not quite, more and less.

A similar condition is the lot of Kimball O'Hara in *Kim*: throughout his own abruptly-ending, gender- and citizen-performance revealing bildungsroman, the Anglo-Indian hybrid Kim is simultaneously extraordinary and utterly ordinary, both Sahib and not Sahib, altogether an ideal servant of the British empire and a de-humanized aspect of it. Born in India to working-class parents from Ireland, the orphan Kim seeks out novelty in the form of experiences and adventures. Drawn for this reason to the Tibetan lama whose disciple he becomes—and whose role presents Kim with another division and multiplication, that of being both spiritual and worldly—Kim, like the Uptons' doll characters, is able to change his identity (or at least perceptions of it) with his clothes: "The woman who looked after him insisted with tears that he should wear European clothes—trousers, a shirt, and a battered hat. Kim found it easier to slip into Hindu or Mohammedan garb when engaged on certain businesses" (5). All in all, his state of being is contemptuously delineated by the novel's Russian and French antagonists, though their reference is the hybridity of Hurree Babu, an English-educated Bengali: "decidedly this fellow is an original. . . . He represents in little India in transition—the monstrous hybridism of East and West . . . He has lost his own country and has not acquired any other" (240). "Not yet European," as Randall phrases it, Kim is also not quite Indian but his ability to pass as such provides him with privileges akin to those offered Mowgli in his own "in-between" state. These include "freedom" greater than that known by the fully white individuals he encounters. Finding himself "newly caught" (137) at a barrack-school, for example, he listens while the white "drummer-boy" ordered to watch him complains that "in this bloomin' Inja you're only a prisoner at large" (105), yet he manages to escape with a change of costume, a feat to which the spy horse-dealer Mahbub Ali comments, "I do not think it is often that a Sahib and the son of a Sahib runs away from there" (133). Like Mowgli in his jungle, Kim, too, can disappear at will (into "his" India), for as he tells Mahbub

Ali, who also relays it to the white Sahib, Colonel Creighton, "once gone, who is to find me again?" (146).

Indeed, much of the text works to cast Kim as "the marvelous boy" cited by Sara Suleri (115) and Don Randall (144). Early on, we are bluntly told "had Kim been at all an ordinary boy, he would have carried on the play" but he knows enough of "human nature" to know when to stop, defer, and curry favor (*Kim* 51). His extraordinariness is repeatedly confirmed by those who either befriend him or wish to use him (or both), as when Lurgan Sahib emphatically tells Colonel Creighton that Kim "is the only boy I could not make to see things," a feature particularly useful to the British government and its espionage department as "it means that he is strong enough . . . to make anyone do anything he wants" (174). Revealingly also, although the Russian and Frenchman are contemptuous of Hurree Babu's hybridity, they see Kim as "a young man . . . of singular, though unwashen, beauty" (240). All of these instances, of course, highlight Kim's gendered identity: not child, adult, or adolescent, he is labeled "boy" and "young man"; as with Mowgli, Kim's performance of good citizenship for the British imperial government is hinged on his performances of gender and sexuality. Predominantly surrounded by masculine figures, often father figures, and at times notably asexual or homoerotic, as some critics have noted, Kim reflects early on that "every time before that I have borne a message it concerned a woman. Now it is men. Better" (40). By the text's end, however, Kim, flourishing in adolescence like Mowgli, recognizes the power of heterosexuality as well, complaining "how can a man follow the Way or the Great Game when he is so-always pestered by women?" (258), but turning his address to the Woman of Shamlegh from "Mother" to "Sister" (257) and surprising her with English and a kiss before leaving, reflecting that "at least she did not treat me like a child" (267). Ultimately, it is only through the aid provided by the Woman of Shamlegh and the Sahiba and her poor relation (277) that Kim is able to return to the search for the Way and service to the empire.[11] In other words, though like *The Jungle Books*, as Plotz elucidates, "the novel stops abruptly . . . as if to cut off any vision of an *adult* Kim living successfully in two worlds, as if such a prospect were unimaginable" ("The Empire of Youth" 127), Kim is still able to use masculinity and sexuality often connected with adulthood to propel native women to help him, reinforcing one of the lessons he learns at St. Xavier's school: "one must never forget that one is a Sahib and that some day, when examinations are passed, one will command natives" (127). It is the seemingly malleable, hybrid child and adolescent (boy/young man) Kim who is valuable to empire, a notion solidified by Mahbub Ali's, Lurgan Sahib's, and Hurree Babu's anxiety and urgency in getting him into the "Great Game" while yet young and Lurgan's own admission, "*I* should have used him long ago . . . the younger the better. That is why I always have my really valuable jewels watched by a child" (174).

The existence of this urgency and anxiety indicates Kim's lack, however, for it is also his very boyhood that marks him as incomplete. Though Creighton is intrigued by Kim, he is still hesitant about him and must be convinced by the others, for as Creighton tells Lurgan, "It's only a boy, after all" (177). Kim's national and ethnic hybridity are also detraction as much as privilege, for as Hurree Babu explains to him when he is allowed to leave St. Xavier's, "if you were Asiatic of birth you might be employed right off; but this half-year of leave is to make you de-Englishized" (186). Despite the text's acknowledgment of his extraordinariness and superiority—his uniqueness exacerbated by the repeated questioning "who is Kim?" (120) and difference highlighted by admission that St. Xavier's school "looks down on boys who 'go native all-together'" though it is precisely his ability and willingness to "go native" that gives Kim and the government he ultimately serves power (126–127)—an undercurrent throughout the text accentuates his absolute ordinariness. Early on in the novel's pages, the narrator affirms Kim's status as but one among many, no different seemingly from other boys with a repetition of the term "boylike": "Boylike, if an acquaintance had a scheme, Kim was quite ready with one of his own; and, boylike, he had really thought for as much as twenty minutes at a time of his father's prophecy" (18).[12] His position as but one undistinguishable in a large mass is repeatedly confirmed, as when he realizes how precarious his life is in the Great Game, reflecting, "for who would miss a boy beaten to death, or, it may be, thrown into a well by the roadside?" (135). At times even his extraordinariness is utterly ordinary. Compared with other boys at St. Xavier's school, Kim's own background is unexceptional: as the pupils he sometimes disdains tell their own stories at bedtime, "Kim watched, listened, and approved. This was not insipid, single-word talk of drummer boys"; instead, just like his own experiences, "the mere story of their adventures, which to them were no adventures, on their road to and from school would have crisped a Western boy's hair" (126).

As with Mowgli, the result of Kim's simultaneous existence—subject of stories both extraordinary and ordinary—is dehumanization along with incompleteness. Kim is described by turns throughout the novel as "wild animal" (105), polo pony or colt (129; 175), and supernatural creature, and reduced to jewel, toy, pawn, charm (or son of), letter and number, machine part, and museum artifact or specimen, an object polished and traded by collectors and players.[13] A refrain of the lama throughout the tale, echoed by Mahbub Ali at least once, is that Kim is an "imp," a term used in teasing for "a mischievous child" ("imp," *OED*) but one that has dark supernatural, de-humanizing, nuances to it, nuances that are reaffirmed in the contexts in which the term is used in the novel to highlight Kim's exceptionality, as when the lama questions in *Macbeth* fashion whether Kim be human-born by stating, "but to none among men, if so be thou art woman-born, has my heart gone out as it has to thee—thoughtful, wise, and courteous; but something of a small imp" (72). Similarly, Mahbub Ali observes, "I have met many men, women, and boys, and not a few Sahibs. I have never in all my days met such an imp as thou art" (146). The extraordinariness of Kim's hybrid status rendering him an object, a "specimen," is overtly suggested by Hurree Babu, who calls him "super-numerary on probation. Quite unique specimen" (186). By the end of the tale, as critics have repeatedly observed, the lama is portrayed as melding into the lifeless "stone Bodhisat" in the Lahore Museum (288), but Kim's own treatment as artifact is consistent throughout the tale. Indeed, both are aligned with religious iconography: just as Kim sets out with the lama for his own larger foray into the Great Game and work for the British government, "an English observer might have said that he looked rather like the young saint of a stained-glass window whereas he was but a growing lad faint with emptiness" (197). Barbara J. Black fascinatingly suggests that "Kipling may have produced *Kim* as his museum piece" (244) and certainly Kim is essentially framed if not formed by his experiences at and among the artifacts on display at the Lahore Museum (which is based on the museum where Kipling's father was curator) and Lurgan Sahib's own dark "Wonder House." Lurgan, whose powers over Kim are thwarted by Kim's Englishness and recurrence to the multiplication table (156–157), casts Kim as object to be collected, polished, traded, and sold by using him to "play the Play of the Jewels" (158) and tellingly admitting, "Yes, my friends, the Kings are very fond of toys—and so am I sometimes" (153). Whether the "toys" meant are the expensive phonograph Lurgan finds "cheap at the price" (153) to break in his failed "testing" (by torment) of Kim or Kim himself (another sort of "jewel" in the crown of empire polished by a renowned jeweler) is left to the reader to determine. However, Mahbub Ali is more forthright, "selling" a de-humanized Kim to Colonel Creighton and the Great Game just as he does—and in the code of—his horses, even suggesting, after forcing Kim to endure what he perceived at the time as "slights," that "my horse is well-trained. . . . Others would have kicked, Sahib" (111). By the last few pages, Kim becomes a machine part loose in a human world, "his soul" described as "out of gear with its surroundings—a cog wheel unconnected with any machinery" until "with an almost audible click he felt the wheels of his being lock up anew on the world without," the "click" presaged by the very phrasing of the de-humanizing identity question, "And *what* is Kim?" (283, my emphasis).

The other prime way the text de-humanizes by objectifying Kim and helping to render him incomplete is through his role as play-thing, toy, or pawn in the Great Game itself, the culmination of the many games and bouts of play ("king of the castle" cannon, prophecy, war, conversation, etc.) the text offers. Indeed, it is his success at various "games" that indicates Kim's fitness for governmental work: the text's opening pages reveal that "what he loved was the game for its own sake," the "game" being "intrigue" (5), and very quickly "he was playing for larger things—the sheer excitement and the sense of power" (49). He respects Creighton after seeing how others treat and speak with him and because of his mastery of Urdu as "no man could be a fool who knew the language so intimately, who moved so gently and silently, and"—taking a page from *The Jungle Books*—"whose eyes were so different from the dull fat eyes of other Sahibs" (120), yet he first admires him as "a man after his own heart—a tortuous and indirect person playing a hidden game" (119). Mahbub Ali comments of Kim that "it is as though a polo-pony, breaking loose, ran out to learn the game alone" (129). Notably, even for Mahbub Ali, Kim is not a player in the game but the vehicle by which the game is played. Indeed, Kim's role as pawn is well-understood. Matthew Fellion suggests that "Kipling presents a vision of India as a chessboard. . . . Yet there are no players who are not themselves also subject to the rules—these pieces move themselves and each other" (904) while Sara Suleri notably argues that

> despite his ostensible mobility and cultural dexterity . . . Kim is an imperial casualty of more tragic proportions than he is usually granted. It is not as though Kim stands outside the colonial system called the Great Game and . . . has the luxury of choosing whether or not to play it: instead, Kim *is* the Game.
>
> (116)

As game-piece, not human player, Kim leaves the pages of the novel torn, incomplete, still divided by his love for the spiritual lama and the worldly responsibilities of empire that weigh him down and break his health as he finds himself caught up in the Great Game. Seemingly restored to health as the novel draws to a close, Kim lacks certainty and resolution regarding his future—even critics disagree whether the novel's (in)conclusion leaves Kim serving the lama and/or the British imperial government, aloof from or still in the midst of the Great Game, freed from or "locke[ed] up anew" (283) on the "wheel of life." Even in—or perhaps because of—his incomplete state, the promises he embodies as cross-cultural imperial subject-cum-citizen, Kim is projected as a "lesson" to other incomplete Western (British, American, perhaps European) boys, particularly boys vested with the legacy of empire. In her analysis of *Kim* and Edith Nesbit's *The Story of the Amulet* (1906), Black indicates that "the represented museum teaches particularly a young and un(in)formed audience about heritage, about what it is . . . to be English, thereby transforming children into citizens and boys into men who will honor the narrative of nationalism" (237). With its frame of museums and recourse to games and play in the spirit of Newbolt's

"Vitai Lampada," Kipling presents Kim as an epitome of malleable—but never complete—British imperial child (boy) citizen, a depiction rein-forced by the text's emphasis on obedience. Although we are told em-phatically that Kim does not wish to be a soldier as "there was nothing in his composition to which drill and routine appealed" (95), he never-theless internalizes the importance of obedience in his role as burgeon-ing imperial servant, loyal British imperial subject, and would-be British imperial citizen: not only does the "Great Game" for Kim "begin" with Lurgan Sahib as "one who is to be obeyed to the last wink of his eye-lashes" and Lurgan's own "school" (158), but he attends St. Xavier's as it "is an order," "blandly" asking Mahbub Ali, "who am I to dispute an order?" (135). With such a question and adherence to "orders," and with Mowgli before him (whose own stories, preoccupied with Jungle law, equally vault notions of obedience), entrenched in a contradictory dis-course of masculinity, games/play, citizenship, performance, and simul-taneous extraordinary superiority and de-humanizing incompleteness, Kim encapsulates his position as ideal boy citizen-in-training for Kipling and, in Robert Baden-Powell's re-tellings, as we will see, both Mowgli and Kim become ideal boy scouts for real-life incomplete boys training to be citizens.

Baden-Powell's extraordinary, incomplete boy scouts and hybrid, liminal citizenship

In one of the few critical analyses of boy scout series books, M. Paul Holsinger counts "more than one hundred full-length novels dealing with the Boy Scouts" "published between 1911 and 1914; well over three hundred different books had appeared in print by the advent of the Great Depression" (178). Though, in the U.S., boy scout headquarters quickly tried to quell problematic portrayals of scouts by, among other things, launching its own approved series (179),

> most of the boys depicted in the Boy Scout novels of the day were fantastic superheroes who were larger than life itself as they took on spies, enemy agents, thugs and murderers of all kinds, and, with relative ease, overcame them all in the name of Scouting and the American Way.
>
> (178)

Such terms—"larger than life" "fantastic superheroes" who "took on spies, enemy agents," etc.—are of course also applicable to Mowgli and Kim, but popular boy scout novels of the period highlight other fea-tures shared by Kipling's boy figures, namely obedience, games-playing proficiency, and hybridity. These features are particularly evident in one notable series book of the period, *The Boy Scouts with King*

George (1915), a tale of a trio of adolescent boys who discover and defeat a group of German spies, culminating with the boys' flying of an airplane and destroying a zeppelin. Aligned with a discourse of incompleteness (with deficiency and de-humanization) also shared by Kipling's boys, these features are prominent in Baden-Powell's scouting materials and especially *The Wolf Cub's Handbook* (1916/1918) as well.

The first few chapters of *The Boy Scouts with King George*, which was penned under the name Major Robert Maitland, serve as exposition for the scouting movement, with the primary protagonist, Harry Fleming, explaining to his friend as well as to the implied reader that Baden-Powell "did a bigger thing for England when he started the Boy Scouts than when he defended Mafeking against the Boers!" (4). While Baden-Powell's original *Scouting for Boys* (1908) was published after the Boer Wars and as Germany began to assert its power more and more, *The Boy Scouts with King George* was published in the midst of World War I, leading it directly to address controversy about militarism that sometimes surrounded the movement: "We Boy Scouts aren't soldiers in any way. But we do learn to do the things a soldier has to do"; even though, as scouts, "we aren't supposed to think of that . . . we learn to be obedient. We learn discipline. And we get to understand camp life, and the open air, and all the things a soldier has to know about, sooner or later" which makes former boy scouts "a lot readier" than others when needed to serve their country in war (5). As the text elaborates,

> you can depend on it that General Baden-Powell had that in his mind's eye all the time, too. He doesn't want us to be military and aggressive, but he does want the Empire to have a lot of fellows on call who are hard and fit, so that they can defend themselves and the country. You see, in America, and here in England, too, we're not like the countries on the Continent. We don't make soldiers of every man in the country.
>
> (6)[14]

Obedience in the first few chapters becomes a pre-condition for and continued requirement of boy scout worthiness. In its introduction of Harry, the text is quick to point out that "as a scout he had learned to be loyal and obedient" (10). The need for these characteristics is reiterated as World War I breaks out and the boy scouts in the story realize that

> there is real work ahead of us . . . work just as real and hard, in its way, as if we all were going to fight for England. Everyone cannot fight, but the ones who stay at home and do the work that comes to their hands will serve England just as loyally.
>
> (23)

Before he leaves for the war, the scoutmaster reinforces this need for obedience and loyalty by asking his troop to "do your duty as scouts" (24). Adherence to duty, loyalty, and obedience, however, serves boys in other ways in the tale. Harry is an American who has a few trying moments of acclimation after moving to England where his father is sent for business, "but his Boy Scout training stood him in good stead. He kept his temper, and it was not long before he began to make friends" (11). His ease of acclimation is further enhanced by another supposed sign of boy scout worthiness: the fact that "he excelled at [sports and] games; even the English games, that were new and strange to him, presented few difficulties for him" (11). Indeed, superior games-sportsmanship as an attribute of an ideal boy scout is indicated almost immediately, with the scoutmaster, John Grenfel, described tellingly as "a big, bronzed Englishman, sturdy and typical of the fine class to which he belonged—public school and university man, first-class cricketer and a football international" (6).

It is Harry's hybridity, however, with its larger connections to Britain's imperial legacy, that helps him finally to succeed. Strikingly, the text opens by toeing the line of empire, referencing pride and humor as "one reason you Britishers are as big an empire as you are. You think it's sort of funny and a bit of a misfortune, don't you, to be anything but English?" (3). As with Kim and Mowgli, the text attempts to offer Harry the best of two identities (in this case, U.S. and British affiliation), muddling its protagonist's subjectivity even as it tries to promote the various "superior" benefits, and maintain the separation, of each identity affiliation. Having excelled in his U.S. scout troop, Harry is allowed to join an English troop, though "it had been necessary to modify certain rules. Harry, of course, could not subscribe to quite the same scout oath that bound his English fellows" (12). Time and again in the opening chapters the text takes pains to keep secure Harry's U.S. national-citizen status (presumably for its American audience) even as he increasingly serves the British government (the text even closes with him being lauded by and reporting to a British colonel). Even as Harry joins in "three cheers for King George!," the text insists that "he was as much of an American as he had ever been" but rationalizes his now divided, multiple (dual) loyalty through analogy to empire: "After all, England had been and was the mother country" (23). As the scoutmaster explains, in words reminiscent of Mowgli's lesson of the "Master Words of the Jungle" for protection and help—"We be of one blood, ye and I" (*Jungle Books* 24)—Harry is non-threatening and able to serve the English in this time of need because "we're of one blood, we English and you Americans. We've had our quarrels, but relatives always do quarrel. And you'll not be asked, as a scout here, to do anything an American shouldn't do" (Maitland 24).

Such British and American blurrings, not being asked "to do anything an American shouldn't do," and even subscribing to the English oath as potential problem are fascinatingly replicated by Baden-Powell's own World War I text, *The Wolf Cub's Handbook*. Like its forebear, *Scouting for Boys*, *The Wolf Cub's Handbook* overtly takes Kipling's boy characters for models. Indeed, Baden-Powell introduces would-be scouts to Kim only a few pages into *Scouting for Boys*, explicitly beginning his section on "Kim" with these words: "A good example of what a Boy Scout can do is to be found in Rudyard Kipling's story of 'Kim'" (14). Within a mere sentence, Kim becomes a boy scout—or, more to the point, the ideal boy scout—a position reaffirmed at the end of the section, when Baden-Powell insists that "these and other adventures of Kim are well worth reading, because they show what valuable work a Boy Scout could do for his country if he were sufficiently trained and sufficiently intelligent" (19). Kim and "Kim's Game" (essentially Kipling's "the Play of the Jewels") make appearances in *The Wolf Cub's Handbook* as well, but in that text Mowgli and Kipling himself are even more prominent. While *Scouting for Boys* begins with Baden-Powell's tale of his experiences in the battle of Mafeking (1899–1900), *The Wolf Cub's Handbook* begins with Baden-Powell's re-telling of Mowgli's adoption by wolves in *The Jungle Books*. Even more notably, the entire handbook is organized by "bites" for "every boy, like every young Wolf, has a hearty appetite" ("Introduction" 7). With that statement, boys reading the handbook and joining the organization are de-humanized, transformed like Mowgli into wolves, with the handbook serving as "a meal offered by an old Wolf to the young Cubs" (7). In it, "there is juicy meat to be eaten, and there are tough bones to be gnawed" (7). At times, the boys' de-humanization verges on the viciously uncomfortable, as in "The Bagheera Dance" of the "Fourth Bite" wherein "each Cub becomes a panther" who pretends to prey on deer, culminating in the cubs leaping onto the pretended deer to "tear him to pieces" and then "biting imaginary lumps of deer meat" (42). In *Jungle Plays for Wolf Cubs* (1928), "arranged by" S. G. Gurney, the violence and de-humanization are even more pronounced, with one cub scout pretending to be the deer, now a doe, while the remainder, the parenthetical "stage" directions indicate,

> spring forward on to the DOE with a yell, seize him, as described in Wolf Cub Handbook, page 43, and apparently tear him to pieces as he disappears amongst the others. Turning outwards they run jumping back to their dens, carrying and biting imaginary lumps of deer meet.
>
> (15)[15]

Citing Baden-Powell's allegiance to G. Stanley Hall's theory of recapitulation in *Adolescence* (1904), Troy Boone explains Baden-Powell's use of the wolf motif and especially of the "howling" exercise that begins meetings of the cub scouts as an instance of letting the child demonstrate its "savage" nature; in so doing, "'recapitulation' of the 'savage' is

supposedly a means of 'elevating' the child to 'civilization'" (118–119).
The overt goal of the scouting movement, of course, was citizenship,
made explicit in the subtitle of *Scouting for Boys: A Handbook for Instruction in Good Citizenship* and in the "Object of Wolf Cub Training"
(Part III) of *The Wolf Cub's Handbook*: "Our object in taking up the
training of the Wolf Cubs is not merely to devise a pleasant pastime
for the Cub-masters or for the boys, but to improve the efficiency of
the future citizens of our Empire" (209). Allusions to empire as part
and parcel of the creation of good citizens were not accidental and form
perhaps the strongest point of agreement between Kipling and Baden-
Powell. Citing Kipling's own *Land and Sea Tales for Scouts and Guides*
(1923), Richard Flynn observes Kipling's direct involvement in the
scouting movement, and suggests "in his association with the Scouting
Movement, Kipling either tacitly approves of or actively endorses Baden-
Powell's attempts . . . to condition the masses to accept Imperialist ideology through Scouting" (56). In his well-known discussion of *Kim*,
Edward Said offers a similar point, elaborating that

> an almost exact contemporary of Kipling, [Baden-Powell,] BP, as he
> was called, was greatly influenced by Kipling's boys generally and
> Mowgli in particular; BP's ideas about "boyology" fed those images
> directly into a grand scheme of imperial authority culminating in
> the great Boy Scout structure "fortifying the wall of empire," which
> confirmed this inventive conjunction of fun and service in row after
> row of bright-eyed, eager, and resourceful little middle-class ser-
> vants of empire.
>
> (137–138)

Moreover, he argues,

> BP and Kipling concur on two other important points: that boys
> ultimately should conceive of life and empire as governed by un-
> breakable Laws, and that service is more enjoyable when thought
> of less like a story—linear, continuous, temporal—and more like a
> playing-field—many-dimensional, discontinuous, spatial.
>
> (138)

Despite Said's emphasis on the "playing field," stories were decidedly
central to Baden-Powell's scouting vision as well. Baden-Powell's use
of Kipling's tales is evidence of that, as are the copious other stories
that make appearances in the guide books, including in *The Wolf Cub's
Handbook* alone, works by Jack London and Juliana Horatia Ewing,
and the very organization of *Scouting for Boys* into "yarns," campfire
stories. As with *The Boy Scouts with King George*, *Kim*, and *The Jungle
Books*, however, games and play were certainly central to the scouting

movement and perhaps the most repeated refrain throughout *The Wolf Cub's Handbook* is acceptance of duty and obedience. Even the very de-humanizing howl itself "means something," for example, which is that the cub scouts "want to welcome" the "old Wolf" or cub-master "and at the same time to show that they are ready to obey his command" (17). The seeming absolute importance of duty and obedience is highlighted again and again in the manual, even made didactically explicit in analysis and re-telling of Ewing's tale of "The Brownies" (which Baden-Powell notably places in "the jungle" [46] so that Ewing's story is re-cast as a jungle tale): Just like cub (and boy) scouts, "Brownies do their work quietly and without wanting to be thanked or rewarded for it. They do it because it is their duty to their father and mother and family" (48). Notably, as is further reiterated throughout the handbook's pages, "it may sometimes be a trouble to them if they are feeling tired or want to be playing, but they must remember that it is their Duty, and Duty comes before everything else" (48). As with *Kim* in particular, games are given as essential to the scouting movement and the wolf cubs because they encourage the understanding and performance of duty for, in Baden-Powell's words, "our method of training is to educate from within rather than to instruct from without; to offer games and activities which, while being attractive to the small boy will seriously educate him morally, mentally, and physically" (210). As such, the conflation of games/play, stories, and obedience is inherent in materials associated with the cub and boy scouts. Indeed, Gurney's *Jungle Plays for Wolf Cubs* makes that conflation obvious. Punning on the word "plays," *Jungle Plays* is both literary endeavor and games manual. Set up as dramatic skits, *Jungle Plays* lets cub scouts "act out" scenes from Kipling's stories even as they play games and dances developed from those stories and outlined in Baden-Powell's *The Wolf Cub's Handbook*, which also encourages "acting" and "make-believe" (*The Wolf Cub's Handbook* 200). Examples in *Jungle Plays* include the cub scouts acting out the "law" as given by Baloo," including the "Master words of the Jungle" and "hunting calls" (7–8), and the cub scout pack reciting at least part of Kipling's poem, "the Law of the Jungle," responding together, "Obey!," to its final lines, "But the head and the hoof of the Law and the haunch and the hump is—" (*Jungle Plays* 10; *Jungle Books* 167).

The conflation of games, obedience, and duty is also manifest in the wolf cub's promise of loyalty, which includes loyalty

> [t]o the King. – I have told you how Wolves in a Pack all obey the chief Wolf. So it is in our nation. The British people are a very big pack, but they have their one chief, His Majesty the King. So long as they look up to him, and obey him, their work will be successful like the hunting of the pack, or the football match, where all obey their captain.

> If everybody started to play the game in his own way, there would be no rules, and there could be no success. But if we 'play the game,' and back up as the King directs, our country will always be successful.
>
> And in the same way, as a Scout Wolf Cub, you must obey the leader of your pack or six.
>
> (32)

Here, as elsewhere, loyalty, duty, and obedience are described as playing a game and following game rules, as when, in repeating the didactic purpose of his use of "The Brownies" story, Baden-Powell informs his readers, "Do not forget that, Cubs. Do your duty, though it may not be pleasant, or it may be unnoticed by other people. Still, you must stick to it, because that means 'playing the game,' not for your own glory or excitement, but that your side may win" (90). Baden-Powell goes on to suggest, after telling of a former scout in the navy who sacrificed his life to "stick to" his duty for his country, that "even a Wolf Cub is not too young to be a hero" (91). As Allen Warren notes, consistent in Baden-Powell's copious and at times conflicting writings is the idea that "each citizen was urged to see him or herself as part of the national team playing the great game" ("Citizens" 238). Games-playing, good citizenship, and empire continuance are one in such portrayals, so much so that Baden-Powell even takes for granted another leisure activity encouraged by empire, collecting, bluntly insisting, "and I am sure that every Cub has got a collection of some sort" (121). Not only can this collecting lead to imperial knowledge but such acts as "drawing and colouring the Medal Ribbons . . . awarded for different wars" can be "an awfully interesting collection to make, because it tells you of glorious fights in which our soldiers and sailors have bled and died for King and Country," which is further useful in showing how "just as" these "soldiers and sailors" "have given up their time and their lives in the Service of the King, Wolf Cubs will be ready when their time comes to follow their good example" (122).[16]

Continued references to king and country, including the loyalty oath, suggest another aspect Baden-Powell's movement shared with Kipling's fictional boys: hybridity. Originally published by Baden-Powell in 1916, *The Wolf Cub's Handbook* was quickly obtained by the Boy Scouts of America, and issued in the U.S. in 1918. This U.S. edition, however, essentially reproduced the British edition with few, if any, changes, leaving intact such things as the oath of loyalty to King George V, a potentially awkward and controversial feature of the British movement already on display in *The Boy Scouts with King George*'s acknowledgment of Harry's not taking "quite the same scout oath that bound his English fellows" (12). Almost if not from the outset, the scouting movement itself was divided and multiple, marked by hybridity formed from its imperial legacy and aspirations. To legitimatize its wolf and scout analogies alone, in addition to freely using *The Jungle Books*, *The Wolf Cub's Handbook* cites the stories of U.S. American Jack London; "the far Western prairies of America" where "the Red Indians were a nation of scouts," the "best" of whom "got the nickname 'Wolf'"; and the "entirely different" people of South Africa who also "called their best scouts 'Wolf'" (18). The "worldly" and imperial theme is extended in the "Sixth Bite," which asks the reader to

> remember, too, that with the boy Wolf Cubs the uniform means something more, it means that you are now one of a big brotherhood. It goes all over the world. There are your brother Wolf Cubs in Australia and New Zealand, in Africa, in Canada, in India—everywhere in the British Empire—all doing the same work as young Scouts, and all wearing the same green sweaters, shorts, and caps.
>
> (56)

With the very emphasis on the "brotherhood" that "goes all over the world," Baden-Powell elucidates gendered aspects of the movement connected also with Mowgli and Kim. As Katherine Magyarody observes,

> part of the trouble in the formation of a Scout-like youth movement for girls was the fact that Scouting—despite its assertion that it was not militarist—used the prospect of both imperial adventure and a pan-European war to catch children's attention[,]

and girls were not supposed to envision their lives with respect to "imperial adventure" and worldliness: in girl guide books, "their vigilance is not oriented toward temporally and physically distant colonial space but toward the local and near-present" (249). With its focus on empire and worldliness cast up from boys' local community groupings, the scouting movement determinedly became a "brotherhood," deliberately and for its time necessarily siphoning girls off into their own separate movement. Don Randall remarks that "the immensely successful Scouting movement . . . confirms and effectively codifies British boyhood as a foregrounded concern in negotiations of national identity and imperial status" and the term "British boyhood" is key (9).

Indeed, the security of wolf cub/boy scout ventures—and of their masculinity—was perhaps even premised, like that of Mowgli and Kim, on their consisting of an all-male (or, really, mostly male) community. Even as and perhaps because they are mostly surrounded by men, the hybrid Mowgli and Kim are at times androgynous and at times hypermasculine, attractive to men and women alike as a result of their superior beauty and strength or skills, with their masculinity tending not to be in doubt. The same was true of the scouting movement, which specifically called upon Kipling in its projections of masculinity, with Baden-Powell's dedication to *The Wolf Cub's Handbook* signifying as much: "To Rudyard Kipling, who has done so much to put the right spirit into our rising manhood" (7). Emphasizing self-sufficiency (particularly in such a seemingly exclusively masculine realm), Baden-Powell insists that every cub must learn to cook (109), should fold his clothes daily/ nightly as a means of "being prepared" (114), and that "a Cub is not much good who does not know how to use a needle" (113). Surrounded by boys, cubs can, it seems, without stigma engage in acts sometimes deemed "feminine." As a result, the handbook confidently puts forth Ewing's domestic tale of "The Brownies," where boys learn to clean up after themselves and for their family, and which likely later contributed to the name "Brownies" being associated with the Girl Guides and Girl Scouts; accepts women as lady cub-masters; and advocates domestic chores for boys, with an entire badge even dedicated to "House Orderly" (192). The description of the tasks for this badge are revealing for the ways in which they blur boundaries of gender and again suggest links between duty, obedience, family, and games. Early on, readers are told that helping one's mother "is a lesson only love can teach" (192) and that "minding baby" and "looking after your little brothers and sisters" is an honor as "it shows great confidence on the part of the Old Wolf to trust its precious Baby Wolf in the care of the Wolf Cub—so live up to it!" (194). Proof for the successful obtaining of a badge for "homecraft" includes whether the wolf cub's headquarters' club room is "a marvel of cleanliness and neatness. It should be the envy and despair of Scout-masters—who will begin to wish the Scouts had a Homecraft Badge, to teach them this, and give them a real keenness about orderly work" (195). Other proofs include "if 'mother,' when she is called on by the Cub-master, says there is nothing in the world like the Cub movement for making little boys helpful and useful and polite" and "that the examiner really *enjoys* the cup of tea [made by the cub]: it will put him in a good temper to pass your boots and your windows and even your greens!" (195). Baden-Powell even comments that "there is scarcely need to suggest any games by which Cubs may practice all this" for "one hears of children 'playing at house.' But Cubs don't really need to *play* at it—they are going to do it really. And it should prove more fascinating than any game" (195).

Of course, even as Baden-Powell suggests worthy domestic tasks for cub scouts, at other points he hyper-masculinizes them. In describing the "Team Player and Athlete" badge (20), for example, *The Wolf Cub's Handbook* emphasizes "self-control and pluck" and insists on a need to "inculcate the Spartan spirit into the boys," who are described as eminently "mouldable" (210). Tellingly, if disturbingly, the "Spartan spirit" includes ignoring hurt team-mates and refusing to cry when hurt (206). Earlier, too, the cubs and would-be cubs are told—prominently, in all capital letters—that "cubs never cry" and "always grin and bear it" despite being "in difficulty, in pain, in trouble, or in danger" (33). To reinforce this sentiment, readers are encouragingly told "that is what our soldiers and sailors do at the Front, so I am sure a Cub can do it" (33). They are also given the story of a German spy who is supposedly outed by a doctor as "not a British soldier" as the doctor has "hardly ever heard one groan or cry, however badly he may have been hurt" (33–34).

As the spy example indicates, too, in its attempt to navigate the waters of British boyhood and citizenship, and even as it advocated a "world brotherhood,"[17] the scouting movement found itself balancing nationality and empire, encouraging national allegiance and patriotism. In other words, the very idea of "citizenship" advocated by the scouting movement was hybrid, divided and multiple. Dieter Gosewinkel notes that with the U.S.' Declaration of Independence, the idea of "citizen/citizenship," as distinct from the idea of "subjecthood to the English Crown," "became core terms of a state order based on democracy and constitutionality" with "the American legal term 'citizen' . . . fundamentally linked to political rights and participation in the political body" (24). Nationality, meanwhile, was a separate entity, conceived of as "duty of obedience or allegiance on the part of the subject and protection on the part of the state" rather than "individual rights and obligations" (25). However, as Baden-Powell's own movement and attempts to encourage "good citizenship" through "duty of obedience" demonstrate, "in the course of the twentieth century, British legal terminology denoting adherence to the state has gradually replaced the traditional concept of subjecthood with the concepts of nationality and citizenship" (27) so that today—and it seems even earlier for Baden-Powell and his cub and boy scouts, if not for Kipling—citizenship is distinguished by multiple, sometimes conflicting, attributes. It is, as Ruth Lister notes, "a contested concept" with "no one single definition" (9). Poised between citizenship and subjecthood with regards to their senses of nationality, affiliation, and duty, Baden-Powell's cub and boy scouts were enmeshed in hybridity akin to that of Kipling's Mowgli and Kim.

As with Kim and Mowgli, too, the cub/boy scouts' portrayals as unrelentingly hybrid, liminal figures reveal fault lines in competing discourses of superiority and incompleteness. Nearly as frequently as it underscores the need for adherence to duty and obedience, *The Wolf Cub's Handbook* depicts wolf cubs and boy scouts as extraordinary. At the same time that it highlights the "world brotherhood" of cub and boy scouts symbolized by their uniforms, for example, the text reiterates their obedience and indicates their extraordinariness, telling readers,

> people think a great lot of a boy who is dressed in this uniform, because they know he is not an ordinary boy, but that he can be clean

and smart and active, and that he can be trusted to do his best to obey orders or to do good turns for other people.

(56)

That cub and boy scouts are "not ordinary boys" is evident from the early pages of the handbook, which in the descriptions of the opening howl and salute with two hands, informs readers that "*Your* best will be twice as good as any ordinary boy's best" (17). Cub and boy scouts' extraordinariness is even remarked on in passing to describe, rather emphatically, seemingly minor things, such as "what duffers ordinary boys are at tying knots!" (87). Simultaneously, however, it is their deficiency that allows cub scouts to be de-humanized into "savages" and "wolves," compared to "primitive" natives, and which leads the handbook time and again to reference the boys as citizens-in-training, not actually "full" or "complete" citizens and to even revert to a discourse of artificiality. Passage after passage of *The Wolf Cub's Handbook* references the cub scouts in opposition to "real scouts," encouraging, for example, its readers to "try hard to pick up all the knowledge you can while you are a Wolf Cub. Try to pass all the tests, and win all the badges that are given for being clever at the game" as "it will be useful to you afterwards, when you want to be a real Scout" (38). The idea of the boy wolf cub's incompleteness is inherent in the very structure of the Wolf Cub organization, where boys begin as mere "recruits" until they earn (through time and examination) the right to be a "Tender-pad" before (after more time and examination) finally being allowed to be a "full-blown Wolf Cub" (59). After they reach "complete" cub status, of course, they can aspire further, for "the Wolf Cub looks up to the Boy Scout and the Boy Scout looks up to the Old Scout or Pioneer" (19), or, in a later analogy, "the boys of the British Empire have the chance of learning how to become its scouts by being Boy Scouts first, just as in the old days the Esquires learnt how to become Knights" and "then, too, the young Scouts, the 'Wolf Cubs,' like the pages of old, preparing to be Esquires, can learn how to become Boy Scouts when they get to the right age for it" (22). "Completeness," it seems, arrives only with the achievement of adulthood and the likely adoption of one of the paths toward "knighthood" (or present-day "real" scouts) Baden-Powell describes. These "real" scouts include "frontiersmen in the wilder parts of our Empire,"

the backwoodsmen, the hunters, the explorers, the map-makers, our soldiers and sailors, the Arctic navigators, the missionaries—all those men of our race who are living out in the wild, facing difficulties and dangers because it is their duty, enduring hardships, looking after themselves, keeping up the name of Britons for bravery, kindness, and justice all over the world.

(22)

But the dangers of fraudulence, of not being "real," extend beyond "adulthood" into masculinity more generally, as the section on swimming ominously indicates: "a fellow is only a 'kid,' and not a real boy until he can swim" (87).

Within the context of official citizenship, of course, only "real boys" were envisioned as stewards of empire and worldly caretakers. Baden-Powell, drawing from Kipling's fictional boys, designed his scouting movement and its performance of daily "good turns" to foster such "real boys," fully aware that, despite the hybrid realities experienced by authors such as Burnett and the Uptons (and their own literary creations), with respect to citizenship, only boys embodied the liminal, transitional potential of hybridity—because only boys could every fully become citizens.[18] Still, boys then as now were subject to views of "childhood as a deficient state," as Courtney Weikle-Mills phrases it (4), echoing many other scholars of citizenship and childhood studies, and this idea of deficiency also contributes to the consistent hybridity of Kipling's and Baden-Powell's depictions of boys, that renders them simultaneously extraordinary and incomplete, marked perpetually by Randall's notion of "not yet"—not yet men, not yet adults, not yet citizens, not yet fully Western or fully human. It is this deficiency that marks Baden-Powell's dedication to Kipling referencing "our *rising* manhood" (7, my emphasis). Kipling's and Baden-Powell's boys are "rising," but "not yet" there, though, unlike girls, their very masculine being embodies the promises and potential of full citizenship: they *can* "get" there—if, unlike Mowgli and Kim, they can achieve adulthood. For a period abruptly delimited by World War I, which took its toll on and of a generation of boys, adolescents, and young men, including Kipling's own son, that was far from certain. Even without the historical context, Baden-Powell, like Kipling before him, bore witness to conflicting notions of boys and growing up. A great admirer of J.M. Barrie's play, *Peter Pan* (1904), Baden-Powell named his son "Peter" after the play's eponymous character and wrote a farewell note to scouts modeling himself after Captain Hook (World Brotherhood 295). Barrie's text not only offers its own generation of "lost boys" but as Baden-Powell could not have been unaware, Peter Pan, even unlike the forever-adolescent Kim and Mowgli, is the exception in "all children, except one, grow up" (*Peter and Wendy* 5). Peter Pan, too, is forever marked not only by his extraordinariness, including his adulthood-defying superiority, but by his incompleteness. By the end of Barrie's novelization of the play, after the Darling children and lost boys return from Neverland, Peter Pan can merely look in at them from the outside: "he had ecstasies innumerable that other children can never know; but he was looking through the window at the one joy from which he must be for ever barred" (141). To be a British or Western boy at the dawn of the twentieth century was also to be looking in a window, imbued with hopes and promises as citizens of the future (not yet) and freighted with the obligations and expectations of empire—and ultimately, it seems, to be contradictorily de-humanized and lauded as superhuman, cast as incipient superhero simultaneously extraordinary and lacking. Fictional, hybrid boys were torn by the struggle inherent in such representations; their real-life counterparts likely found it little easier.

Notes

1 See "Oh, Golly, What a Happy Family!," where I compare the series with two later twentieth century series for children, Enid Blyton's *Noddy* books (1949–1963) and Allan Ahlberg's "Happy Families" books (1980–1997), the latter of which is based on the nineteenth century card game.
2 Exacerbating the doll's racist legacy (the name "golliwog" is still used as a racist slur) is Florence's own admission of abusing the doll in a way not dissimilar to the racist game of "Aunt Sally," where cudgels were thrown at a figure made to look like a black woman, and reminiscent of Robin Bernstein's descriptions in *Racial Innocence* of the treatment of black dolls, such as Frances Hodgson Burnett's portrayal in *The One I Knew the Best of All* of herself as a child whipping a black doll while playing a game of pretend based on Harriet Beecher Stowe's *Uncle Tom's Cabin*. Depictions of "savage" natives and other black figures as iterations of "Sambo" also do not help attempts to reclaim the Uptons' series from racism, though it is true, as the few critical appraisals of the Uptons' works note, that Golliwogg is not only generally the leader in the books but one of the first generally positive black figures in children's literature.
3 Andrew Hagiioannu observes additional "hybrid" features of these texts in that not only is it well known that *The Jungle Books* were written in the U.S., "*Kim* was originally conceived in Vermont" (106).
4 Winnie Chan, for example, calls Kipling "the Bard of Empire" (134), while Don Randall suggests Kipling is "arguably, *the* representative voice" of the period, particularly with regard to imperialism (12).
5 Notable scholarly work on the boy scouts and girl guides of this period include Katherine Magyarody's recent reading of early girl guide handbooks and the creation of potential space for "odd girls" and "odd women"; Laureen Tedesco's analysis of the "Americanization" of immigrants embedded in the U.S. girl scouts (350); Troy Boone's exploration of class politics and hygiene in *Scouting for Boys* and the movement itself; Allen Warren's analysis of the "complex[ity]" of the "imperial origins" and "cultural sources" of the movement ("Citizens of the Empire" 237) and the "Rovers" aspect of the movement ("Popular Manliness"); Richard Flynn's early consideration of Kipling's scouting connections which concludes that, "even translated into other cultures, Scouting is explicitly designed to uphold cultural hegemony" (58); and Björn Sundmark's connecting through the lens of citizenship *Scouting for Boys* and Selma Lagerlöf's *The Wonderful Adventures of Nils*.
6 Connections between the schoolboy ethos, games and sports, and empire during the period are well known. For further considerations of masculinity and sports at the time, see (for instance) Mike Huggins, Dennis Brailsford, Richard Holt, and J.A. Mangan.
7 Deana Stover offers a similar point in her analysis of little lord Fauntleroy, Cedric Errol: "Cedric's future as an earl and his separation from his American friends and mother—in other words, his status as an adoptee—are essential

to understanding him as neither wholly American nor wholly British: he is both and neither" (348).

8　A similar physical/animal and emotional/human confusion for Mowgli occurs just before he leaves the jungle for the first time: as he prepares to say his good-byes, "something began to hurt Mowgli inside him, as he had never been hurt in his life before, and he caught his breath and sobbed, and the tears ran down his face." Not knowing what is going on, he turns to Bagheera, asking "What is it? What is it? . . . I do not wish to leave the jungle, and I do not know what this is. Am I dying, Bagheera?" Bagheera replies, "No, Little Brother. Those are only tears such as men use. . . . Now I know thou art a man, and a man's cub no longer" (19). Though Bagheera here conflates humanity and adulthood, the continuing Mowgli stories call Mowgli's full-fledged adulthood, rather than childhood or adolescence, into question.

9　Contrasting Kipling's work with that of aesthete and decadent writers and figures of the time in his analysis of masculinity in *The Jungle Books*, Wynn Yarbrough points to Raksha in particular as an example where "Kipling constructs gender performances that are unstable and though seemingly traditional reveal the transgressive spirit of the fin-de-siècle" (219). Identity, including gender identity, is consistently blurry throughout *The Jungle Books* and *Kim*.

10　His wife is similar. In today's terms she is a child-bride at the age of thirteen (334), yet Kipling has Gisborne view her as "a maid no more" (347) in a discomfiting scene: "This was not at all the girl that Gisborne had seen with a half-eye slinking about the compound veiled and silent, but another—a woman full blown in a night as the orchid puts out in an hour's moist heat" (346).

11　The at times mocked but respected Sahiba outlines the importance of women—as nurturers—to the empire through her care for Kim and in her comment that a District Superintendent of Police (later revealed to be a British agent as well), who she discovers was nursed by a native woman, is "the sort to oversee justice. They know the land and the customs of the land. The others, all new from Europe, suckled by white women and learning our tongues from books, are worse than the pestilence. They do harm to Kings" (77–78).

12　Matthew Fellion offers a fascinating gloss on this passage, observing, "as Kim eludes the categories applied to him throughout the narrative, failing continually to be fully explicable, he reveals that the category of 'boyhood' is more stable and knowable than the individuals it encompasses" (901). As individuals, Kim and Mowgli are extraordinary; rendered into "categories" as servants of empire, they become part of a seemingly "ordinary" mass.

13　For another consideration of the use of objects throughout *Kim*, see Jesse Oak Taylor's "Kipling's Imperial Aestheticism."

14　That the boy scouts were often connected with militarism is overtly on display in McLoughlin Brothers' *Battle Game with Boy Scouts* (circa 1910), which features twenty-four cardboard scout figures depicted with guns. The figures are placed into two (or four, depending on number of players) facing lines and are then "fired upon" by provided "cannon": "When a Scout is knocked down, from any cause whatever, he shall be considered dead" ("Directions for Playing").

15　The theme of animals and animality is reinforced in the period's related material culture, with, for example, Parker Brothers' *The Game of Boy Scouts* (1912) presented as a pack of cards divided into five "patrols" indicated by animals: wolf, bull, lion, owl, and curlew.

16 For further analysis of collecting and its relationship to empire as well as museums and *Kim*, see Black.
17 The idea of a boy scout brotherhood is of course resiliently persistent, with a "world brotherhood" edition of *Scouting for Boys* even published in 1946.
18 Though girls could be hybrid with respect to nationality affiliation (as are Burnett's Mary Lennox and Sara Crewe), this rarely seems problematic in the literature as girls/women were not destined to actual full citizenship rights and their hybridity could be used to bolster the health of and thereby the imperial ruling/maintenance work of the men/boys in their lives (as Mary helps "heal" Colin and Archibald Craven in *The Secret Garden* and Sara similarly helps heal Carrisford in *A Little Princess*).

4   "'Art for art' is their motto"

Aesthetic citizenship, children's play, and class politics in the eyes and hands of Burnett and Nesbit

In 1909, Jessie H. Bancroft, assistant director of physical training for the New York public schools and the first woman in such a position, published *Games for the Playground, Home, School, and Gymnasium*.[1] This games manual highlights many of the considerations at the heart of discussions of play at the end of the nineteenth and beginning of the twentieth centuries, including, with its very authorship, the increasing acceptance of women and girls in those discussions and in play activities. It also demonstrates play's tendency to defy definition, to be ultimately "irreducible," as Johan Huizinga claims (7), or how "it is impossible to keep ambiguity from creeping into" considerations of play, as Brian Sutton-Smith suggests (216). In her introduction, Bancroft attempts to distinguish between definitions of "games" and "play," clarifying that "a marked distinction has been made between games, on the one hand, and, on the other, the unorganized play and constructive activities included in many books of children's games" even as she acknowledges that "the term 'play' includes games, so that we 'play games,'" and that "in a strictly scientific sense, games do not always involve the element of sport or play" (7). For her own work, she insists that "no game has been included that has not been considered to have strong playing values, by which term is meant, in addition to other qualities, and above all others, the amount of sport and interest attending it" (8). She also takes pains to address the claim that "many principals object to recesses because of the moral contamination for which these periods are often responsible" by averring that "the author has had repeated and convincing testimony of the efficacy of games to do away with this objection" (17–18). Perhaps most tellingly, however, she explains her choice of games for the manual through comparisons to English ballads and Homeric epithets and by asserting,

> there is an aristocracy of games, classic by all the rights of tradition and popular approval . . . these standard games are amply represented, mingled in the true spirit of American democracy with strangers from foreign lands and the new creations of modern athletic practice.
>
> (6)

She describes games as akin to "painting, poetry, music, or any other field of spontaneous imitative or creative expression" (8–9) and yet as offering "the most valuable training of all . . . of inhibition—the power for restraint and self-control" (11). For Bancroft, even as they encourage democratic sentiment and creative, literary, and aesthetically-inspired moral behavior, games ultimately provide the discipline and obedience so vaunted in the period—ideas Dieter Gosewinkel, as I observed in the previous chapter, also links to nationality, which in Britain became connected with citizenship and the two together "gradually replaced the traditional concept of subjecthood" (25–27), for like play, citizenship tends to defy "single definition" (Lister 9).

In this way, Bancroft echoes late nineteenth and early twentieth century contemporaries' senses of play as productively aligned with citizenship, as a way of encouraging child welfare, discouraging delinquent behavior, and teaching other aspects of "good" citizenship through continual nods at notions of beauty and associations with "good" literature. Robert Louis Stevenson, writing on "Child's Play" in 1881, describes a similar relationship between aestheticism, play, and literature, asserting:

> "art for art" is [children's] motto; and the doings of grown folk are only interesting as the raw material for play. Not Théophile Gautier, nor Flaubert, can look more callously upon life, or rate the reproduction more highly over the reality; and [children] will parody an execution, a deathbed, or the funeral of the young man of Nain, with all the cheerfulness in the world.
>
> (233–234)

According to Stevenson, "the true parallel for play is not to be found . . . in conscious art," but in literature, in romance, fiction, or what might be considered play-dreams as children actively find themselves needing to "act" out whatever it is they are reading and thereby transform stories into games and play (234). Around the same time Bancroft published her manual, Edward B. DeGroot, general director of field-houses and playgrounds for the South Park commission of Chicago, issued a report clearly linking art, beauty, and improved citizenship: the report states that

> dirt upon the hands and faces of the children of the streets rub off when it comes in contact with the bathing facilities of the park. Likewise do art and beauty "rub off" in contact with young folks in the park and are no doubt carried to homes in expressions of home improvement.
>
> (qtd. in Russell 189)

As games manuals and playground-promoting documents repeatedly indicate, at the turn of the nineteenth and twentieth centuries aesthetic associations occurred simultaneously with an increased attention to concerns over childhood delinquency and citizenship, with fears over the working and lower classes' development in Britain and waves of immigration in the U.S. helping to initiate child-saving movements, including movements advocating improved environments for children through play and play spaces. As Douglas Mao observes,

> solicitude about dangerous children and children in danger . . . was leading to unprecedented philanthropic and state-sponsored intervention in the lives of minors. Axiomatic for proponents of such action was that it must be possible to make better citizens by changing the environments in which young people mature.
>
> (3)

In other words, for many on both sides of the Atlantic, surrounding children with beauty would have the effect of creating beautiful citizens— beautiful souls craving only that which is beautiful and therefore somehow inherently good and moral and leading to a beautiful, ideal world. Tellingly for some, as we will see, this beautiful world also rested on obligations as an ideal citizen to know and adhere to aspects of established class hierarchy.

As Stevenson's consideration of children's play shows, those advocating for and making connections between literature, play, art, and beauty included not only public servants but children's writers. Strangely, however, outside of a few critical works hinting at links to Oscar Wilde (or discussing Wilde's own fairy tales, which were not necessarily intended for children), works exploring Kenneth Grahame's connections to aestheticism, and works detailing aesthetic writers' interest in the figure of Pan, little attention has been given to intersections between children's literature and the aesthetic movement.[2] Jennifer Sattaur's consideration of the figure of the child at the fin de siècle primarily references (young) adulthood and texts for adult audiences, as does Kevin Ohi's *Innocence and Rapture: The Erotic Child in Pater, Wilde, James, and Nabokov* (2005).[3] Yet, as various critics like Diana Maltz, who addresses "the comprehensive influence of Victorian aestheticism upon philanthropy" (2–3) alongside "working-class life and culture" (3), and Ruth Livesey, who explores "the development of the modern British socialist movement in the early 1880s [as] marked by a particular preoccupation with aesthetics as well as politics" (5), observe, aestheticism involved women as well as men, and working class people as well as elite artistes, and arts and crafts décor and aesthete clothing styles found their way into middle class tastes even as only a few individuals espoused decadent lifestyles. A movement that, in its varied permutations, affected upper, middle, and working-classes and their politics and women as well as men could not entirely avoid influencing children and their culture.[4] Indeed, in his work charting the period's fascination with the unconscious and its links to aestheticism, particularly for the young (the idea that "what lends beauty its special influence over the soul is precisely its capacity to slip in and improve the child without the child's being aware of it at all," which he traces by beginning with Wilde's lecture on "The Decorative Arts" delivered in 1882), Mao argues that

> the scarcely registered workings of environment on the developing human being were a preoccupation of many kinds of people, from artists to scientists, from writers of fiction to crafters of policy, from experts pondering national problems raised by juveniles to parents gnashing their teeth over domestic ones.
>
> (5)

This chapter seeks to begin to fill a gap in the scholarship of aestheticism and children's literature by pointing to ways in which two authors today seen almost exclusively as writers for children, Frances Hodgson Burnett and Edith Nesbit, participated, in their children's literature, critical-autobiographical texts, and philanthropic and political activities regarding childhood, in the period's discourse on child welfare not only by privileging children's play as a site of citizenship-building but by drawing on notions of aestheticism to do so. For both authors, notions of child citizenship were intricately bound up in matters of class, beauty, and play. Fitting in with Bancroft's rhetoric of "aristocracy of games" balanced alongside "true spirit" of "democracy," Burnett's and Nesbit's portrayals of games and play betray some of the contradictions inherent in notions and definitions of citizenship (and play) and tensions between the potential of children's citizenship, with its implied citizens-in-training, for "beautiful" change and conservative notions of "inhibition—the power for restraint and self-control"—or ultimately knowing and keeping to one's place (and class) as a player, as a child, and in the world.

Burnett, playful children as art, and benevolent class systems

Burnett's participation in late-nineteenth century social and spiritual movements is well-known: though she wasn't a convert, Christian Scientist ideas infuse many of her texts, and Theosophic and New Thought ideas, especially the power of the mind and positive thinking, are prominent in texts such as *The Secret Garden* (1911) and *The Land of the Blue Flower* (1909). It seems unlikely that someone who was so in touch with contemporary fads that she attended séances (Gerzina 83) and who was in love with dress, fashion, and home decoration as much as Burnett was (78) was oblivious to the influence and discourse of the aesthetic movement—and especially when we know that Burnett was entertainingly visited by Oscar Wilde in Washington, DC, and attended a banquet in London in her honor where he was present and where she commented that he unfortunately did not "gyrate and have some species of aesthetic convulsion" but "bore himself like the ordinary nineteenth century civil man" (qtd. in Gerzina 121).

Burnett's likely debts to Wilde are in fact generally apparent. Among the most famous scenes of *Little Lord Fauntleroy* (1886) may be those where Cedric Errol, the titular little lord, lies reclining, often though not always asleep, including a notable scene in which he is prostrate on a tiger skin rug (65).[5] As Anna Wilson, Anna Maria Jones, and others acknowledge, it is difficult to read the book without being aware of its erotic, if not homoerotic, gaze, of its repeated passages of beautiful boy body as spectacle and of the seeming influence of Wilde and aestheticism with Cedric's infamous black velvet suit likely modeled after Wilde's own clothing. The book dwells lovingly and longingly on Cedric's beauty: when we are first introduced to him we are told that "he was so beautiful to look at that he was quite a picture" (6), "he was so handsome and strong and rosy that he attracted everyone's attention" (7). Through its emphasis on the spectacle of Cedric's beautiful body, the text reflects a central tenet of aestheticism, with Cedric's beauty serving to transform the characters who view him, particularly his curmudgeonly grandfather, and ultimately paving the way for society's benefit and its own beautification: through Cedric's guidance his grandfather begins improving his tenants' houses and lives. As Talia Schaffer and Kathy Alexis Psomiades outline it,

> beginning in the 1870s the word *aestheticism* came to be used to indicate not only a certain style of painting, or way of writing, or set of ideas but also popular manifestations of a belief in art's ability to make life more beautiful and to allow the beholder to achieve transcendence.
>
> (2–3)

Or, as Ohi phrases it, "the consequences of a rapt gaze at a beautiful male form," "the beautiful child," are those "of the unnerving power aestheticism gives the work of art to alter its viewer or reader" (11).

The phrase describing Cedric's beauty as "quite a picture" is particularly revealing of Burnett's depictions of her child characters. Cedric Errol's role throughout *Little Lord Fauntleroy* is to act as the catalyst for his grandfather's change, in Ohi's sense "the beautiful child" as "work of art" "altering" its beholder, Cedric's grandfather. Throughout her texts, including *Little Lord Fauntleroy*, Burnett consistently portrays child characters as akin to art. Yet she is also eager to insist that her child characters are playful beings influenced by beauty or at least beautiful ideas. In other words, they are both works of art capable of transforming others and figures shaping and being shaped by the forces around them. They are simultaneously passive figures of beauty and active players, dependent subjects and liberated citizens. By considering *Little Lord Fauntleroy* alongside Burnett's other children's works, both more famous works like *The Secret Garden* and *A Little Princess* (1905) and more obscure works such as her *The Lost Prince* (1915), *The Land of the Blue Flower*, and the semi-autobiographical *Children I Have Known* (1892), I will suggest that it is to the influence of aestheticism that Burnett's child characters and especially beautiful boys—Fauntleroy included—may owe their transformative power.[6] Active play augments that transformative passive beauty for Burnett, who ultimately, if paradoxically, deploys the two together to offer a view of ideal citizenship and patriotism that reflects traditional adherence to a supposedly benevolently beneficial class hierarchy.

Voyeurism, with seeing as knowing and transforming, is a recurrent theme in text after text of Burnett's works. In *The Secret Garden* Martha peeks at the sleeping Mary, while Colin's healing body with its "sharply chiseled ivory-white face . . . and the black lashes rimmed so startlingly the close-shut eyes" is observed in its sleeping form by his father and by his mother's portrait and in its recovery by Ben Weatherstaff and Susan Sowerby alongside Mary and Dickon (202). In *A Little Princess* Sara watches the sleeping Becky and looks in at windows at the Large Family just as the Large Family, the shop woman, and Ram Das watch her. Like Sara, Marco in *The Lost Prince* looks at the people and things around him and, as before Sara lost her fortune and its elegant trappings "the sight of her bright, eager little face and picturesque coats and hats had often caused people to look after her" (*A Little Princess* 90), so even in shabby attire, Marco "was the kind of boy people look at a second time when they have looked at him once" (*The Lost Prince* 4–5). Throughout the pages of *Little Lord Fauntleroy* Cedric can hardly fall asleep without someone gazing at him and whether at play, in thought, or simply eating, someone is bound to be watching, as when we are told his grandfather, upon their first meeting, "kept looking at him across the table" (92). Soon his grandfather can "scarcely endure to have him out of sight" (171) and he is even intentionally placed "on view" at a notable dinner-party (175). In each of these examples, the characters involved are either transformed or serve to transform (or both)—learning to become kinder, healthier, and/or a better parent, or gaining a friend or overcoming loneliness. Often, as we will see, this transformation involves accepting one's "natural" place in the class hierarchy and serving in that class position admirably and benevolently.

It isn't enough for Burnett's child characters to be objects of a transforming gaze, however. Time and again throughout Burnett's works children and their potential to transform and be transformed are aligned with actual works of art: Cedric shows his grocer friend the formidable gallery of paintings of his ancestors (231); Mary Lennox stumbles upon an ancestors' painting gallery in *The Secret Garden* and is drawn to a painting of a girl she feels she resembles (42), while Colin, who "looked rather like a picture himself" is watched over by a portrait of his deceased mother (103); and in *The Lost Prince* Marco frequently visits art galleries and his status as long-lost royal heir is revealed through his resemblance to a revered painting (358–359). In *Children I Have Known*, Burnett even compares herself to an "artist" who "sees almost everything as a picture" (vii) and offers readers a collection of "descriptions of real children [she] has seen in different countries" (xi) out of which she has "ma[de] some sketches as artists often do when they are preparing to paint a picture" (xii) so that she has her own "gallery of children" (37). *The Lost Prince* even makes explicit the importance of art and its connections to play, beauty, "story," and citizenship. Early in the book, as the culmination of a chapter titled "A Young Citizen of the World," we are told that Marco's "father could not often go with him, but he always took him for the first time to the galleries, museums, libraries, and historical places which were the richest in treasures of art, beauty, or story" (18). Taking advantage of free days at such sites and

> having no playmates and nothing to play with, [Marco] began when he was a very little fellow to make a sort of game out of his rambles through picture-galleries, and the places which, whether they called themselves museums or not, were storehouses or relics of antiquity.
> (19)[7]

This *Kim*-reminiscent "game" consists of trying to remember as much as he could about what he saw in the galleries and describing it to his father afterwards, whereupon his father would explain to him the "story" behind notable objects (19–20). As with Stevenson, art, story, and game here are linked: beautiful things become part of a game and a story. Moreover, through attention to detail and history, they help to shape an ideal patriotic citizen. Not only does knowledge of the beautiful objects make Marco "a young citizen of the world," the game he begins to play as "a very little fellow" forms the foundation for the later other Kipling-esque "game" he plays as a child-spy for his father and the fictional country of Samavia, traveling in secret from country to country to deliver the important message that paves the way for his father to become king.

The notion of children as art is particularly evident at Burnett's 1892 opening in London of the Drury Lane Boys' Club, an organization founded a few years earlier by a small group of working-class boys. The club's popularity and success had grown so quickly that, by the time of the opening of its new site, it included seventy-five boys, a games-room, a gymnasium, and a library reading-room, the last of which was Burnett's most prominent contribution and which she made in honor of her son Lionel, who died of consumption two years earlier. Burnett's history of the club, published both on her son Vivian's own printing press and for a wide audience in *Scribner's Magazine*, expresses her delight in thoughts of the boys' active play and games and their supplemented moments of quiet reflection and reading, but does so by connecting the boys' play pursuits with aesthetics and their importance as future citizens. In a letter she had printed up and given to each boy, and which she reproduces in her history, she presents the boys with the *Dorian Gray*-esque comparison she says she frequently told her own two young sons:

> you are like a block of marble which is to be made into a statue. You yourselves are the sculptors. It depends upon you whether you chisel it into a figure which is beautiful and noble, or one that is distorted and base. Every ungenerous act, every hurtful word, every unmanly thought is a false stroke of the chisel and mars the stone.
>
> (69)

For Burnett, in literature as in life, the child's body itself becomes a work of art meant for beauty, greatness, and "noble" citizenship.

Perhaps the most striking example of children as art, and their supposed transformative potential, appears in her chapter on "Eight Little Princes" in *Children I Have Known*. In that chapter, she describes her sense of eight young royal boys she has never met. Basing her account of them on various photographs she has seen, generally in shop windows, and moved by their (to her) particular and endearing beauty, she concludes,

> These are the eight Princes I feel as if I know though they do not know me, and even in the most Republican country in the world— even in America which does not believe in Kings—I am sure there is no one who will not say in thinking of these boys, "God keep the little princes and help them to care for their people, and God bless the Queens who are their Mothers."
>
> (64)

Her hopes did not quite bear fruit: the five German princes she describes were the sons of the very last German monarch, the Serbian prince was assassinated in his early twenties, the King of Spain experienced exile and witnessed his country succumb to dictatorship and civil war, and the Italian prince contended with the assassination of his father, two world wars, fascism, abdication, and ultimately the loss of the monarchy. Yet Burnett's conclusion underscores themes prevalent in much of her writing: the beauty and promise of boyhood, idolization of mothers, and a consistent privileging of class, with nobility and aristocracy arising alongside seemingly more democratic sentiments. Even as she proclaims the existence of a "love which makes every mother a Queen and every Queen only a sweet woman" and writes for an audience she presumes is at least partly "American," admitting that "America does not believe in Kings," Burnett implies that she at least does—believes in their hope, their boyhood, and especially their beauty (64). Simply seeing them, or seeing their proxies in photographs or in written descriptions of those photographs, Burnett suggests, will transform even Americans who do "not believe in Kings" into well-wishers supportive of the princes' supposed "car[ing] for their people." For Burnett, children, even her own sons, who not only provide models for characters in stories (most famously Vivian as the prototype of little lord Fauntleroy) but whose portraits provide inspiration in essays such as "The Boy Who Became a Socialist," are or must be made into works of art—novels, paintings, photos, sculptures—to create ideal citizens (*Children* 117). The impossibility of that ideal is perhaps manifested in the reality that the actual humans captured in the art forms soon become unrecognizable to the art, which essentially remains frozen in time: in her essay on "How Fauntleroy Occurred," for example, Burnett admits that at sixteen Vivian no longer physically resembles the child Cedric Errol (*Piccino* 219) and, as Wilson points out, she revealingly subtitles her essay "and a very real little boy became an ideal one" (247).

The idea that simply seeing a beautiful figure, particularly a beautiful youth, in real life or in proxy is a transformative experience remains consistent throughout Burnett's works. Not only do followers of the long-lost King Ivor of Samavia keep his portrait on an altar in reverence (*Lost Prince* 356), at the end of *The Lost Prince* "Samavians had a strange and superstitious worship for [Marco], because he seemed so surely their Lost Prince restored in body and soul—almost the kingly lad in the ancient portrait—some of them half believed when he stood in the sunshine, with the halo about his head (412). Likely based loosely on the situation of Serbia at the outbreak of World War I, *The Lost Prince* tells the romantic story of Marco's discovery that he is a long-lost heir to the Samavian throne. His father and his father's fathers have long known their history and have, while in exile and hiding, trained and prepared themselves for the day their civil war-torn country is ready—really fit—to have them return. Because of their noble lineage, as the book makes clear, Marco and his father are unbelievable specimens of regal masculine beauty. When Marco's father

> walked down a street, people turned to look at him even oftener than they turned to look at Marco, and the boy felt as if it was not merely because he was a big man with a handsome, dark face, but because he looked, somehow, as if he had been born to command armies, and as if no one would think of disobeying him.

(17)

We are told that in general Samavians in the past were "of such great stature, physical beauty, and strength, that they had been like a race of noble giants," a fact important because Marco's and his father's resemblance to Prince Ivor's portrait confirms their being even more splendid as Ivor is described initially as "bigger and stronger for his age than any man in the country, and . . . as handsome as a young Viking god" (22–23).[8]

The text's end fulfills the transformative—and in Burnett's hands ultimately fantastically traditional and conservative—potential of gazing on beautiful, young male bodies. Once the people of Samavia catch sight of the long-lost heirs to the throne and their phenomenal beauty, they realize that it is in their best interest for the monarchy to be restored and willingly submit to it, so that the end of the tale supports an English child character's vehement exclamation that "what the civilized countries [like England] have got to do is to make [the Samavians] choose a decent king and begin to behave themselves" (100). In this way, *The Lost Prince* echoes Burnett's earlier fairy tale, *The Land of the Blue Flower*, which tells of the restoration of a young king, Amor, who, as his guardian admits, "when he stands before his [people] they will think he is a young god" (24). When Amor returns to his people as their king, "the light shining upon his beautiful face and his crown made him look more than ever like a young god and giant" (30). Ultimately, the tale tells of how King Amor's beauty and his laws that require his people to beautify the kingdom (by planting and gardening) transform that kingdom and save its inhabitants from misery produced in great part through ugly thoughts.

Still, as much as Burnett presents child and youthful figures as epitomes of transformative beauty and akin to art, she also strives to proclaim their childishness, particularly through active games and play. In *Little Lord Fauntleroy*, for example, she portrays Cedric as a passive work of art with the potential for aesthetic influence while also ensuring early on that Cedric's seemingly impossibly good mother reminds the reader of Cedric's active child status by telling Mr. Havisham, Cedric's grandfather's lawyer, that Cedric is "very fond of childish play" and "a very boyish little boy sometimes" (30). Her statement is confirmed when Mr. Havisham encounters Cedric for the second time and watches him win a race. Mr. Havisham notices that "his young lordship . . . was shouting and making as much noise as the noisiest of his companions. He stood side by side with another little boy, one little red leg advanced a step" (31). The scene is primarily conveyed through the detail of these very active legs, notably adorned with the red stockings, the color at that time being very masculine, which I suspect Burnett included, like the later determined pony riding passages, in an attempt to counteract what is sometimes perceived as the "feminine" aesthetic passivity of the little lord.[9] Mr. Havisham "really never remembered having seen anything quite like the way in which his lordship's lordly little red legs flew up behind his knickerbockers and tore over the ground as he shot out in the race at the signal word" and "the way in which the red legs flew and flashed up and down, the shrieks of the boys, the wild efforts of Billy Williams whose brown legs were not to be despised as they followed closely in the rear of the red legs, made him feel some excitement" (31).[10]

Burnett consistently uses moments of play in *Little Lord Fauntleroy* symbolically: while the race serves to reinforce Fauntleroy's active boyish—masculine and child—status, the baseball parlor game Cedric plays with his grandfather (based on actual baseball parlor games available through companies such as McLoughlin Brothers around that time) confirms his patriotic and citizenship potential. The very evening of his arrival at his grandfather's estate in England, Cedric proclaims, "I'm an American!," "you have to be an American if you are born in America," and that "if there was another [Revolutionary] war, you know, I should have to—to be an American!" (87). His grandfather "hated America and Americans, but it amused him to see how serious and interested this small patriot was. He thought that so good an American might make a rather good Englishman when he was a man" (88). When Cedric tells him he "should *like* to be a president," his grandfather remarks, "we'll send you to the House of Lords instead," a compromise to which Cedric replies, "well . . . if I *couldn't* be a president, and if that is a good business, I shouldn't mind" (97). The very next morning—after incidence of beautiful spectacle where the grandfather and others gaze at the boy's sleeping form—Cedric introduces his grandfather to the baseball game, which has its own complicated British and U.S. lineage through the game of Rounders, and which in the text immediately gets likened to cricket and enthralls boy and grandfather alike, combining aesthetic spectacle and transformation with childish play. Cedric "showed all the attitudes of pitcher and catcher and batter in the real game" so that "his vigorous, graceful little body, his eager gestures, his simple enjoyment of it all were pleasant to behold" (108–109). His grandfather enjoys himself so thoroughly that he finds himself in a congenial mood and his first beneficial action towards a tenant behind on rent (Higgins) takes place over the game table (119–120).

Play and games are deployed similarly in other Burnett texts, serving to emphasize precocious characters' actual child status, moldability, and influence. As I suggest in Chapter 2, the storyteller Sara Crewe has her "quaint," "old-fashioned," adult-like seriousness undercut—and her orphaned, impoverished situation's pathos heightened—by her love for and imaginary play with dolls (7) and Mary Lennox learns to become more childlike throughout *The Secret Garden*, even acquiring child playthings to do so, such as a skipping rope and "two or three games" in addition to books (122). The race against Mary out of the garden and into his father's arms that Colin wins highlights not only his gendered class position ahead of Mary's as heir to the landed estate but his full recovery as a healthy child (208).[11] In *The Land of the Blue Flower*, children learn to banish fear, hate, and ugly thoughts by focusing on such things as beautiful gardening, balancing work and leisure so that "they finished their task early and played games" (33). Marco and his English friends, particularly the disabled Jem Ratcliff (called "The Rat"), fill their days with the "game" (as they call it) of drilling and being drilled, learning to obey without hesitation or question the orders of their superiors and particularly Marco's father as "commanding officer" (137).[12] Presented initially as amusement to pass the time or children playing at being soldiers, the "game" takes on the stature and meaning of the "Great Game" in Rudyard Kipling's *Kim* (1901) and highlights the children's roles as citizens-in-training: what seems to the children initially to be play, arbitrary games for fun, is actually greater preparation for their futures, even as children, as spies, soldiers, and leaders. At the end of the chapter where they first meet, The Rat, who hangs around barracks and watches and learns from soldiers and has created and leads his own drill club for working-class boys, expresses his admiration of Marco by remarking, "he's been drilled himself. . . . He knows as much as I do" (53).[13]

As Cedric's baseball parlor game and Marco's and The Rat's drilling/spy "game" especially illustrate, Burnett's depictions of play become wrapped up in her visions of patriotism and good citizenship inspired by beautiful specimens of childhood. In these visions—fantasies, really, at times—ideal patriotic citizenship frequently is divided from an actual country, reminding us that ideas of citizenship developed alongside, and even at times separate from, ideas of nation and nationality, as Tom Cockburn, Gosewinkel, and other scholars of citizenship also observe. Many of Burnett's child characters, like Burnett herself and other child characters and children's writers of the time, are hybrid figures: Sara and Mary, for example, are Anglo-Indians (Sara with an additional French background) who have little knowledge of England before their arrival to it and, even then, little national allegiance. In *Little Lord Fauntleroy*, being a patriot is not ultimately dependent on firm allegiance to either the U.S. or England: one of these nations would work as well as the other, baseball and U.S. sentiments of democracy can infuse Britain without significantly changing British cultural and class traditions, and an altered allegiance in no way affects one's "patriotism." Patriotism separated from nationalism is even more striking in *The Lost Prince* as the very word "patriot" appears repeatedly in its pages. The English Rat swears allegiance to Marco, his father, and the Samavian cause, and Marco believes his father garners the attention he does in England and elsewhere because "they know he is a patriot and patriots are respected"; Marco "himself wished to be a patriot, though he had never seen his own country of Samavia" (7). That Burnett's discussion of patriots seems to participate in thoughts current at the time is attested to by a circa 1890 Parker Brothers *Game of Famous Men* card game, which offers a category of "Patriots" that includes figures from several different countries (Poland, Hungary, as well as the U.S.).

Rather than being dependent on nationalist notions of citizenship, "patriotism" in Burnett's view seems defined by being a good model and benefactor to the people—and knowing and making the absolute best of your class position, often at the expense of democratic, class-equalizing sentiments. Cedric's primary achievements, through the pride and charm presented by his beauty, are the conversion of his grandfather into a benevolent aristocratic ideal (so that, through cajoling, his grandfather tears down buildings of "ugliness and slovenliness" on his land and replaces them with new "model" cottages) and making himself beloved by all, with, in the last chapter, the entire village coming out in homage to him on his birthday reminiscent of a fantasy of feudal fidelity (161). He is so successful that the text's most ardent democrat, a U.S. grocery-man, refuses to return to the U.S. in part due to its lack of ancestors and nobility, a respect which he has gained through Cedric and Cedric's aristocratic inheritance (237–238). Colin's recovery and its positive effect on his long-absent father—as owners responsible for a large country manor and estate—can be argued to have a similar purpose in *The Secret Garden*. Despite the frequent democratic proclamations embedded in *A Little Princess* about different class statuses being merely an accident of birth, with Sara early on telling Becky that despite Sara's own wealth and privileges, "we are just the same—I am only a little girl like you. It's just an accident that I am not you, and you are not me!," the restoration of Sara's wealth at the end of the book reasserts her upper-class benefactor power, which she uses to give Becky a better but still servant position and to provide food for the hungry poor via Anne and the shop woman (41). *The Lost Prince* also consistently undercuts its democratic tendencies: though we are told that Marco "would never let [The Rat] forget that they were only two boys and that one was of no more importance than the other," Marco's royal lineage is alluded to frequently and it is evident that, though the The Rat's drilling, soldierly bearing, loyalty, and leadership potential help prove him to be a worthy companion for Marco, The Rat's being the son of an actual (though fallen on hard times) gentleman in no small way contributes to that worth as well (362).

Though the upper classes, through the espousal of democratic sensibilities, offer a pretense of denying it, the behavior of the lower classes throughout Burnett's texts underscores the idea that it really is one's duty as a patriotic, good citizen to adhere to traditional class values to foster a supposedly beneficially reciprocal system. Despite poverty, Marco's and his father's elderly servant, Lazarus, remains with them to patch their clothes and wait on them so that "however plain and scant the food they had to eat, it was always served with as much care and ceremony as if it had been a banquet" (101). Lazarus is in fact "very obstinate and particular about certain forms of manner. Nothing would have obliged him to remain seated when Loristan or Marco was near him" (15). It is precisely this proud servant behavior that The Rat quickly learns to emulate: on the second day after he has been invited to live with Marco after the death of his alcoholic father, The Rat seeks out Lazarus to confess that he can't stop looking in admiration at Marco's father, Stefan Loristan, and to inquire whether there is anything he can do for him. Lazarus concedes that he can shine Stefan's boots "perhaps once a week" (139). For The Rat, this isn't serving enough, but when he suggests that he will start watching for other ways to help, he finds himself in competition, as Lazarus bluntly tells him, "anything any one else did for him would be interfering with me" (140). The Rat recognizes this as a serious problem, concedes to tell Lazarus before doing anything, and enviously admits, "you served him first," to which Lazarus replies, "I have served him ever since he was born" (140). When The Rat comments, "he's—he's yours," he is "stern[ly]" reprimanded: "I am his—and the young Master's" (140). As Lazarus comprehends the extent of The Rat's devotion, however, he softens enough to admit that The Rat, upon good behavior, will likely someday soon have the privilege of also being "his," of "belonging" to Stefan and Marco. Over time, Lazarus and Stefan allow The Rat to serve more, so that when he is honored by being allowed to accompany Marco on the spy mission (and make sure Marco doesn't carry himself too much like the noble gentleman he is by birth), he

> begged Loristan to let him come with Marco as his servant, and his servant he had been more than willing to be. When Loristan had said he should be his aide-de-camp, he had felt his trust lifted to a military dignity which uplifted him with it. As his aide-de-camp he must serve him, watch him, obey his lightest wish, make everything easy for him.
>
> (229–230)

Marco does not always appreciate this behavior, but characters throughout the text make clear that it is appropriate. As The Rat reflects, one of the elderly women to whom they delivered their message had a

> sort of reverence in her manner when she spoke to [Marco]. She reminded him of Lazarus more than once. When she gave them their evening meal, she insisted on waiting on him with a certain respectful ceremony. She would not sit at table with him, and The Rat began to realize that she felt that he himself should be standing to serve him.
>
> (298–299)

Similar behavior is present in Burnett's other texts. Not only do Cedric's future tenants pay him homage, his mother's and his U.S. servant makes the long voyage to England to help them out, and the kindly house-keeper sends his mother a cat to help with her loneliness (64) even as, as Mr. Havisham reflects, Cedric "would scarcely be allowed to make playmates of the gate-keeper's children" (73). After Sara's loss of fortune in *A Little Princess*, the scullery-maid Becky makes it a point "before daybreak . . . to slip into Sara's attic and button her dress and give her such help as she required before she went down-stairs to light the kitchen fire," an act of assistance repeated at bedtime (75).[14] Though Becky's situation is just as dire as Sara's is, it is Sara's attic room alone that is decorated and Sara alone to whom new clothes and other items are given by Ram Das and Mr. Carrisford—only because Sara thinks of her, likely because of her continued serving kindness, is Becky given some of her castoffs, leftovers, and extras and finally "command[ed] by "the sahib" "to be the attendant of Missee Sahib," Sara (181). This "reward" frees Becky from the clutches of Miss Minchin but retains her class servant status just as Anne's being taken in by the shop woman frees her from the streets but not the lower or working classes. In *The Secret Garden*, the servant Martha's moor family repeatedly make sacrifices for the chil-dren of the great manor: it is Martha who gives Mary the skipping rope, bought by Mrs. Sowerby with Martha's own pennies, though she's "got four places to put every penny" (53) and, though early on Martha is scandalized by Mary's lack of appetite and the wasted food she wishes she could bring to her own young siblings (but won't because it isn't theirs) who somehow, in typical Burnett logic, grow fat simply by eating air and grass and laughing (25–26),[15] Mrs. Sowerby later manages to send Mary and Colin, well-fed at the manor, eggs, potatoes, bread, milk, and butter to indulge their pretending to be invalids (177). The children do remember that the Sowerbys would struggle to afford the extra food and send shillings to help, but Mrs. Sowerby freely offers even before the children provide payment (180–181). Tellingly, too, throughout the novel class and childhood are startlingly conflated through play: as de-scriptions of the Sowerby moor cottage family serve as substitutes for Mary's Ayah's stories in India, the cottage's inhabitants are compared to playful animals, with "the children seem[ing] to tumble about and amuse themselves like a litter of rough, good-natured collie puppies" (40). It is through the playful, animalistic, "childish" lower-class that Mary in fact learns to become a child. Not only does Martha insist she go outside and learn to play and give her the skipping rope, she must learn to print rather than write to communicate with Martha's brother Dickon, and it is through Martha and Dickon that she initially acquires her gardening seeds and tools (63).

The overlaying of traditional, limiting class values onto aesthetic ide-als of beautiful children at play makes it difficult to indulge completely

the temptation—offered through their cross-cultural, transatlantic sentiments and refusal to accept easy national allegiances—to read Burnett's
works in general, as Katharine Slater fascinatingly does *The Secret
Garden*, as "translocal," "hybrid" "assemblage[s] of cross-border concerns and accessible identifications that transcend national constructs"
(4). Their translocality, as Slater hints for *The Secret Garden*, is tempered
by connections to colonialism and Western perspectives, such as late
nineteenth century aestheticism, and they do not, as Slater suggests for
translocal texts generally, defy "the nation's"—or, at least, a—"relentless
interpellation of . . . subjects into a particular model of citizenship"
(4). Burnett's characters seem, through their aestheticism, patriotism,
and periodic democratic sentiments, at times to defy borders but the
ultimately conservative notions of citizenship as subjecthood they advocate also call that defiance into question: beauty is transformative
and promotes benevolent citizenship but that citizenship is predicated
on traditional English class values where everyone knows his or her
place and makes the best of it. Burnett's "young citizens of the world"
know what Marco reminds himself: "when one was very young, one
must remember orders first of all" (166). Adherence to obedience, that
consistent refrain in notions of citizenship throughout the period, is
linked to notions of nationality and citizenship, but prominent among
that obedience, those "orders," for Marco and Burnett's characters in
general is class hierarchy, knowing one's place in ways that even games
played among, with, and to the benefit of varying peoples and classes
cannot disrupt.

Nesbit, playful children imagining beautiful places, and vanishing class concerns

Though Burnett often seems the more "old-fashioned" and Nesbit the
more "modern" writer, they were actually contemporaries, influenced
by many of the same movements and ideas (Nesbit passed away a few
months before Burnett). Two years after the publication of *The Secret
Garden* and two years before *The Lost Prince*, and just beyond the
height of her own popularity as a children's author, Nesbit introduced
Wings and the Child (1913), an autobiographical treatise on children's
play and education, "as an attempt to contribute something, however
small and unworthy, to the science of building a magic city in the soul
of a child, a city built of all things pure and fine and beautiful" (vii).
Described also in her children's novel *The Magic City* (1910) as well
as in a *Nine Unlikely Tales for Children* (1901) short story and put on
display at the Children's Welfare Exhibition in Olympia in the winter of
1912–1913, "magic cities" were for Nesbit creative miniature buildings
made from household objects; they were also ways, in literary and physical examples of play, to promote notions of aesthetics and citizenship.

Indeed, in *Wings and the Child* Nesbit appears at moments to channel Wilde, such as in the following passage:

> To show a child beautiful things, and to answer as well all the questions he will ask about them, to charm and thrill his imagination with pictures and statues and models of the wonders of the world, to familiarize the child with beauty, so that he knows ugliness when he meets it, and hates it for the outrage it is to the beauty he has known and loved ever since he was very little—this is worth doing. If we would make beauty the dear rule of a man's life, and ugliness the hated exception, we should make beauty as familiar to the child as the air he breathes, and if we associate knowledge with beauty the child will love both.
>
> (53)

Nesbit, like Burnett, was certainly familiar with the aesthetic movement and its key figures. As Julia Briggs, Nesbit's primary biographer, shows, Wilde wrote Nesbit at least one letter of admiration, Nesbit ran in some of the same socialist circles as William Morris, and she grew up "at a time when Ruskin's reputation was at its height: his social criticism had provided the foundation of her own socialist beliefs, and the phrases and titles of his are deliberately redeployed throughout her work" (323). She even, as M. Daphne Kutzer notes, "affected . . . aesthetic clothing" as part of her alternate beliefs (63). Her notions of aesthetics, citizenship, and even "magic cities" and play are strongly embedded in her socialist views: one of the two child sibling protagonists of the magic cities short story, "The Town in the Library in the Town in the Library," is likely not coincidentally named "Fabian," the name of the socialist society of which she famously was a founding member. Unlike with Burnett, however, Nesbit's notions of aesthetics and citizenship have less to do with the supposedly transformative beauty of individual playful children and more to do with their roles in creating beautiful places and societies. In establishing such societies, Nesbit's works concerning "magic cities" and play exploit traditional senses of place and identity—childhood, rank, gender, class—to promote an idealized version of beauty through "good" (and literary) citizenship that seeks to dismantle those very traditions. In typical conflicting Nesbit fashion, however, her works are reliant on and even return her child protagonists to worlds that actually, like Burnett's, confirm the dismantled traditions.

In her acknowledgment of Nesbit's literary "thieving" (Nesbit's allusions and debt to other authors is well known), Marah Gubar quips that "Nesbit's biographers and critics have had no end of fun exploring how she teetered back and forth between conventional and radical stances" (*Artful Dodgers* 131), an oscillation Raymond E. Jones notes when he says that "Nesbit the writer was at odds with Nesbit the woman" (viii). As he observes,

> A romantic whose children's books celebrated traditional home and family life, and the values upon which that life was based, she herself was something of a bohemian who not only refused to wear corsets, dressed in knickers, cut her hair short, rode a bicycle, and smoked in public—actions calculated to attract attention, if not scandalize the *bourgeoisie.*
>
> (ix)

Her marriage was unconventional, with affairs on both sides, and despite her Fabian membership and the fact that she "supported that society's utopian ideals in some of her fiction, she consciously addressed her novels to middle-class children and frequently revealed a conservative's nostalgia for idealized versions of the past" (ix).[16] Indeed, such nostalgia is a grounding force of *Wings and the Child*, which premises its arguments on two ideas: firstly, that the only way to understand children is to remember what it was like to be a child, to be one of those "few who have managed to slip past the Customs-house with their bundle of memories intact" (5), and who therefore remain "children, disguised by grown-up bodies" (7), and secondly, that "the world is much uglier than it was" with "ugliness," like "the airship," proposing to be "the hallmark of a really advanced nation" (43).

Indeed, though Burnett's texts like *The Secret Garden* seem "Victorian" in feel and setting, it is Nesbit who openly defends "old-fashioned," "Victorian" positions, chastising "clever young people [who] find it amusing to sneer at the old-fashioned ideal of combining instruction with amusement—a stupid Victorian ideal, we are told, which a progressive generation has cast aside. Too hastily, perhaps— too inconsiderately" (42). She claims that "in the Victorian days we sneer at," "our fathers could not see that there was any quarrel between knowledge and beauty, both of whom they loved" (47). The bulk of *Wings and the Child* is devoted to this rose-tinted Victorian past (despite Ruskin's own sense to the contrary), despairing of the downfall of civilization through ugliness and the present state of its factories, consumer goods, and education. In a chapter notably titled "The One Thing Needful," Nesbit insists that

> the most ardent advocate of our present civilisation, the blindest worshipper of what we call progress, can hardly fail to be aware of the steady increasing and brutal ugliness of life. Civilisation, whatever else it is, is a state in which a few people have the chance of living beautifully—those who take that chance are fewer still—and the enormous majority live, by no choice or will of their own, lives

which at the best are uncomfortable, anxious, and lacking in beauty, and at the worst are ugly, diseased, desperate, and wretched.

(94)

Her solution for this unfortunate state of civilization is faith in the power of imagination and particularly children's imaginations and possibilities, their potential as "future" citizens and ability to be shaped as citizens-in-training. In a *Daily News and Leader* newspaper piece she published in conjunction with the 1912–1913 exhibition and which she later used (at times verbatim) in *Wings and the Child*, Nesbit claims "the child's memory becomes a storehouse of beautiful and wonderful things which are or have been in the visible universe, or in that greater universe, the mind of man," while

> of the immeasurable value of imagination as a means to the development of the loveliest virtues, to the uprooting of the ugliest and meanest sins, there is here no space to speak. But the gain in sheer happiness is more quickly set forth. Imagination, duly fostered and trained, is to the world of visible wonder and beauty what the inner light is to the Japanese lantern.
>
> ("The Magic World," *Daily News and Leader* 5)

Play, as indicative of children's imaginative capacity, therefore becomes fundamental to Nesbit's citizenship-training schemes for the future and reflects her similarities to the Victorian Stevenson. Just as he acknowledges children's tendencies to "act" out what they read in play, she insists that children's play is colored "according to the measure of your dreams and the nature of the latest book you are reading" (*Wings* 107–108). For Nesbit, as with Stevenson, and reflecting the conflicting and contradictory nature of attempts to define play, if not the challenges or impossibility of fully defining it,

> the prime instinct of a child at play—I do not mean a child at games—is to create . . . he will make as well as create, if you let him, but always he will create: he will use the whole force of dream and fancy to create something out of nothing—over and beyond what he will make out of such materials as he has to hand.
>
> (17)

Imagination is essential to what she terms "active games," or, as she explains, in contrast to games such as cricket, racquet, and football, "the games without bought accessories should perhaps rather be termed 'plays' than games. And the more highly cultivated the imagination the more intensely joyous are the games" (112). Though she portrays in her fiction and defends as "precious on wet days, or when other people have headaches," games such as croquet, badminton, chess, draughts, "halma, the poor relation of draughts and chess," and "dominoes, which we all love," she singles out for condemnation those games "bought at a shop, games in boxes," which "heroic," "self-sacrific[ing]" aunts "settle themselves down to play, in cold blood, with their nephews and nieces" (118).[17] These she describes as

> meaningless games with counters and dice: ill-balanced dice and roughly turned counters and boards that look like folding chequerboards till you open them, and then you find all the ugliest colours divided into squares or circles or slabs, with snakes or motors or some other unpleasing devices on them.
>
> (119)

Still, imagination reigns triumphant: for games with "bought accessories" or "toys" imagination "supplements or corrects the suggestion of the toy" while for games without these items "the child's imagination has to supply everything" and "in both, as in every movement and desire of the natural child, it is imagination which tints the picture and makes the whole enterprise worth while" (107).

Possibilities for this imagination at play in the establishment of good citizenship are envisioned in *The Magic City*. The premise of the book is a fantasy adventure where two children, Philip and Lucy, adjusting to their new family situation, find themselves transported to a living version of magic cities created out of everyday objects, including playthings (chess pieces and dominoes figure prominently), books, and figures and items literally made alive from literature, as well as cities conceived of in dreams and in the imagination. Consistently throughout the text play prefaces inspiration and the solving of a personal or civic problem, including the seven deeds Philip and Lucy must accomplish and which become a "pursuit of their duty" in which "all citizens were bound to help" (75). Worried and trying not to think about the reasons behind Lucy's disappearance early in the book, Philip plays chess and spellicans (43); as they wait in preparation for their deed helping the dwellers by the sea, Lucy and Philip play noughts and crosses (90). As Philip tries desperately to think of a way to help those dwellers ("happy" "gentle islanders" who are children served by M.A.s taking vacations), Lucy and Billy, the "Lord High Islander," play cat's cradle for, as Billy admits of the islanders, "of course we play games and all that" (95–97). When Philip still can't think of anything to solve the "government['s]" problem of the islanders' fear, Billy tells him "well, don't swat over it any more . . . just stay with us and have a jolly time. You're sure to think of something. Or else Lucy will. We'll act charades tonight" (97–98). His advice turns out to be sage: after six pleasant days of playing games such as hide-and-seek and rounders, in addition to swimming and dancing, Philip unexpectedly comes up with a solution.

Emphasizing in particular the need to balance work (such as solving societal ills) and play for ideal citizenship is the deed involving the Great Sloth. The sloth is so lazy that he sleeps all the time and forces his subjects—living figures from the game of *Halma*—not only to serve him but to sleep when he sleeps. As a result, the *Halma* people's "once . . . great and beautiful city" lies in ruins (139). Lucy frees the *Halma* people from their bondage by tricking the sloth into wishing for "a machine to draw up water for eight hours a day" as "that's the proper length for a working day" (141). According to the law of the land (actually a "dreadful" one "made by mistake"), "if any one asks for machinery they have to have it and keep on using it" (81). So, the sloth discovers he must work eight hours a day in service to the *Halma* people and the *Halma* figures immediately settle back to being "a most energetic and industrious people" who, through their very nature as playthings, certainly know how to play as well as work (145). Reinforcing this view—the need for play as well as work for successful societies and healthy citizens—is the punishment delivered to the book's "villain": at the end of the book she is sentenced in part to "teach the Great Sloth to like his work and keep him awake for eight play-hours a day" (154).

Despite the deeds the children must undertake to improve the city, Polistopolis, and area, Polistarchia, Nesbit's fictional magic cities world is in many ways a utopia of the sort Morris or Ruskin might imagine: created out of "a mixed crowd of all nations" (58), it has factories "where people of all nations made beautiful and useful things, and loved making them. And all the people who were making them looked clean and happy" (79). The people's cleanliness and happiness are attributed to the factories' being more than just "money factories" and the requirement that "every one" "has to make something that isn't just money or *for* money—something useful *and* beautiful" (79). Even laws are expected to be simultaneously "useful and beautiful" (80) in this community where "*making's* the thing" and workers and craftsmanship are respected (54). The inhabitants of Polistopolis are all of the workers who had a hand in some way in creating the objects out of which the city is composed—"if it was no more than the lad that turned the handle of the grindstone to sharp the knife that carved a bit of cabinet or what not, or a child that picked teazle to finish a bit of the cloth that's glued on to the bottom of a chessman" (54). Above all, Polistarchia is a world where ugliness (as defined by Nesbit's personal and political views) is abhorred: until one is wished for out of necessity, there are no motor cars in Polistarchia, "nor yet phonographs, nor railways, nor factory chimneys, nor none of them loud ugly things. Nor yet advertisements, nor newspapers, nor barbed wire" (57). Lack of ugliness is also implicitly connected to notions of good literature. Buildings in *The Magic City* are constructed at least in part out of books, which (particularly poetry) lend the world much of its variety as a book's contents can come to life if the book is opened. In "The Town in the Library in the Town in the Library," which has a premise similar to *The Magic City*, the magic city the children visit is made with, in addition to the usual playthings and everyday objects, "the Beauties of Literature," which include and are acknowledged alongside works by Shakespeare, Macaulay, and Milton, Gibbon's *Decline and Fall of the Roman Empire*, and renowned British periodicals (253–254). Briggs describes *The Magic City* as

> peculiarly concerned with the creativity and the permanence of works of art. At the centre of *The Magic City* lies the fantasy of an alternate world where everything made in the world has an independent existence, even after it has been destroyed and dismantled.
>
> (331)

Belief in the importance if not permanence of art and imagination, or lasting beautiful citizenship crafted out of creative and literary-influenced play, in fact underlies all of Nesbit's "magic cities" works and incarnations.

As Jenny Bavidge observes, Nesbit's views of art and imagination, and the permanence at least of their influence, fit in well with ideologies underpinning the Children's Welfare Exhibition which, modeled after a similar 1911 exhibition in Chicago, strove to compete in the belief that "the city which cares most for its children will be the greatest city" (qtd. in Bavidge 125). As Bavidge asserts,

> Nesbit's Froebel-influenced philosophy of children's literature and child development was at home in the atmosphere of the Exhibition, which for all its interest in modern systems, often speaks in a language of magic, beauty, and retreat from the modern world.
>
> (133)

Nesbit, however, does not ultimately wish for children to retreat, but argues that they should take center stage in the world: developed throughout *Wings and the Child* is the view that children as well as adults have responsibilities and public obligations as good citizens, though children's obligations are framed according to their roles as citizens-in-training, with active instruction in good citizenship. Children, Nesbit suggests, "may well begin with the lesson that it is part of the duty of a citizen to help to keep his city, his country, clean and beautiful" (86). She insists in fact that "the duties of a citizen should be taught in all schools: they are more important than the latitude of Cathay and the industries of Kamskatka" (86). For such lessons class distinctions are irrelevant, as she argues, it is time, indeed, that certain of the finer duties of citizenship were taught in all schools, Harrow as well as Houndsditch, Eton as well as Borstal. And one of the first of these is the keeping of the beauty of beautiful places unsmirched, the duty of preserving for others the beauty which we ourselves admire.

(88–89)

In her view,

if there is not time to teach geography as well as the duties and decencies of a citizen, the geography should go, and the duties and decencies be taught. For what is the use of knowing the names of places if you do not know that places should be beautiful, and what is the use of knowing how many counties there are in England unless you know also that every field and every tree is a precious gift . . . to be cared for as one cares for one's garden and loved, as one should love every inch of our England, this garden land more beautiful than any garden in the world?

(89)

The patriotic reference to England as Burnett-esque beautiful garden, and as especially beloved, begins to indicate the limits of Nesbit's idealism, ways in which her utopian vision of play and magic cities falls back on the very traditions it seeks to disdain and overturn. As Philip completes his tasks throughout *The Magic City*, he steadily rises in rank: he is knighted to fight a dragon (as any who "have read any history will be aware that no mere commoner can expect to conquer a dragon"), then made a baronet, earl, and duke before finding himself crowned king (58). These various traditional English ranks are occasionally mocked throughout the text, as when it is suggested by Polistopolis' leader, Mr. Noah, that "the existence of baronets . . . has always seemed to the thoughtful to lack justification" (80) and the denouement of the novel attempts to shed them altogether: Mr. Noah abruptly tells Philip and Lucy directly after the coronation, "I regret to inform you that we must part. Polistarchia is a Republic, and of course in a republic kings and queens are not permitted to exist" (155). Yet the very use of the ranks in completing the tasks and even the existence of Mr. Noah and his position in the republic defy the text's attempts at class/rank-leveling. Mr. Perrin, a carpenter known to Philip who becomes a citizen of Polistarchia when he is asleep and dreaming (having contributed to its building through the products of his carpentry), describes Mr. Noah as belonging to the "aristocracy" of "our old families. Very much respected. They're all very high up in the world. Came over with the Conker, as the saying is" (55).

The allusions to "the Conker" and beautiful garden land of England emphasize the text's underlying imperial and patriotic ideology, which its glorification of the colonizing Julius Caesar (who frees Polistarchia of book-released barbarians near the novel's close) also highlights, and which is reverted to frequently through nationalist leanings meant to inspire good citizenship. As Philip considers whether to undertake the seven deeds, Mr. Perrin chastises him: "come, Master Philip, sir, don't talk as if you wasn't going to be a man and do your duty for England, Home and Beauty, like it says in the song," "The Death of Nelson" (56). Philip's first task is symbolically patriotic as well: Like St. George, the patron saint of England, Philip's first duty is to "slay" a dragon (a clock-work one). In good citizenship fashion, Mr. Perrin, Lucy, and Mr. Noah even find a Union Jack flag to fly over the ark they sail. Nationalist ideas don't escape Nesbit's texts entirely without ridicule: perhaps riffing on the interest in "flags of all nations" that formed many card games at this time, the children, when in another boat, use such flags, including the Union Jack, as wraps to keep warm (128), and in "The Town in the Library in the Town in the Library" red-coated British soldiers are of lit-tle help as "they knew nothing but drill, and even the Red Captain said he really couldn't advise" (263). Still, both flag and soldiers provide com-fort: as the short story explains, once they were in the town that "now had red soldiers in it" rather than blue ones, the children "felt quite safe, and the Union Jack was stuck up over the gateway" (261–262).

Gender roles, as Mr. Perrin's encouraging Philip "to be a man" suggests, also become central to Nesbit's portrayals of good citizenship. Through-out *The Magic City* Nesbit represents females such as the villain-nurse and Lucy as having courage and being as capable of solving civic and other problems as males such as Philip, and even outright indicates that males are sometimes simply wrong, as when Philip initially thinks "girls always keep to paths" and "they never explore," to which the narrator remarks, "which just shows how little he knew about girls" (51). Yet despite the tendencies of the aesthetic movement itself to offer gender deviance, especially for boys (such as Burnett's Cedric Errol), traditional notions of gender consistently surface in Nesbit's works to puncture such ideas—especially for girls. Lucy is portrayed, like Cedric's mother in *Little Lord Fauntleroy*, as too good, always being kind and hopeful and wanting Philip to like her and be friends even when he behaves terribly towards her. Tolerating such behavior, it is implied, may be part of her duty as a good female citizen for, as she tells Philip, "Napoleon was cross sometimes, I believe . . . and Julius Caesar" (124). Moreover, we are told the seven deeds would be different if the deliverer was a woman (59) and as part of the first deed where Philip becomes proxy for Sir George, Lucy becomes a princess terrorized by the dragon, the damsel in distress whose saving renders her Philip's property (64). While male civic duties are to become like St. George and Caesar (Lucy's father lit-erally becomes Caesar incarnated at the end of the book), female civic duties are to be "motherly," nurturing and supportive, echoing the ideas of female "citizenship" I explore in Chapter 2 (154–155). Helen, Philip's older sister who marries Lucy's father, is primarily a motherly figure, in Lucy's terms "a perfect duck" (122), and even though Philip tells Lucy "to be a man" (130) and later apologizes for calling her "only a girl" (144), she shows "real heroism" by making cocoa and in "motherly accents" instructing others to drink it (132). In *Wings and the Child* Nesbit disparages women as too frivolous as regards to new clothing and ornaments so that, she claims, "the passion for ornaments—not ornament—is another of the unsettling factors in an unsettling age" but "men are far more sensible. Every man knows the appeal of an old coat. So long as women are insensible to the appeal of an old gown, they need never hope to be considered, in stability of character, the equals of men" (37). Such views of women as not, in key respects, "the equals of men," also influence her presentation of the villain in *The Magic City*. As the villain vies for the position of "deliverer," she is given the title "Pretender-in-Chief to the Claimancy of the Deliverership," which she insists be called the "Pretenderette" (59). The likely allusion, as both Briggs and Bavidge note, is to suffragettes, whom Nesbit did not actually support.

Similar seeming sympathy at times for progressive ideas and yet lack of actual support arises in Nesbit's consideration of class concerns. Though she argues that ideals of citizenship in keeping places beautiful should be taught in "Eton as well as Borstal," for fortunate children as well as delinquent ones, for upper-class children as well as working-class ones, her treatment of lower class figures, generally sympathetic at major moments, tends finally to fall short and back on more conservative, traditional beliefs. Workers in *The Magic City* are given eight hour working days (with the encouragement of a similar number of play hours) and lovely working conditions, including beautiful buildings as factories. Telling sympathy, too, is offered to the villain, the "destroyer," Lucy's working-class nurse, who reveals at the novel's conclusion,

> you don't understand. You've never been a servant, to see other people get all the fat and you all the bones. What you think it's like to know if you'd just been born in a gentleman's mansion instead of in a model workman's dwelling you'd have been brought up as a young lady [sic].
>
> (154)

The "punishment" the book bestows upon the nurse, however, ignores if not belittles the class-based conditions that have led to her situation: Caesar (epitome of patriarchal, imperial leadership) sends her to the sloth and the *Halma* people with the requirement that her freedom depends on making herself "beloved" and therefore undoing the "sentence" "life has pronounced" on her wherein "nobody loves you," an act which would actually deprive her of her supposed freedom, for as she protests, "you know well enough . . . that if that ever happened I shouldn't want to go anywhere else" (154). Reducing class inequalities to a matter of loving and being loved—the final moral of the tale, for the nurse as well as Philip and readers is bluntly given as "learning to be fond of people— which is the only way to be happy"—is not too dissimilar to Burnett's equally conservative sense that if everyone just did their duty and kept to their (class-based) place, everyone would appropriately care for and provide for each other and happiness would abound (158).[18]

Though her attempts to do so are numerous, Nesbit does not in her works transform or even transcend class and inequality-based realities. Even descriptions of what she believes to be "ugly" toys that "outrage the child's inborn sense of beauty" veer into prejudice and racism, as the "worst outrage of all" are "ugly toys, monstrosities, deformities, lead devils, grinning humpbacked clowns, 'comic' dogs and cats, hideous misshapen pigs, incredible negroes, intolerable golliwogs" (*Wings* 19). She is aware of the plights of poorer children, acknowledging

> that poor children live in such crowded houses that there is no room for the building of cities, and in the courts and streets where they play they cannot build, for the passers-by would tumble over their cities, and the policemen would call it an obstruction. So if they have a city at all it must be where they have most of their pleasant plays— at school. Besides, the children I have in mind are so very poor, that no one child could possibly collect enough materials for a city.
>
> (180)

Although she strives to find ways poorer children might be able to pool resources (perhaps better spent on other things) and use "inferior" items such as pegs in place of chess pieces, Nesbit bestows only slight attention to children of the lower classes—in *Wings and the Child* only one penultimate chapter—and presumes that, given their home environments, naturally "most of their pleasant plays" would happen elsewhere, at school. The bulk of her treatment of play is for, like the audiences to which she primarily addressed her novels, middle and upper-class children, such as Philip and Lucy in *The Magic City*, whose great manor house with its glass chandeliers provides much more attractive and seemingly easy to obtain supplies for building magic cities.

Indeed, the very materials and play items her child protagonists use to create their fantastical magic cities betray foundations of the class system she otherwise seems to wish to dismantle: as mentioned earlier, among the residents of Polistopolis are child workers such as "a child that picked teazle to finish a bit of the cloth that's glued on to the bottom of a chessman" (54). For this teazle-picking working-class child, the chessman is work, not play. And play is repeatedly aligned with work for Nesbit—even her depiction of magic cities building in *The Magic City* blurs distinctions between work and play and reads as if it could be lifted from Burnett's *Land of the Blue Flower*: Philip "worked hard and he worked cleverly, and as the cities grew in beauty and interestingness he loved them more and more. He was happy now. There was no time to be unhappy in" (14).

Perhaps most revealing, however, is Nesbit's proposal for play for citizens-in-training, for helping children learn and know their places. Not only are Lucy and Philip obsessed with "manners" throughout *The Magic City*—in other words, societal conventions of "good behavior"—and are taught not to ask too many questions of adults (it bothers Mr. Noah [105] just as it seems to be a point of contention with Nesbit herself, who observes of children in her "The Magic World" piece, "Heaven knows they ask questions enough" [5]), Nesbit suggests in *Wings and the Child* teaching "very little children" obedience in "the form of a game, in which a series of orders were given" for "there is no position in life where the habit of obedience to your superior officer is not of value" (87–88).[19] Play, in Nesbit's view, as in Burnett's and others of the time, can promote order and obedience as well as inspire imaginative possibilities, and both are pivotal to good citizenship. In this way, Nesbit's works on magic cities and play revert to traditional undercurrents just as her texts' ends tend to restore and confirm the traditional status quo. "The Town in the Library in the Town in the Library" returns its children to a non-magical status quo by giving them measles—were the adventures merely illness-induced delusions?—while *The Magic City* overturns its senses of progress by returning Lucy and Philip to their well-off world, "the most beautiful house" Philip "had ever seen," filled with Lucy's toys summarized as "every kind of toy or game that you have ever had or ever wished to have" (9–10). Surrounded by servants, the motherly Helen, and the Caesar-esque Peter, Lucy's father, the children certainly know their manners—and their places, just as the nurse has learned hers, for as the narrator concludes the tale, "at any rate no one that I know of has ever seen her again anywhere else" (158). The problem of the nurse's unequal working-class social conditions is solved, as in so many of Nesbit's texts, by simply removing the problematic figure from the world—in other words, the problem really isn't solved at all, for though the figure is gone, the problematic social conditions remain.[20] Out of sight, out of mind, the nurse is learning or has found her place loving, serving, and teaching the sloth and *Halma* people just as she previously (minus the love of course) served and taught Lucy and Philip. Obedience, discipline, and still knowing and remaining in your place and thereby recognizing your inherent gendered, classed, and "citizen"-bound duty are ultimately as important for Nesbit's conceptions of citizenship as beauty and play are—and in this way she echoes her contemporaries, aligning herself with individuals such as Bancroft and Burnett, and as outlined in previous chapters, Kipling and Baden-Powell, if not writers of girls' fiction. Together, perhaps, they remind us of aestheticism's conservative tendencies.[21] Though often perceived today as radical through its socialist links and its queer potential, particularly in its treatment of (generally male) youth and the erotic gaze, aestheticism at the turn of the nineteenth and twentieth centuries, as both Burnett and Nesbit well illustrate, was just as capable of being used to limit and inhibit, to attempt to define citizenship and good behavior in conventional ways, especially for youthful figures, playful children.

Notes

1 For Bancroft's biography, see Mary L. Remley's entry in *Notable American Women* (1980).
2 U.C. Knoepflmacher (in "Oscar Wilde at Toad Hall"), Holly Blackford, Miles A. Kimball, and Wynn Yarbrough (in *Masculinity in Children's Animals Stories*), are among the few who have considered links between children's literature and aestheticism, particularly with respect to Wilde and to representations of Pan.
3 As Kenneth Kidd observes, too, "queer theorists seem more drawn to canonical writers who are preoccupied with beautiful, erotic children but who do not write for children" (184).
4 The aesthetic movement certainly, as the work of Walter Crane, for example, makes clear, influenced illustrations in children's literature.
5 Tiger skin rugs are notable markers of wealth and imperial connections for Burnett. Sara Crewe and the Large Family in *A Little Princess* each also have tiger skin rugs (68; 165).
6 Burnett's fascination with beautiful boys reflects late nineteenth century aestheticism's fondness for the masculine, and particularly male youth, form; however, it also reflects her own personal circumstances as mother of two boys and tendency towards autobiography even in her fiction. In "How Fauntleroy Occurred" in *Piccino and Other Child Stories* (1894), she makes it well known that the character of Cedric was modeled directly on her youngest son, Vivian, who was friends with an actual president and who, like Cedric, had divided U.S. and British allegiance through his parents. The story "Giovanni and the Other," appended to *Children I Have Known*, is also transparently autobiographical: published just two years after the death of Burnett's son Lionel, it tells in part the story of a mother grieving the loss of her son meeting and understanding the grief of a similarly bereaved mother.
7 Marco's affiliation with art galleries and museums at the beginning of the book is one of several striking similarities to Rudyard Kipling's *Kim*, which of course begins with Kim outside the "Wonder House," the Lahore Museum.
8 The impressions suggested here of being in a state of constant preparation are reminiscent of Baden-Powell's boy scout ideology just as Burnett's depictions of superhuman beauty are reminiscent of Kipling's extraordinary boys, Mowgli and Kim.
9 Many scholars, such as Wilson, Jerry Griswold, and Lorinda Cohoon, strive to align the book, the tale of a young U.S-born boy who moves to England to prepare for his future as heir to a British earldom, within a tradition of

American boyhood but are given pause by the text's portrayals of gender—
not by Cedric's integration into British life and likely assumption of British
citizenship or by Burnett's own hybrid U.S. and British national and
citizenship status. The feminized or androgynous lord Fauntleroy (often,
like Peter Pan, played by a woman or girl in dramatic productions) is no
Huck Finn, who appeared essentially simultaneously with the little lord.
The text's erotic gaze and spectacle of the beautiful boy—aestheticism's
at times defiance of traditional and heteronormative notions of gender—
seem to mystify many readers in regards to *Little Lord Fauntleroy*'s notions
of citizenship and patriotic legacy and may be the reason why Cohoon
claims "Fauntleroy [is] remembered neither for his boyishness nor for
his Americanness" (121). In her own compelling analysis of the "textual
citizenship" of Burnett's play version of *Little Lord Fauntleroy*, in which
she "explore[s] Burnett's portrayal of familial reading practices as a means
of creating political communities through which members can perform citizenship," Deanna Stover similarly observes that "so far, modern criticism
has not moved much beyond Cedric's gender identity" (339).

10 In her obsession with the beauty of young boys, Burnett relies heavily on the
adjective "little" and seems particularly fascinated by legs and stockings,
adding as a parenthetical to her description of one of the German princes in
her chapter on "Eight Little Princes," "I cannot tell you how pretty Eitel's
bare legs in his short socks look drawn together in that grand military way.
They are quite war-like" (53–54). In addition to highlighting aestheticism's
interest in male figures and Burnett's own biases as mother of two boys,
Burnett's portrayals of children also tend to confirm James Kincaid's notions
of Victorian child-loving.

11 For discussions of some of the gender, class, and imperial politics undergird-
ing *The Secret Garden*, see Jerry Phillips' "The Mem Sahib, the Worthy, the
Rajah and His Minions" and Elizabeth Lennox Keyser's "'Quite Contrary.'"

12 Like Colin in *The Secret Garden*, The Rat essentially "heals" himself
through positive thinking and sheer willpower so that he ultimately is
healthy enough to go with Marco on their spy mission. Both Colin and The
Rat teach themselves to walk, though the Rat uses crutches. Burnett's texts
in general offer possibilities for intersections with disability studies today,
a critical need Alexandra Valint has begun to fill with her recent article on
"disability and Colin's wheelchair" (263). For work in disability studies that
has been done on masculinity and literature from earlier in the nineteenth
century, see Karen Bourrier's *The Measure of Manliness*.

13 Drill (40), "playing soldiers" (12), and "getting up a company" (40; 73) are
also "play" activities Cedric Errol expresses strong interest in in *Little Lord
Fauntleroy*.

14 Mavis Reimer makes a similar observation in considering Sara's roles as
"princess" (115–116).

15 One of the strangest exchanges in *The Lost Prince* may be when Marco,
discussing strained economic circumstances, says, "we know how to go
hungry. One does not die of it," to which Lazarus agrees, claiming that
"the insult" of the landlady speaking to Marco about rent is instead "not
endurable" (383).

16 Burnett's marriages were also unconventional for the period and did not
last.

17 In addition to the requirements of creativity for completion, an advantage
of her magic cities as play, she argues, is that "grown-ups suffer a great
deal in playing with children: it is not the least charm of a magic city that a

grown-up can play it and suffer nothing worse than the fatigue incidental to the bricklayer's calling" (*Wings* 119).

18 Such a focus on loving and being loved as a solution to the challenges of un-equal social class conditions is also not dissimilar to Burnett's promotion of Cedric Errol's success in *Little Lord Fauntleroy* as being primarily a result of his loving and being loved, notably by his faithful tenants.

19 Examples of an interest in manners in *The Magic City* are almost too nu-merous to trace. Two examples are when Philip, responding to a statement by the parrot that uses an extensive vocabulary, says "Eh? ... which is not manners, and he knew it" (129) and when Mr. Perrin refuses to help Philip build the ark without Mr. Noah's approval and advice: "carpentry's one thing and manners is another. Not but what I know manners, too, which is why I won't be a party to no such a thing" (100).

20 Making the figure vanish rather than actually solve the conditions of her or his social class concerns notably also occurs in *The Story of the Amulet* (1906) where Imogen, an orphaned working-class girl, finds a mother (a queen no less) to love her in ancient Britain's past, as Julius Caesar is about to invade, and in *The Phoenix and the Carpet* (1904), where a cook and a burglar, sent to a tropical island, marry and become the island's queen and king.

21 My thanks to a Midwest Victorian Studies Association 2015 conference participant who reminded me that, despite its seeming radical potential through gender and sexual deviance and association with Socialist movements, late nineteenth and early twentieth century aestheticism also has a conservative, tradition-inclining base: some wealth and privilege are needed to adopt an aesthetic lifestyle and such a focus on art and beauty tends to necessitate certain requirements of consumerism if not conspicuous consumption (requirements today also conflated with citizenship in some conceptualizations).

Conclusion—"playing houses"

Citizenship, play, and domestic adventure in Enid Blyton's *The Famous Five* series and the adventure playground movement

About a third of the way into *Five on Finniston Farm* (1960), the eighteenth book of Enid Blyton's popular *The Famous Five* twenty-one book series, the eldest of the main characters, Julian, reflects on the experience he, his siblings Dick and Anne, and their cousin Georgina (George) have just had in touring a centuries-old farm: "That was good. . . . Very good. I somehow feel more English for having seen those Dorset fields, surrounded by hedges, basking in the sun" (69). The emphasis on Englishness that results from the excursion might be viewed as an undercurrent in the entire series. As Rashna B. Singh suggests, "throughout Blyton's books we are insidiously reminded of the connection between individual character and national character. Acts of courage or fortitude, which seem to come naturally to the children are reflective not only of their individual character or their upbringing, but also of their very Englishness" (213). In *Five Go Down to the Sea* (book twelve, 1953), it is pointedly noted that a performance concluded when "the fiddle struck up 'God Save the Queen,' and everyone rose loyally to stand and sing every word lustily" (111). The tenth book, *Five on a Hike Together* (1951), ends with an Inspector telling the four child protagonists to "Shake! . . . All of you! You're the kind of kids we want in this country—plucky, sensible, responsible youngsters who use your brains and never give up! I'm proud to meet you!" (193). Tellingly, while this tenth book sees the children locate the jewels of a fictional queen and country ("the Queen of Fallonia"), the only time the series seems to resort to outright fantasy over realism, the twelfth book acknowledges the actual queen and the eighteenth book seeks to defend Britain's own history and property (182).

In its defense of history and property, *Five on Finniston Farm* reveals another preoccupation of Blyton's works also often cited by critics, including Singh: frequent skepticism of foreigners. Americans are at times given more mixed portrayals in the *Famous Five* books, as when Anne admits in *Five on Finniston Farm*, "I've met heaps of fine American children" (68). Still, they are not immune to dismissive treatment or to bouts of disdain, as when Julian scolds the American girl, Berta, in *Five Have Plenty of Fun* (book fourteen, 1955) by telling her, "Come on, kid. . . .

Be your age! Remember you're a guest here and put on a few of your best manners. We like American children—but not *spoilt* ones!" (54). Berta is also consistently mocked for her pronunciation, particularly her tendency to say "wunnerful" for "wonderful" (a jibe repeated in the characterization of the Americans in *Five on Finniston Farm*) for, in George's words, "It's got a D in the middle, you know" (42). Unlike the majority of the other books in the series, *Five on Finniston Farm* does not include the police or clear crime, though dubious practices are certainly afoot. The crux of the story involves foiling an unpleasant American and his inconsiderate son (portrayed, unlike Berta, as irredeemably spoiled), who are bent on acquiring English antiques. The text's position on their attempts to purchase relics of British history is certain: the elderly antique store proprietor exclaims that he's "*always* upset when people want to buy our beautiful old things and take them away to a country they don't belong to" (74) while a respectable grandfather argues that it is "selling our birthright, that's what we're doing—for a mess of potage!" (88). Making matters worse, the American derides the grandfather and his family by referring to the antiques he wishes to purchase ("made," readers are told, "before the first American was born") as "junk" and insists that "you ought to be glad that a poor, run-down, back-dated country like Britain has got anything to sell to a fine upstanding one like America!" (88–9). While, as I noted in Chapter 1, an often one-sided transatlantic rivalry (generally betraying fears of a young U.S. nation) flourished in children's and family games and cards and their frequent literary and historical contents late in the nineteenth century and the beginning of the twentieth, as the middle of the twentieth century approached, Blyton's texts show, a renewed transatlantic rivalry appeared. The rivalry this time, however, placed Britain on the defensive, with play again at stake and even on the offensive.

As I have suggested throughout these pages, the end of the nineteenth century saw a transatlantic wave of interest in children's play. In the U.S., this interest was notably reflected in the child study movement, including in particular the U.S. playground movement, which I have explored in detail elsewhere, that influenced the British play center movement championed by individuals such as Mary Ward.[1] In the U.S., the playground movement gained momentum throughout the end of the century and at the beginning of the twentieth, leading to the establishment of playgrounds in cities and towns throughout the country, often on disused and abandoned sites, including sites that were once burial grounds. In Britain, as mid-century approached, a new play movement arose, the adventure playground movement, also established frequently at disused and abandoned places, particularly sites bombed in the second world war. Generally eschewing conventional playground equipment such as swings and slides, the adventure playground movement envisioned play sites as open spaces for children to create, build, and do whatever they want (within reason) as play, with the site offering wood, tools, and other building and surplus materials (donated or scrounged up) with which to create and play. In many of its tenets and goals, including those connecting play, childhood, and citizenship (and viewing children primarily as citizens-in-training), this new primarily European movement echoed that of the earlier U.S. movement. Strikingly, while the earlier U.S. movement did not gain firm hold in England, the later movement did not make many inroads in the U.S. While Ward, a prominent British author, overtly took on the cause of play at the end of the nineteenth century and the beginning of the twentieth century, Blyton, another prominent British author—who also did not make many inroads in the U.S., despite her name and signature (like Walt Disney's in the U.S.) being at times synonymous with childhood in England and well-known in the commonwealth—implicitly reinforced values inherent in the later play movement. Indeed, Blyton's literary texts highlight views of childhood, citizenship, and play on display in the British adventure playground movement and in play discourse of the period, with *The Famous Five* series offering a notable symbolic crystallization of such views. More broadly, I will argue, Blyton and her *Famous Five* books can be seen as heirs to the nineteenth century ideas of playful literary citizenship I have traced throughout the pages of this book. In Blyton's texts and in the adventure playground movement that paralleled them surface not only a renewed uneasy transatlantic rivalry but a continuation if not evolution of thought on ideas of what play and good citizenship are for children (and where they take place), on gender and the possibilities for play (and adventure and citizenship), and even on aesthetic notions surrounding childhood play and citizenship potential. Though still frequently and generally envisioned, particularly at play sites, as citizens-in-training, children in Blyton's figurations and in the adventure playground movement also illustrate shifts in thinking about citizenship and child citizenship, with views of citizenship increasingly reflecting notions of nationality and interiority rather than worldly or transatlantic sentiments just as play itself turned more "internal" and "domestic" despite continued desire for "adventure."

Blyton's place as heir to the various threads of discourse on transatlanticism, children's literature, play, and citizenship on display in this book seems fitting. David Rudd, who has perhaps written on Blyton and her works more than any other critic, overtly titles Blyton "English Disney" ("From Froebel" 251), specifically calling out her Noddy figure[2] as a means for Britain to "retaliate" against and "combat" "fear of 'Disneyfication,'" and reminds us that "not only was Blyton regarded as useful for the promotion of Britain abroad [after the second world war], but she was congratulated as standing against the encroachment of American popular culture" (262). Born in 1897, at the end of the aesthetic movement, Blyton made use of the Uptons' Golliwogg figure in her own texts (which are not free from racist and other stereotypes and prejudices) and was certainly familiar with play discourse, having trained as a Froebel-inspired kindergarten teacher. Her *Famous Five* books (and others) make use of the four child protagonists structure Edith Nesbit effective deployed,[3] while as critics time and again have noted, class concerns—and conventional and not infrequently problematic class portrayals—plague her works.[4] Notably, for example, the villains (thieves, smugglers, kidnappers) of the books early in the *Famous Five* series are all lower or working-class individuals (foreigners become more prominent as villains as the books progress), with the child of working-class parents, Edgar Stick, targeted for especial condescension in *Five Run Away Together* (book three, 1944). The fisher-boy, Alf, keeps Timmy the dog for George in the opening book, *Five on a Treasure Island* (1942), but never seems to be invited to play with the other children and is forgotten and re-named (or replaced by?) "James" in later books, such as in *Five Have Plenty of Fun*.[5] Singh wide-rangingly connects Blyton's works to Frances Hodgson Burnett's *The Secret Garden* (213) and to Robert Baden-Powell's boy scout movement (207) and considers, with respect to ideas of character at least, Blyton as "actually writing in the tradition of the Victorians" (203). Still, Blyton's depictions of play and gender in the *Famous Five* books in particular demonstrate the changing paths considerations of good child citizenship took in the twentieth century, the ramifications of which we continue to experience.

Ideas of play in the *Famous Five* series are fairly uniform, likely reflecting the formulaic nature of many of Blyton's plots. As Robert Druce rather drily remarks,

> three plots recur and account for the entire series. In five books the children find buried treasure (often, as in other buried treasure stories within Blyton's oeuvre, through the intervention of an animal); in seven they release kidnap victims; in twelve they capture smugglers, counterfeiters or thieves.
>
> (124)

He also points to "seven adventures" "in which foreign agents steal secret plans or kidnap scientists" (124). The series' persistent focus on buried treasure, smugglers, counterfeiters, thieves, and kidnappers highlight again the texts' interest in British property (and people, particularly valuable children and brilliant scientists who tend to be prone to such kidnapping). It also, however, underscores the insularity and interiority of the adventures. While Kim, Mowgli, and the boy scouts have India or the entire British empire as terrain for their play, games, and adventures—and children playing parlor, board, and card games at the end of the nineteenth century were given similar imaginative and often colonial realms—the children of Blyton's fictions look inward and to domestic realms, and do not leave the United Kingdom. For their play and adventures, Julian, Dick, Anne, and George venture underground and inside, exploring castles, dungeons, ruins, caves, tunnels, and secret passages in book after book. Their excursions also take them to simulacrums of Britain and its senses of itself: the children camp out in tents or caravans to explore and live on or in islands, lighthouses, farms, fields, and moors. In Blyton's depictions, girls are now free to leave their physical homes and gardens to play across the country (in ways an earlier writer like Charlotte Yonge would have found unfathomable) but as the British empire began increasingly to unravel after the second world war, play and adventure returned home for Blyton's boy figures. Tellingly, too, just as they were for Lewis Carroll's nineteenth century Alice, adventures for Blyton's famous twentieth century quintet of siblings, cousin, and dog are strikingly domestic affairs. Anne is frequently affectionately teased for her love of "playing houses" but in nearly every book of the series (and, as we will see, just as on nearly every adventure playground) the children set up their own houses and housekeeping, delighting in procuring food, water, shelter, beds, and other domestic comforts and in taking on "adult" roles in running and keeping a house, whether that "house" be a borrowed or makeshift cottage, caravan, tent, ruin, barn, or cave.

The books' focus on "domestic affairs" is clear on another level as well. Written in the midst of and after the second world war, the *Famous Five* books depict threats increasingly as dangers to English safety, sovereignty, might, and prowess. As in the actual world of the period, Americans are both friend and foe, collaborators with regards to science, technology, and prestige, as well as potential usurpers and liabilities (Berta's dad is a scientific collaborator with George's scientist father, though his willingness to put his daughter before his scientific findings makes him vulnerable to kidnappers and extortion). Dangers, moreover, abound from foreigners or foreign or mercenary allegiance: spies and treason, as Druce hints, are real concerns and form part of the plot of several of the books which center on the theft of scientific papers (or scientists or their children). Book eleven, *Five Have a Wonderful Time* (1952), involves the kidnapping of one scientist by another who is described by the kidnapped scientist as "dangerous. He's a traitor, and must be caught before he gives away all that he knows about the work he and I have been doing" (190). Early in the book George sets the tone by reflecting on news of the scientists' disappearance as "just two more of those silly scientists who are disloyal to this country, and disappear to another country to sell our secrets!" (8). In other words, even as they are influenced by foreigners, the threats the narratives hinge upon are nevertheless frequently internal or have the potential to be. Book sixteen, *Five Go to Billycock Hill* (1957), surrounds two pilots who disappear along with their aircraft, "two valuable ones, into which had been incorporated new devices" (107). Luckily, the stolen aircraft crash into the ocean and the two pilots turn out to have been kidnapped and left in a cave to be found by the Five, but the specter of treason—the domestic internal threat of a friend or relative being "a traitor . . . flying off with a plane of ours to sell to an enemy," as Julian explains it—looms over the book and often the series (107). Hints of home-grown and foreign-empowering nuclear or other weapons threats are also evident: the only winter tale, *Five Get Into a Fix* (book seventeen, 1958), sees the children stumble upon strange metal and technology described in ways reminiscent of atomic bomb tests:

> Suddenly the loud rumbling stopped and the light disappeared as if someone had turned off an electric switch! Then, in the darkness, a glow formed, a strange glow that came upwards and outwards, and seemed to go right through the roof itself! Dick clutched at Julian.
> That's the kind of glow we saw the other night!" he said. "My word—it begins down here, goes right up through the hill in some strange way, and hangs above it! That shimmering must come from here too—some kind of rays that can go through anything—like X-rays or something!
>
> (179)

Julian's gloss on the science behind the metal serves well as a stand-in for the author's own: "so much shuddering and shimmering and rumbling. . . . Funny that that hill should always have been so peculiar, isn't it. . . . Must be some kind of iron, I suppose, that magnetizes things. Oh well—it's all beyond me!" (197–198). The threat is persistent, internal but frighteningly vulnerable to foreign interests: as one of the ruffians explains, telling the children that a man is tricking his mother to get access to the metal under her property, which she wouldn't agree to sell,

> well, if *he* wants to sell it, why shouldn't he? But what I say is this— he shouldn't sell it to foreigners, no, that he shouldn't! If I'd have known that—well—I wouldn't have taken money from him to act like I did.
>
> (167)

Rather than training or deploying children as future citizens to lead the world and serve as models of citizen-subjecthood to colonized peoples, by mid-twentieth century good child-citizens were needed—at least in fiction—to secure Britain itself from internal as well as external threats, to show child readers what good citizenship entailed (suspicion of foreigners, loyalty to Britain, horror at notions of treason, and a sharp awareness of and look out for traitors).

The series' consistent focus on internal adventure and danger also surfaces in the startlingly recurrent appearances of travellers (Roma and fair/circus folk), who in the United Kingdom were subject to legislative scrutiny with their caravans in the 1950s and especially 1960s, and who tend to be used in the *Famous Five* series to reinforce allegiance to traditional class values and advocate for intervention in ways hinted at by the adventure playground movement and reminiscent of the earlier turn of the century playground movement. In several of the books, *Five Go Off in a Caravan* (book five, 1946) and *Five Go to Mystery Moor* (book thirteen, 1954), for example, the travellers are a disreputable lot, although their children (such as Nobby in *Caravan* and Sniffer in *Mystery Moor*) are redeemable, capable of good citizenship, if given the right opportunities and companions, attitudes also prevalent in the playground movements. As promising citizen-in-training candidates, both Nobby and Sniffer help the Five in their adventures to thwart Nobby's and Sniffer's guardians' criminal plots and to bring the guardians to justice (and prison). Nobby's and Sniffer's rewards for their good citizen attempts maintain the characters' class placements (and at times suggest limited aspirations) even as they emulate values of the middle classes. In both cases, the children are required—and desire—to leave the travellers' way of life. At the end of book five, Nobby is given a position at a farm working with horses (212), while Sniffer is poised at the end of book thirteen "to get his wish and leave the caravan life to live in a house," with the Five persuaded "we might be able to get him a good home," complete with a well-earned bicycle (194). While Sniffer admits he wants a chance to go to school, Nobby is older than he looks ("he seemed more like twelve by his size") and takes gleeful pride in his lack of learning: when asked by a police Inspector whether he should be in school, he "grinned" and exclaims "Never been in my life, mister. . . . I'm just over fourteen, so I reckon I never will go now!" (*Five Go Off in a Caravan* 210). Even before their fates are determined by the resolution of their adventures, however, Nobby and Sniffer emphasize their worthiness (if not citizenship potential) by their willingness to acknowledge the supposed superiority of the other children, particularly their perceived cleanliness. Both Nobby and Sniffer are repeatedly impressed by the other children's cleanliness (especially with respect to things like caravans and handkerchiefs) and betray their supposed class affiliations through their ignorance of tokens of comfort: "Nobby doesn't sleep in sheets" or even know what they are (*Five Go Off in a Caravan* 94) and Sniffer refuses to use the handkerchief George gives him, instead treasuring it and keeping it as "carefully" "as if it were made of glass" (*Five Go to Mystery Moor* 63). Even Sniffer's name suggests his "unclean," lower class status and background: it is derived from his habit of sniffing his nose, with the text emphasizing "it was certainly a good name for him; but what a horrid father he must have!" (26). Sniffer has, moreover, completely "forgotten" his "proper name" and doesn't seem to mind either the nickname or the disparaged habit of sniffing, which he compounds by using his sleeves instead of his handkerchief when he does wipe his nose (26). As with her portrayal of Americans, however, Blyton does offer a nuanced sense of the travellers and the internal threat they otherwise ostensibly pose: viewed warily and as disreputable by many in the texts, travellers are also considered traditional, even at times traditionally "English," and can, therefore, be good folk, with strong claims to—and displays of—good citizenship. In this way, the travellers in *Five Have a Wonderful Time* are instrumental in helping to rescue a kidnapped scientist and the travellers in *Five Are Together Again* have camping and passage rights stemming from around the Battle of Hastings and unchangeable even by Oliver Cromwell (48). The thief of property and secrets who connects himself to them remains a separate entity, not a familial descendent from 1066 but a bad apple who keeps to himself and takes advantage of his relationship with the circus.

Similar class-based views—even, as we will see, considerations of travellers—and internal threats mark the discourse of the adventure playground movement. Echoing the nineteenth century playground movement's calls for play spaces free from the dangers of the streets (including the physical dangers presented by cars as well as the moral dangers associated with juvenile delinquency), adventure playground movement organizers and play leaders—today re-named play workers in acknowledgment of the goal of promoting child-directed play—also highlighted adventure playgrounds as sites to encourage democracy and good citizenship for child citizens-in-training, particularly for children in the lower and working classes, who, along with perceptions of juvenile delinquency associated with them, represented another sort of internal threat to the nation, democracy, and notions of good citizenship.[6] Only a few days after the Crawley Adventure Playground, one of the first in Britain, opened in August 1954, "two or three mothers came up to say how grateful they were, because the playground kept their children occupied and off the streets" (Crawley Community Association 6). A "resident in a nearby council house estate" suggested that "our street isn't the same since the playground opened; we don't hear any fights or see the children mucking aimlessly around as they used to" (9). Creating better "citizen-worthy" social behavior was an overt goal of the adventure playground, evident for instance in The Crawley Community Association Adventure Playground Committee's argument for

> the playground to be more secluded from outside adults; the fence boundary with the football ground has led well-meaning adults to argue with the children on their activities. In one instance this provoked one tough youngster into anti-social behavior—just to 'show 'em!'.

(16)

The diary of the first Crawley Adventure Playground play worker also reveals some of the senses of class difference underpinning the initial forays of the movement. Her entry for Monday, 30 August observes,

> I find the children very interesting to talk to, they often confide in me when there are only one or two in the hut. Both boys and girls are so very sensible and talk just like adult people. They seem to have missed their babyhood. I should say as soon as they learn to talk and walk, there is no pampering, they have to fend for themselves and it makes them so old in their heads [sic].
>
> (13)

"Tough," unpampered youth who "missed their babyhood" are the primary targets of the early adventure playground movement just as they were of the late nineteenth century playground and play center movements, which specifically sought out the working and lower classes in Britain and immigrant populations in the U.S. As Roy Kozlovsky has observed, "playgrounds are very much about censoring and restricting types of play deemed undesirable and displacing them from places deemed dangerous or corrupting, such as the street" (171). Thomas H. Russell argued in 1914 that the play movement arose because "thousands of children were found to be growing up in the streets, coming into conflict with the police, and their hope of useful manhood and womanhood being destroyed" (174) "Tough gang leaders" with criminal records could even, he elaborated, be "transformed into forces for good" through playgrounds (176). Mary Ward advocated for her play centers through pleas in London's *The Times*, one of which she in 1914 tellingly titled "Evening Play Centres: A Better Playground than the Streets." Lending credibility to their concerns, Viviana A. Zelizer concludes that "by 1910 accidents had become the leading cause of death for children ages five to fourteen" as "railroads, street-cars, and automobiles emerged as fiercer killers of children than communicable diseases, which were rapidly being controlled by medical research and improved public health" (32–33).

The opening page of The Crawley Community Association Adventure Playground Committee's report about its adventure playground explicitly highlights the goals of good citizenship often assumed by adventure playgrounds, citing as one of "the questions asked when interested adults discuss adventure playgrounds" "will it help to produce good citizens?" (2).[7] Similarly, Jørgen Andersson suggests in his component of the report on adventure playgrounds offered by the sixth international conference of the International Playground Association (1975) that "it is our duty to believe in our children so they can believe in themselves and so be responsible for democracy in the future" (11). Lady Allen of Hurtwood, who brought adventure playgrounds to England, also argued for adventure playgrounds not only as deterrents to juvenile delinquency but to help "in fostering a 'democratic community,'" a view aligned with Kozlovsky's sense of adventure playgrounds as "aimed at promoting an egalitarian mode of citizenship through the activity of play . . . as an antidote to collective and individual misconduct" (177; 180–181). Ideals of playgrounds as harvesting good (future) citizens for democracy were also explicit in the late nineteenth century playground movement as title after title and article after article in materials put forth by the Playground Association of American indicate. In but one example, in February 1909, *The Playground*, a monthly journal published by the association, overtly recommends playgrounds through the understanding that the playground "stands for body and character building and produces better children, homes, morals, and citizens" ("The Philadelphia Grand Jury" 4).[8] Yet, as Kozlovsky discerns, the adventure playground movement reflected changes in views of citizenship by and just after the second world war, a shift that, like Blyton's texts, reflects a focus on the internal. Drawing from Foucault as well as Nikolas Rose's notions of a "shift from the contractual model of citizenship to one that stresses the subjective aspects of citizenship," Kozlovsky points to a new focus on individuality—and for the adventure playground movement, child—"interiority," observing that, by means of adventure playgrounds, "the welfare state brought children's interiority under observation and indirectly shaped it from the outside, while consenting subjects experienced this employment of power as a space of freedom and agency" (172–173). He argues that "the adventure playground's democratic and participatory model of collectivity" "was rooted in a psychological notion of political citizenship . . . predicated on the not-so-liberal notion that society has a right, even the obligation, to know and govern the interiority of its subjects to advance the greater common good" so that adventure playgrounds help to "[govern] subjects from the inside, by inducing them to change their everyday conduct to act as active citizens, ardent consumers, enthusiastic employees, and loving parents, as if they are realizing their own intimate desires" (187). Observing that the adventure playground was seen by some of its advocates such as Marie Paneth as a way to thwart fascism, Kozlovsky underscores the contradictions inherent in the movement and in conceptions of play and citizenship: deployed as a means of social control, the adventure playground nevertheless cast itself as an epitome of independence and freedom (183–184). As he ironically concludes, "the playground was one of these institutions where children were made into subjects, precisely because in play they felt themselves to be autonomous and free" (187).

Given the persistent focus on class and the interiority and internal, domestic "threats" on display throughout Blyton's mid-century texts and the origins of the adventure playground movement, it perhaps should be of little surprise that travellers appear to be of note in the early days of the Crawley Adventure Playground. Indeed, by September, the play worker's diary reveals, members of the "Fair Community" arrive to play (15). She reflects that "they were very keen and thought the playground a very good idea, wishing there were more of them near the sites at which the Fair encamped" (15). The day after their first appearance at the adventure playground, one of the Fair Community children's grandmothers came to look at the playground and told the play worker, "I don't know how you stand it, love," later clarifying the "it" as "all the noise and kids," a response which gave the play worker pause and made her consider the likely noise of fairgrounds (15). Compared with the regulars of the neighborhood—the Crawley Adventure Playground, like others beginning at the time, was beset by (generally adolescent) hooligans who periodically tended to destroy overnight what had been built or created—the traveller children seem nearly unremarkable and even praiseworthy: upon their arrival at the adventure playground, they complete a house wherein "the building time was a record and the finished product was very well done" (15).

Acknowledgement of the traveller children's "building time" highlights other aspects of the adventure playground movement reflected in or paralleled by Blyton's texts. Both the *Famous Five* novels and the adventure playground movement reinforce the idea of adventurous play occurring locally, on local sites convenient to children's homes and families. The early play movements, including the "worldly" boy scouts, still existed and exist, but as Joe Benjamin comments in his 1961 study of the beginnings of the adventure playground movement, in places such as Bristol, "in spite of the other playground, the green spaces, the community centre, the Cubs, Brownies, and Cadets, a number of parents were of the opinion that there was nowhere for [their children] to go" (44). The boy scouts and its affiliations, as Troy Boone discerns, were frequently middle-class leisure pursuits, even as their discourse at times seems directed at the lower and working-classes (126). Certainly, too, the pull of the empire and sense of being in charge of the world was waning in considerations of child play by mid-century: as with Blyton's child characters and reminiscent of the earlier Alice in her Wonderland, the children on mid-century adventure playgrounds tend to indulge in strikingly domestic activities rather than, for instance, the military-inspired "drills" which mark The Rat's play in Burnett's *The Lost Prince* and which were also common as citizen-inspiring play on nineteenth century playgrounds. Just as the Five enjoy establishing houses and procuring and cooking food, the craze for children at the adventure playgrounds in the middle of the twentieth century was also to make houses and cook using bonfires. In his portrayal of the case made for opening an adventure playground in Grimsby, Benjamin points to a photographic exhibit displayed "in the window of a prominent local store" in 1954 by the National Playing Fields Association. In the display were photographs of (then seemingly transatlantic, though that quickly faded) adventure playgrounds in "Copenhagen, Minneapolis and Clydesdale. All of them showed children at work with hammers, spades, or wheelbarrows, digging, building, cooking and generally playing house, and it can be reasonably assumed that it was this type of activity that was forseen" (57).[9] A few days after the opening of the Crawley Adventure Playground that same year, the play worker described various groups at play, writing typically, for example, of "one little family consisting mainly of girls [who] lit their fires and cooked boiled potatoes and chips, enjoying a good lunch together with fried bread" (6). In his depiction of adventure playgrounds, Andersson expounds upon the role of such domesticity, arguing,

> we must have house building—it is one of the most important things for children. Every child whether it is Spring or Autumn should have his own house. Therefore they must be allowed to build their own houses with their own ideas and learn to take care of these houses.
> (9)[10]

They must, it seems, learn to embrace the domestic and learn to view "adventure" and "play" as local and home-based if not home-inspired.

Adventure playgrounds' tendency to foster "playing houses" renders more ironic a corollary to the ideas of play and adventure as local and domestic that asserted (or re-asserted) themselves as the mid twentieth century approached: alterations in notions of middle class play that produced the "backyard playground movement" in the interwar period. Lisa Jacobson has observed that the period from about 1920–1940 saw notable shifts in views of play, with "commercial" forms of entertainment ("movies, amusement parks," etc.) at times appearing to rival familial influence (581–582). As a result, playrooms and eventually family rec rooms were promoted within the home and the backyard playground movement became prominent in the 1920s and 1930s with "recreation reformers promot[ing] backyard playgrounds as a way to tie children's play to the safety of the home" (590). These backyard play sites conveniently "addressed a number of parental anxieties about the dangers of street play amid car traffic and unwholesome influences" while "using veiled language that betrayed fears of race and class mixing in public play spaces" (591). In other words, as the mid-century approached, play became even more literally home-centered and home-based than it was for many late nineteenth and early twentieth century children, particularly boys. As the adventure playground movement began to flourish, it had to compete—at least for those, especially in the middle and upper classes, whose families could afford things like swing sets and separate spaces in houses designated primarily for play beyond "nurseries"—with at-home play for local play adventure possibilities.

The prevalence of "playing houses" on adventure playgrounds resulted in early adventure playground documents sometimes highlighting girls' domestic overtures on the playground, and the presence of girls as well as boys on adventure playgrounds, as well as the success of the back-yard play movement, offer reminders that by mid-century girls' play and adventure were much less controversial than they were for, say, Yonge, Alcott, and Carroll nearly a century earlier. Yet gender was still a signifi-cant concern, with adventure playground documents frequently offering perceptions of gender differences even as they acknowledge children of both sexes enjoying the activities the adventure playgrounds invited, and with lingering effects of such views still present today, a fact hinted at by merely the title of Christine Johnson's study, *Sexism on the Adventure Playground: Making Sense of Practice* (1990). Perhaps even more fasci-nating is Blyton's series' portrayals of gender, which interrogate gender concerns through a surprisingly unconventional but generally uncontro-versial figure. In an early critical appraisal of Blyton's works (and girls' fiction in general), Mary Cadogan and Patricia Craig address Blyton's creation of George, a girl who identifies as/wants to be a boy and who, throughout the *Famous Five* series, dresses in boys' clothes, adopts and emulates perceptions of boys' behavior, and insists on being called by the male version of her name (rather than Georgina).[11] As Cadogan and Craig fairly accurately observe, "for Enid Blyton the whole complex business of social roles and attitudes is thoroughly simple, on the sur-face. George wants to be a boy and behaves as if she were one, and that is the end of the matter" (338). Though characters occasionally tease George about "girlish" behavior or appearance and dismiss her identity or identity desires by hinting that trying to be a boy is something George will outgrow, there is altogether little concern in the series about a girl's desire to be a boy; it is generally just accepted as a fact, so much so that the local villagers take to calling George "Master," to George's great delight, as the fisher-boy does in the first adventure (*Five on a Treasure Island* 46). George's parents are essentially nonplussed about the situ-ation as well, with George's mother introducing the figure to the other children in the opening book relatively matter-of-factly: "But George hates being a girl, and we have to call her George, as if she were a boy. The naughty girl won't answer if we call her Georgina" (10). George's "naughtiness" here is due as much to her temperament (a fiery one, like her father's) as to her insistence on being a boy: in the opening book, wary of strangers, she has disappeared instead of waiting to meet her cousins as her mother asked, which is what makes her mother initially label her "naughty" (9).

The few critical considerations of *The Famous Five* series tend to gloss over George's likely being transgender to focus on whether or not the series is ultimately conforming with respect to gender conventions or even sexist. Singh approaches George's transgender possibility the most directly, suggesting that "George, one of Blyton's most famous and best-loved characters, is far more than a tomboy" and that in the series "gender roles are strictly defined, yet consistently crossed, though only from female to male—never in the other direction" (210). She observes that, "in her firm insistence on freedom and flexibility in the assignment of gender roles and identity, George offers young girls a role model that was nothing short of avant-garde at the time of her creation," though she later qualifies that assertion with the view that "what George is doing is appropriating these [masculine] traits, rather than owning them. This is less radical than degendering traits of a character" (210–211). Singh's analysis of George is a notable departure from Cadogan's and Craig's earlier notions that tomboys and George suffer inherently from a sense of "basic deficiency" (338) and that "the author has withheld complete approval from George, and for this reason George is one of her most interesting creations" (342). In their view, the series has "one fairly strong character, and it is this girl, George, who has carried the series; the other three children are as unmemorable as the author can make them" (338). As a part of the other characters' "un-memorability," Cadogan and Craig maintain that

> Anne, as a foil to George, is the archetypal "feminine" girl, fond of dolls and cooking and "playing house." She is "babyish" to begin with, but becomes less so. In George, on the other hand, there is something for the reader to come to grips with: fierceness, resentment, the wish to have been a boy.
>
> (338)

While they cite another of the series' possible transgender figures, Henry (short for Henrietta, who also desires to be a boy and dresses and strives to act like one), as existing "for comic effect," they claim that "George is not quite fairly treated: there is no suggestion that her fantasy of being a boy is just as 'normal' as Anne's acceptance of a 'housewifely' role" (342). Rudd addresses some of Cadogan's and Craig's criticism while aiming to defend the series and Blyton from charges of sexism, "questioning," for example, "whether Blyton's views were as orthodox" as charges of sexism (and criticism like that of Cadogan and Craig) imply (*Enid Blyton* 111). Even as he makes a case for "George's overall triumph" (116) and defends the treatment of Anne and her implied power—"it would be wrong, therefore, to belittle Anne's behavior, particularly as it still represents a reality for many women" (118)—he insists that "what needs emphasizing, however, is a gradual downplaying of George's power," generally in favor of "the growing control of the boys," as "the undermining of George's independence is increasingly characteristic of the

Five books, read in chronological order" (115). He does find it odd that Cadogan and Craig

> omit to mention Jo, who is the main alternative tomboy in the series, and clearly a favorite of Blyton's, given her record three appearances. She effortlessly surpasses the Five in daring and capability—rescuing them all, boys included, from various scrapes.
>
> (117)

What is additionally odd, I would suggest, is how consistently the *Famous Five* criticism in general overlooks the series' potential transgender youth, the sheer number of children presented as girls who actually identify as or wish to be boys (or, in one case, are forced to disguise themselves as a boy).[12] Indeed, if one read just the *Famous Five* books, Anne would seem to be the "odd" one out: far more common are girls who are really or wish to be boys. These include the already mentioned George, Henry, and Jo (who is perhaps even more spunky than George and Henry but who is of a lower class, affiliated with travellers, and to her dismay required by her guardian to wear skirts and dresses, though she does manage to do such things as keep her hair short). They also include one of the "Harries" in *Five on Finniston Farm* and the American girl, Berta, who is threatened by kidnapping, prompting her father to insist that she disguise herself as a boy. When she briefly—and against her initial objections—becomes "Lesley" (her androgynous boy name), we are told she actually makes surprisingly "a jolly good-looking boy!" (*Five Have Plenty of Fun* 67). The Harries are "the most twinny twins," "*exactly* alike!" (*Five on Finniston Farm* 11), described by their mother in this way, in a conversation with Dick:

> "We called the boy Henry, and he became Harry, of course—and we called the girl Harriet, and *she* calls herself Harry for short—so they're known as the Harries."
> "I thought they were both *boys*!" said Dick in amazement. "I wouldn't know which is which."
> "Well, they felt they *have* to be alike," said Mrs. Philpot, "and as Harry can't have long hair like a girl Harriet has to have shorter hair to be like Harry! I very often don't know one from the other myself."
> Dick grinned. "Funny how some girls want to be boys!" he said, with a sly glance at George, who gave him a furious look.
>
> (15)

Dick's "glance" and mention of "some girls" single out George, yet simultaneously emphasize—along with the proliferation of such figures in the series—that she is not actually exceptional in her behavior, that it may be "funny" but yet a reality. Singh points out that "Blyton revealed that George was her favorite character" in a January 13, 1963 BBC interview with Marjorie Anderson (211), an admission that also helps to undermine Cadogan's and Craig's view that "the author has withheld complete approval from George," at least personally (342). Moreover, in the interview, Blyton noted that "although as a rule her characters were imaginary . . . George was based on a real girl she once knew" (Singh 211). Not only, then, are potential transgender children normalized within the scope of the series, they are observed to be a "normal" fact in real life.

Rudd considers Jo's "daring and capability" (*Enid Blyton* 117) and defends Anne and (seemingly) conventional notions of womanhood as definite power centers in the series, but the series goes even further in its interrogation of—if not challenges to—traditional notions of gender behavior. George herself plays a notable rescuing role in the sixth book, *Five on Kirrin Island Again* (1947), which Rudd suggests was originally conceived of as the end of the series (*Enid Blyton* 114). In the actual final book, George is given, as Rudd also discerns, much narrative space, going against Julian's wishes to single-handedly bring a dangerous thief to justice (*Enid Blyton* 115–116), and her success forces Julian to recognize that he "should *never* have thought of doing all the things [she] did" (*Five Are Together Again* 170). Yet it isn't just girls-who-should-be-boys who manage such daring and adventurous feats in the series. In the penultimate book, *Five Have a Mystery to Solve* (1962, book twenty), Anne markedly defies expectations. She is teased by Julian early on that "a mouse can't suddenly turn into a tiger! Anyway, one tiger's enough. *George* is the tiger of our family—my word, she can put out her claws all right—and roar—and rant and rave!" (5). Before the page is out, however, Anne shows herself to be equal to George in "tiger"-ness, lashing out at Dick for his bumping his bicycle into hers, a response which not only amazes Julian but prompts Dick, after hearing his sister explain that she was "being a tiger for a moment—putting out my claws! I thought Dick and you might like to see them!," to exclaim that he "never heard you yell like that before" and to add his own telling analysis of her behavior: "Surprising—but quite pleasing!" (5). Anne soon uses her new-found tiger prowess to tame a little boy prone to being a pest, throwing a bucket of water on him, an action which inspires him to refer to her as "like a tiger!" and prods Julian to remark that indeed "the mouse has turned into a tiger! Well, you said you might one day, Anne—and you haven't lost much time!" (43). The Anne-as-tiger theme continues throughout the book, culminating when Anne herself foils the men (foreigners, of course) who are removing valuables from the island on which the children are temporarily stranded. As the men attempt to set the children's boat adrift, further stranding them, she confronts them alone—an action virtually unimaginable earlier in the series for the at times seemingly timid character—"yelling to Timmy to bite the men, and dancing about in a rare old temper!" (167). She hurls a stone at them and succeeds in frightening them off, with Julian arriving in time to witness the event and confirm "You've scared them stiff! . . . You even scared *me*!" (167). He calls her a tiger yet again, a title that makes Anne "glad" as she "hated you all thinking I was a mouse. You'd better be careful now, I *might* turn into a tiger again!" (167–168), a sentiment re-affirmed at the book's end, with the closing page dwelling for a moment on the "half asleep" figure of "quiet little Anne who *can* turn into a tiger if she has to!" (170). Anne, who does not wish to be a boy and is not transgender, Blyton forcefully and explicitly insists, also has remarkable strength and other powers, a commentary, it would seem, taken together with her portrayals of George and other characters, on the capabilities of all women and girls, if not children, whether they prefer to "play houses" and identify with domesticity or femininity or not.

Anne's "tiger" capacity, alongside the power Rudd discerns her do-mestic management inspires, also calls attention to the books' treatment of boys and domesticity. In her discussion of gender in the series, Singh insists that, in the books, "when a boy takes on the female role, it is only in jest" (211). Though it is true that the series doesn't present its readers with any boys who wish to be girls and though it would be incorrect to suggest that the series never offers "traditional" gender views in line with the time of the writing of the books, it is striking how frequently the presentations of traditional gender roles and duties interrogate those very views by overtly questioning them, defying or challenging them, or even calling attention to their potential ludicrousness. At the end of *Five Go to Mystery Moor*, after overhearing George and Henry comment to each other on being "as good as" or even "*better* than a boy" (195), Dick chimes in, saying, "I say, do let me share in these compliments! . . . Just tell me I'm as good as a girl, will you?" (196). They respond by throwing a hairbrush and a shoe at him, but the idea is planted in readers' minds that the entire rationale for the conversation—or the sense of "as good as"—is absurd: moreover, Dick's response has the potential to imply, the idea of being "as good as a girl" may offer a "comic" moment but why shouldn't a child want to be as good as a girl, as well as, as good as a boy? (196). Or, if a girl can aspire to be as good as a boy, why couldn't a boy aspire to be as good as a girl? Earlier in the book, the children's host insists that the "girls must wash up for me afterwards . . . [as] I've such a lot to do today," a request George immediately recognizes as an instance of inequality: "'Why can't the boys help?' said George at once" (87). In resolving the situation, Anne teases that she'll do the washing up and all the "boys"—including George and Henry—"can go out to the stables" (87). But the other children recognize the inequality as well, with Dick "g[iving Anne] a good-natured shove" and empha-sizing "You know we'll help, even if we're not good at it" (87). The "even if we're not good at it" may seem to be giving "boys" an "out," or highlighting that domestic activities are not their forte, but the fairness of boys taking part in domestic obligations—and their full capability of doing so—is a recurrent motif of the series. In *Five Go Down to the Sea*, Anne offers to help a farmer's wife shell peas, a suggestion the farmer's wife meets with pleased agreement but with a notable exception, "but the boys needn't help" (43). Again, George has none of it, immediately querying, "indignantly" and with the preamble "how unfair!," "why shouldn't they, just because they're boys?" (43). Dick again also responds promptly, telling George "we're going to help, don't worry! We like podding peas, too! You're not going to have all the treats!" (43). One of his goals, according to the text, is to calm George's famous temper but the subtext is clear and consistently reaffirmed: just because they are boys doesn't mean they can't engage in acts of domesticity or be domestic. This is particularly evident in *Five on a Secret Trail* (1956, book fifteen). Waking up one morning while camping out/sheltering in a ruined cottage, Julian exclaims,

> "Hey, George! Anne! Sleepyheads! Get up and get us breakfast!"
> George sat up, looking furious, as Julian intended. "You jolly well get your own b . . ." she began, and then laughed as she saw Julian's amused face.
> "I was only striking a little match to set you alight!" said Julian. "Come on—let's all go for a swim in the pool!"
>
> (95)

Julian uses the idea of expected female domesticity to tease George and spur her to waken more quickly but his very teasing and confirmed expectation of George's resistance demonstrate that he understands the unfairness of certain gender expectations and some of the effects of that unfairness. His "striking a little match" comment and proposal of a swim imply strongly that he will indeed get his own breakfast and was always intending to do so, that his being a boy actually does not prevent him from being able—or needing—to do such a thing.

The various takes on "housekeeping" and gender offered by Blyton and the mid twentieth century adventure playgrounds—where both boys and girls built and maintained houses and engaged in such activities as cooking and preparing meals—help perhaps ironically to reveal another defining aspect of the mid twentieth century playground movement and its links to past views of childhood, citizenship, and play. While late nineteenth and early twentieth century figures like Burnett and Nesbit sought to align notions of play, childhood, and citizenship with a discourse of aestheticism, privileging notions of beauty, the mid twentieth century playground movement quickly found itself straying from such ideals. Kozlosvksy points to views of "the playground as a landscape, making art into a useful part of everyday life" (173), but notes that, particularly for adventure playgrounds, such a viewpoint is at odds with "children's activities inside the playground's premises" that do "not correspond with the artistic status of the playground as a landscape," with "the anti-aesthetic portion of the playground . . . most pronounced in its appropriation of junk as desirable play material" (174). Though semblances of housekeeping were on display at adventure playgrounds, notions of tidiness and beauty were frequently put to the test, as is indicated well by one of "the questions asked when interested adults discuss adventure playgrounds": "Surely it must be an eyesore to people in adjoining houses?" (Crawley Community Association 2). A refrain in many early adventure playground documents is neighbors wanting fences built to block the view of the playground and all the messiness inherent to it: scraps of wood, metal, and other supplies filling the space, along with the children's own creations which of course varied considerably and were not always the most aesthetically pleasing (to adult eyes) in design. The early alternative name for the adventure playground— "junk" playground—conveys well its differing ideology. Carl Sørensen, who designed the first adventure playground (it was located outside of Copenhagen), is frequently cited for remarking that "of all the things I have helped to realize, the Junk Playground is the ugliest; yet for me it is the best and most beautiful of my works" (qtd. in Chilton 2). Not envisioned as infusing children with the beauty otherwise evident in their surroundings, as Nesbit might have suggested, or even made beautiful simply by the transformative presence of extraordinarily beautiful children, a favorite theme of Burnett, the adventure playground is yet envisioned as aligned with beauty through the idea that play—and children's creativity—is internal, capable of being drawn out, and inherently beautiful. Beauty, in this sense, is hidden, inside, invisible, a product of children's interiority and aligned with the very sense of the importance of the internal that looms large in Blyton's *Famous Five* series as well as in the adventure playground movement.

Ultimately, however, just as adults on both sides of the Atlantic—and their play movements and trends—as I have shown in this book often sought to employ games and play in tandem with notions of "good" literature to solidify idealized and generally gender-based expectations of child citizenship, and the "tough" youngster at the early Crawley Adventure Playground uses "anti-social behavior" to defend his activities along the football field boundary, so do the children of Blyton's Famous Five demonstrate time and again that children are equally capable of defiance—and even of employing games, play, and senses of "good" literature for their own purposes and often as subterfuge against problematic adults and their authority. Early on in *Five Go to Billycock Hill*, George reflects on the power of childhood, the potential for pleasure it offers, and while Baden-Powell earlier conceived of himself as akin to

Captain Hook, she connects herself to the similarly androgynous Peter Pan: "I don't want to grow up . . . There can't be anything nicer in the world than this—being with the others, having fun with them. No—I don't want to grow up!" (38). By book's end, Anne resembles another classic model of children's literature, the ostensibly domestic Alice, for holding a little boy's pet pig, she "look[s] like Alice in Wonderland. She carried a pig, too!" (182). The pig, which goes "to sleep, just like Alice's pig," offers its own path for deviance (182). Even as the pig in *Alice's Adventures in Wonderland* defies Alice's expectation by turning into a pig from a baby and then running away, so this pet pig constantly runs away. It is clear throughout *Billycock Hill*, though, that the pig's habit of running away is really an excuse to allow its owner, a small boy, free reign—he goes where he wishes under the pretense of having to find his lost pig. In *Five Go to Billycock Hill*, in other words, Alice—and her surprising pig—are reminders of child power and the power of defiance just as Peter Pan is a reminder of the potential power of childhood and youth.

While nineteenth century card, board, and parlor games were meant to inspire transatlantic child citizens-in-training with notions of good literary and colonial citizenship even as they betrayed tensions of a transatlantic rivalry; croquet was re-cast as duty to mitigate some of the potential of playful girls; boys like Mowgli, Kim, and the boy scouts were perceived as incomplete but extraordinary hybrids, pawns as much as players in the Great Game of empire and realities of citizenship; and children, still citizens-in-training, were ultimately seen as moldable through the alignment of play and beauty; so the Famous Five children emblematize the potential of interiority—hidden depths—also on display in the adventure playground movement. Entwined, like the discourses of citizenship and play in general, with contradiction—"free" play "supervised" by watching adult "play" "workers," balancing safety with needs and desires of risk-taking—the adventure playground movement, through the very name it adopted, sought to provide children with adventure through play—but adventure that is contained, bound, limited by borders, local, and ultimately internal, aligned inextricably with domesticity. The children of the Famous Five, depicted simultaneously as getting older in the series and yet as staying children, half-adult and yet cast constantly as kids, know well how to take advantage of such contradictions—to, for example, enjoy youth, Peter Pan-like, even while insisting they are old enough (or Julian is or they all are, with Timmy the dog along) to be on their own and stay safe. Within the realm of the texts, these claims work: despite continuing to have adventures and dangerous escapades in book after book they are allowed again and again to be on their own and have even more adventures.

Just as they recognize the importance of good literature for defiance, they know, too, the importance of games and play for deception, subterfuge, and power. Games upon games—an alphabet game (*Five on a Secret Trail* 59), traditional Snap (cited in many of the books), trans-atlantic Scrabble (*Five Are Together Again* 149), even soldiers in 1948's *Five Go Off to Camp*, though it is notably disparaged (95)—mark the pages of the *Famous Five* books. Julian makes a point of packing both "books and a few games to play in case it's rainy" when they go ad-venturing in caravans and Blyton even offers readers a list of the spe-cific games: "snap cards, ludo, lexicon, happy families, and dominoes" (*Five Go off in a Caravan* 22–23). Though villains sometimes play cards and though the children sometimes play games merely to pass the time, just as notable (and perhaps just as frequent) are those instances when games-playing is cast as the children's especial purview, deployed to ac-complish a particular aim (often at the expense of adult authority) or as a form of deception against adults. In this way, in *Five Go to Smug-gler's Top* (1945), the children can malign the brilliant scientist Uncle Quentin's ability to play games—"he really wasn't much good at all, not even at such a simple game as snap" (6)—while using games to delay the inevitable bed time, with George taking advantage of a game to cajole her mother and get her own way: in response to her mother's suggestion that she and Anne head to bed, George insists "just one good game of Slap-Down Patience, all of us playing it together, Mother! . . . Come on—you play it too. It's our first evening at home. Anyway, I shan't sleep for ages, with this gale howling round! Come on, Mother—one good game, then we'll go to bed" (8). In *Five Fall into Adventure* (1950, book 9), Snap is used to deceive watching villains into believing all the children are present in a room. Class biases surface again as the chil-dren trick the paper-boy, Sid, described as "not that bright," into sitting and playing the game with them to allow Dick to sneak away disguised as Sid to spy on the thieves who are after Uncle Quentin's papers and who have kidnapped George (70). As the cook, Joanna, exclaims, "we'll never hear the last of it, down in the village—him being invited here to supper" (75).[13] Still, the children of the Famous Five have their way: the only official adult present, Joanna, is not told of the children's plans until they are in process (Sid has himself essentially already been kidnapped by the children, with Dick grabbing his cap, bike, and papers and ped-dling off). She nevertheless accedes to the display of childhood power, agreeing to the ploy, and the children use the game to buy Dick more time. The card game is also effectively used as deception later in *Five Go to Smuggler's Top* when the children use the pretense of games-playing to hide Timmy. Realizing that someone is eavesdropping outside their door, George tells the other children to "all talk loudly and pretend to be playing a game" (88). To trick the villain listening in, "they began to play snap" and as "they yelled 'snap' nearly all the time, pretending to be very jolly and hilarious," "anyone listening outside the door would never guess it was all pretence" (88).

The children of Blyton's *Famous Five* series reveal the ability and strategy of using games and "good literature" for one's own ends are not confined to adults. Real as well as fictional children over the last few centuries undoubtedly knew that, too—and found ways to carve out spaces for their own aims, within and against the at times conflicting views of ideal playful literary citizenship, almost-citizenship, and citizenship-in-training embedded, conveyed, and reinforced throughout the long nineteenth century in adult projections and couplings of play and literature. Neither play nor literature ultimately are exclusive adult realms, nor ultimately is citizenship—and particularly future citizenship—entirely controllable or shaped by adults. Just as children create their own rules and strategies for games and play, even at times ignoring those rules set forth by adults, so do they too—even at times out of the literature and notions of citizenship given to them by adults, complete with notions of national and cultural rivalry, takes on gender, and senses of beauty—create their own stories and narratives, their own adventures, and ultimately their own expectations of play, literature, and citizenship.

Notes

1 See my article, "Recycled Stories: Historicizing Play Today Through the Late Nineteenth Century Anglo-American Play Movement," in the *Journal of the History of Childhood and Youth* (2014).
2 I also analyze the Sampson Low Noddy books with regards to their sense of the "outside" and foreigners in "Oh Golly, What a Happy Family!"
3 Though Blyton's texts, unlike Nesbit's, tend to eschew first-person narration.
4 Bob Dixon prominently underscored some of the class (and other) concerns in Blyton's works in *Catching Them Young: 1. Sex, Race, and Class in Children's Fiction* (1977); nearly every critic since then (if not before) has at least acknowledged those concerns, with even Jacqueline Rose mentioning it and referencing Dixon in her brief reference to the *Famous Five* books (69) in her groundbreaking *The Case of Peter Pan* (1984).
5 Blyton's books are often disparaged for poor writing; she was a prolific writer—she wrote over six hundred books—and the quantity of her output may well have affected its quality. So, too, might have her writing process which, she explains in *The Story of My Life* (1952), supposedly involved typing out her stories immediately as they spontaneously came to her: "they came all ready made, pouring out complete. . . . If I sit in my chair and shut my eyes for a minute or two, in comes the story I am waiting for, all ready and complete in my imagination" (87). Slips in names and even at times prominent ideas are evident throughout the *Famous Five* series, which begins by suggesting that George's dad is brother to Julian's, Dick's, and Anne's father while Kirrin Island where sits the remains of Kirrin Castle in Kirrin Bay belonged to George's mom (who passes it down to her). As George explains in the first book,

> Years ago my mother's family owned nearly all the land around here. Then they got poor, and had to sell most of it. . . . All that's left of what Mother's family owned is our own house, Kirrin Cottage, and a farm a little way off—and Kirrin Island.

(*Five on a Treasure Island* 20–21)

With this lineage, then, it is striking that Blyton frequently refers to the children by the surname "Kirrin" in the books, as in *Five on Finniston Farm*, where they are introduced to their host as "The Kirrins" (13). This is especially notable as, in *Five Get into a Fix,* the mother of Julian, Dick, and Anne is referred to as "Mrs. Barnard" (3). As Druce bluntly suggests, plot devices and themes recur a bit too consistently throughout the series (particularly those involving travellers and/or fair folk as well as smugglers, kidnappers, and hints of wreckers). Both *Five Go Down to the Sea* and the last book *Five Are Together Again* (book twenty-one, 1963) involve two-person costumes used to impersonate either a donkey or a horse, yet by the later book Julian and Dick appear not to remember that they are already the possessors of such a suit (the "Clopper" horse costume was given to them at the end of *Five Go Down to the Sea* [195]). A potentially striking feature for readers throughout the series is that one of the reasons George agrees to attend an all-girls boarding school with Anne is that the school has a kennel and allows her to take Timmy. The final book of the series, *Five Are Together Again,* however, strangely suggests that Timmy is at home waiting for George to return from school for her holidays, that she has "missed old Timmy so *much* this term," and that he always seems to know when she is coming home from school and meets her at the train station (1). Blyton's memory for details, in other words, is not perfect throughout the series, which may be another reason why the fisher-boy Alf suddenly seems to become the fisher-boy James. It may also explain the children's sudden desire for orangeade and lemonade over ginger beer later in the series (as in many of Blyton's books, food appears prominently in the *Famous Five* series).

6 Though often viewed as necessary for such things as child safety through supervision if not to foster play, play leaders/play workers (and their need) have been controversial throughout the history of the playground movements. Both the late nineteenth century playground movement's and the adventure playground movement's focus on the streets are of course telling regarding notions of citizenship in the U.S. and Britain. According to Tom Cockburn, "with the exception of the modern western city, cities are pervaded with the energy and noise of children"; it is only through "recent developments" that "children (certainly unaccompanied children) have been virtually removed from the public spaces of cities" with "children on the streets … seen by adults and the state both as a source of concern and as a potential danger" (6). As Cockburn ultimately observes, "the absence of children from public spaces begs the question of what has happened to children's citizenship" (6).

7 In a sense of how successful the adventure playground movement has been in Britain as compared to the U.S., Crawley alone now appears to have four adventure playgrounds; in the U.S., only a few such playground exist (there is one, for example, in Berkeley, California, and another in New York City).

8 Another subtheme of both the late nineteenth century playground movement and the adventure playground movement (and indeed at times prevalent in discussions of play today) is a sense of rural/urban divide, with some believing (and others contesting) that rural areas "naturally" provide children with more opportunities for play. As Tony Chilton observes, "few Adventure Playgrounds were established in rural areas because of the general misconception that children living in such areas had free and easy access to more adventurous play opportunities. This is a fallacy that persists even today" (6). In addition to concerns over safety and the streets, concerns over safety at adventure playgrounds (which allow for such things as tools and fires) are prominent in adventure playground discourse and, though advocates argue that properly organized adventure playgrounds are quite safe and that risk

is a requirement for play and child development, safety concerns (real or perceived) are one of the primary reasons why adventure playgrounds are not more common in the U.S.

9 The adventure playground established in Minneapolis early in the movement (1950, though referenced still in the 1954 exhibit) was short-lived: in Joe Benjamin's words in 1961, "the playground itself has long ceased to exist" (21) and

> all that is known is that the experiment was not repeated. It is known, however, that city departments in America regard it still with the same sort of suspicion that was the reward of early efforts in this country [Britain].
>
> (23)

10 Citing Marie Paneth's Branch Street study and play center experiment, Kozlovsky offers an alternate analysis of domestic sorts of activities on adventure playgrounds,

> such as making fires, cooking mid-day meals, and dwelling in self-made homes and tree houses. Although these phenomena are all too readily explained as an expression of the child's desire to imitate the world of adults, Paneth's work suggests the strategic purpose of defining the playground as a second home [as] the second home allowed the social worker access to the first and to pin the pathologies of the slum child on inadequate mothercraft [and to use the] second home [to] rescue . . . children's attitude toward society and authority.
>
> (184)

11 For consistency with the books and critics I will throughout follow the series' convention of using the "she" pronoun for George, who was governed by mid-century rules; however, today, a transgender George would warrant the pronoun "he" or "ze."

12 Strikingly, Sally Mitchell notes a similar theme from around the time of Blyton's childhood: "many women who were girls at the turn of the century had longed intensely not to be," so that "while nursery children played boy games in boy clothes during holidays, working-class girls longed for trousered freedom in public" (103). As she remarks,

> dreams of boyhood are hardly unique to the period. Given the cultural valuation of male as better and the visible privileges granted to boys, many girls have envied their brothers. In this period, however, girls' boyishness developed a publicly acceptable face.
>
> (103–104)

Blyton's later portrayal of George and the other girls-who-would-be-boys in *The Famous Five* books, (and in other works in her oeuvre) made that "publicly acceptable face" even more commonplace.

13 Though Sid's lack of games-playing ability—in his terms, he got "muddled" in his attempts "to learn draughts" and Joanna admits "he's never got much beyond Snap and Happy Families" (75–76)—is attributed in some degree to his being "not that bright," there seems to be a class element as well. Though Joanna does suggest she'll play cards with the children, how well she plays isn't indicated; however, the traveller-affiliated child Jo does play cards in *Five Have a Wonderful Time*, with readers informed, "Jo was very bad at cards, and soon stopped playing" (130).

Works cited

Abbot, Anne. *Game of Dr. Busby*. Salem, W. & S.B. Ives, 1843.

Adams, Jennifer. *The Adventures of Huckleberry Finn*. Layton, UT, Gibbs Smith, 2014.

———. *Alice in Wonderland: A Colors Primer*. Layton, UT, Gibbs Smith, 2012.

———. *Anna Karenina: A Fashion Primer*. Layton, UT, Gibbs Smith, 2013.

———. *A Christmas Carol: A Colors Primer*. Layton, UT, Gibbs Smith, 2012.

———. *Emma: An Emotions Primer*. Layton, UT, Gibbs Smith, 2015.

———. *Frankenstein: An Anatomy Primer*. Layton, UT, Gibbs Smith, 2014.

———. *Jabberwocky: A Nonsense Primer*. Layton, UT, Gibbs Smith, 2013.

———. *The Jungle Book: An Animals Primer*. Layton, UT, Gibbs Smith, 2014.

———. *A Little Princess: A Friendship Primer*. Layton, UT, Gibbs Smith, 2017.

———. *Little Women: A Playtime Primer*. Layton, UT, Gibbs Smith, 2016.

———. *A Midsummer Night's Dream: A Fairies Primer*. Layton, UT, Gibbs Smith, 2016.

———. *Moby-Dick: An Ocean Primer*. Layton, UT, Gibbs Smith, 2013.

———. *The Odyssey: A Monsters Primer!* Layton, UT, Gibbs Smith, 2016.

———. *Pride and Prejudice: A Counting Primer*. Layton, UT, Gibbs Smith, 2011.

———. *The Secret Garden: A Flowers Primer*. Layton, UT, Gibbs Smith, 2015.

———. *Sense and Sensibility: An Opposites Primer*. Layton, UT, Gibbs Smith, 2013.

———. *Treasure Island: A Shapes Primer*. Layton, UT, Gibbs Smith, 2015.

———. *The Wonderful Wizard of Oz: A Colors Primer*. Layton, UT, Gibbs Smith, 2014.

———. *Wuthering Heights: A Weather Primer*. Layton, UT, Gibbs Smith, 2013.

Alcott, Louisa May. *Eight Cousins*. Mahwah, NJ, Watermill Press, 1985.

———. *Little Women*. 1868. Peterborough, Canada, Broadview, 2001.

Allen, Warren. "Citizens of the Empire: Baden-Powell, Scouts and Guides and an Imperial Ideal, 1900–40." *Imperialism and Popular Culture*, edited by John M. MacKenzie, Manchester, Manchester University Press, 1986, pp. 233–256.

———. "Popular Manliness: Baden-Powell, Scouting, and the Development of Manly Character." *Manliness and Morality: Middle-Class Masculinity in Britain and America, 1800–1940*, edited by J.A. Mangan and James Walvin, New York, St. Martin's Press, 1987, pp. 199–219.

American Card Company. *Union Playing Cards*. New York, circa 1863.

Andersson, Jørgen. "The Adventure Playground in Theory and Practice." *Adventure Playgrounds and Children's Creativity: Report of the Sixth*

International Conference. Sheffield, UK, International Playground Association, 1975, pp. 9–15.

Armstrong, Nancy. "The Occidental Alice." *Contemporary Literary Criticism: Literary and Cultural Studies*, fourth edition, edited by Robert Con Davis and Ronald Schleifer, New York, Longman, 1998, pp. 537–564.

Auerbach, Nina. "Alice in Wonderland: A Curious Child." *Victorian Studies*, vol. 17, 1973, pp. 31–47.

BabyLit. "About Us." babylit.com/pages/about-us.

Baden-Powell, Robert. *The Wolf Cub's Handbook*. 1916. New York, The Boy Scouts of America, 1918.

———. *Scouting for Boys*. 1908. Mineola, NY, Dover Publications, Inc., 2007.

———. *Scouting for Boys*. World Brotherhood Edition. Boy Scouts of America for the Boy Scouts International Bureau, 1946.

Bancroft, Jessie H. *Games for the Playground, Home, School, and Gymnasium*. New York, The Macmillan Company, 1909.

Banet-Weiser, Sarah. *Kids Rule!: Nickelodeon and Consumer Citizenship*. Durham, Duke University Press, 2007.

Barrie, J.M. *Peter and Wendy*. *Peter Pan*, edited by Jack Zipes, New York, Penguin, 2004.

Battiscombe, Georgina. *Charlotte Mary Yonge: The Story of an Uneventful Life*. London, Constable, 1943.

Bavidge, Jenny. "Exhibiting Childhood: E. Nesbit and the Children's Welfare Exhibitions." *Childhood in Edwardian Fiction: Worlds Enough and Time*, edited by Adrienne E. Gavin and Andrew F. Humphries, Houndmills, Basingstoke, UK, Palgrave Macmillan, 2009, pp. 125–142.

Beckley, Welcome L. *Game of Quotations*. Chicago, 1889.

Beissel Heath, Michelle. "Oh, Golly, What a Happy Family!: Trajectories of Citizenship and Agency in Three Twentieth-Century Book Series for Children." *Jeunesse: Young People, Texts, Cultures*, vol. 5, no. 1, Summer 2013, pp. 38–64.

———. "Recycled Stories: Historicizing Play Today Through the Late Nineteenth Century Anglo-American Play Movement." *Journal of the History of Childhood and Youth*, vol. 7, no. 1, Winter 2014, pp. 107–133.

Benjamin, Joe. *In Search of Adventure: A Study of the Junk Playground*. London, The National Council of Social Service, 1961.

Berlant, Lauren. *The Queen of America Goes to Washington City: Essays on Sex and Citizenship*. Durham, Duke University Press, 1997.

Bernstein, Robin. *Racial Innocence: Performing American Childhood from Slavery to Civil Rights*. New York, New York University Press, 2011.

———. "Toys Are Good for Us: Why We Should Embrace the Historical Integration of Children's Literature, Material Culture, and Play." *Children's Literature Association Quarterly*, vol. 38, no. 4, Winter 2013, pp. 458–463.

Benson, J.K. *The Book of Indoor Games for Young People of All Ages*. London, C. Arthur Pearson, Ltd., 1904.

———. *The Book of Sports and Pastimes*. London, C. Arthur Pearson, Ltd., 1907.

Bhabha, Homi K. *The Location of Culture*. London, Routledge, 1994.

Black, Barbara J. "An Empire's Great Expectations: Museums in Imperialist Boy Fiction." *Nineteenth-Century Contexts*, vol. 21, 1999, pp. 235–258.

Blackford, Holly. "Childhood and Greek Love: Dorian Gray and Peter Pan." *Children's Literature Association Quarterly*, vol. 38, no. 2, Summer 2013, pp. 177–198.

Blyton, Enid. *Five Are Together Again*. 1963. London, Hodder & Stoughton, Ltd., 1997.

——. *Five Fall Into Adventure*. 1950. London, Hodder & Stoughton, Ltd., 1997.

——. *Five Get Into a Fix*. 1958. London, Hodder & Stoughton, Ltd., 1997.

——. *Five Go Down to the Sea*. 1953. London, Hodder & Stoughton, Ltd., 1997.

——. *Five Go Off in a Caravan*. 1946. London, Hodder & Stoughton, Ltd., 1997.

——. *Five Go Off to Camp*. 1948. London, Hodder & Stoughton, Ltd., 1997.

——. *Five Go to Billycock Hill*. 1957. London, Hodder & Stoughton, Ltd., 1997.

——. *Five Go to Mystery Moor*. 1954. London, Hodder & Stoughton, Ltd., 1997.

——. *Five Go to Smuggler's Top*. 1945. London, Hodder & Stoughton, Ltd., 1997.

——. *Five Have Plenty of Fun*. 1955. London, Hodder & Stoughton, Ltd., 1997.

——. *Five Have a Mystery to Solve*. 1962. London, Hodder & Stoughton, Ltd., 1997.

——. *Five Have a Wonderful Time*. 1952. London, Hodder & Stoughton, Ltd., 1997.

——. *Five on a Hike Together*. 1951. London, Hodder & Stoughton, Ltd., 1997.

——. *Five on a Secret Trail*. 1956. London, Hodder & Stoughton, Ltd., 1997.

——. *Five on a Treasure Island*. 1942. London, Hodder & Stoughton, Ltd., 1997.

——. *Five on Finniston Farm*. 1960. London, Hodder & Stoughton, Ltd., 1997.

——. *Five on Kirrin Island Again*. 1947. London, Hodder & Stoughton, Ltd., 1997.

——. *Five Run Away Together*. 1944. London, Hodder & Stoughton, Ltd., 1997.

——. *The Story of My Life*. 1952. London, Grafton Books, 1986.

Boone, Richard G. "History Games: General Statement to Teachers." *The Game of United States History: Illustrated*, by Bryant Venable, edited by Wilbur F. Gordy, Cincinnati, OH, The Cincinnati Game Co., 1903.

Boone, Troy. *Youth of Darkest England: Working-Class Children at the Heart of Victorian Empire*. New York, Routledge, 2005.

Bourrier, Karen. *The Measure of Manliness: Disability and Masculinity in the Mid-Victorian Novel*. Ann Arbor, MI, University of Michigan Press, 2015.

Brailsford, Dennis. *British Sport—A Social History*. Cambridge, Lutterworth Press, 1992.

Briggs, Julia. *A Woman of Passion: The Life of E. Nesbit, 1858–1924*. New York, New Amsterdam Books, 1987.

Bruce Nadel, Ira. "'The Mansion of Bliss,' or the Place of Play in Victorian Life and Literature." *Children's Literature*, vol. 10, 1982, pp. 18–36.

Buckingham, David and Verbjørg Tingstad. "Introduction." *Childhood and Consumer Culture*, edited by David Buckingham and Verbjørg Tingstad, Houndsmills, Basingstoke, Hampshire, UK, Palgrave Macmillan, 2010, pp. 1–14.

Buckner, W.T. *Game of National Finance*. Wichita, KS, 1895.

Burdette, J.W. *The Anarchist: A Game Devised and Intended to Illustrate in an Interesting and Amusing Manner the Destructive and Subversive Influence of the Anarchist in the Community*. Burlington, IA, Burdette Company, 1886.

Burnett, Frances Hodgson. *Children I Have Known and Giovanni and the Other*. London, James R. Osgood, McIlvaine & Co., 1892.

———. "The Drury Lane Boys' Club." Washington, DC, Press of "The Moon" (Vivian Burnett), 1892.

———. *The Land of the Blue Flower*. 1909. Tiburon, CA, H.J. Kramer, Inc., 1993.

———. *Little Lord Fauntleroy*. 1886. London, Penguin Puffin, 1994.

———. *A Little Princess*. 1905. New York, Penguin, 2002.

———. *The Lost Prince*. New York, A.L. Burt Company, 1915.

———. *The One I Knew Best of All: A Memory of the Mind of a Child*. New York, Charles Scribner's Sons, 1893.

———. *Piccino and Other Child Stories*. 1894. New York, Charles Scribner's Sons, 1899.

———. *The Secret Garden*. 1911. Oxford, Oxford University Press, 2011.

Burns, Robert. "To a Mouse." *Poems, Chiefly in the Scottish Dialect*. Edinburgh, William Creech, 1797, pp. 202–205.

Cadogan, Mary and Patricia Craig. *You're a Brick, Angela!: A New Look at Girls' Fiction from 1839 to 1975*. London, Victor Gollancz, Ltd., 1976.

Carr, S.W. *Presidential Electoral Game*. Crestline, OH, 1892.

Carroll, A.B. *A New Game of Authors*. Rev. ed., Chicago, A. Flanagan, 1889.

———. *The New Game of Authors*. Burlington, IA, Bishop Brothers, 1885.

Carroll, Lewis. *Alice's Adventures in Wonderland* and *Through the Looking Glass*, edited by Richard Kelly, Peterborough, Canada, Broadview Press, 2015.

———. *Alice's Adventures Under Ground* (1864) [Appendix A]. *Alice's Adventures in Wonderland* and *Through the Looking Glass*, edited by Richard Kelly, Peterborough, Canada, Broadview Press, 2015.

———. *The Diaries of Lewis Carroll*, edited by Roger Lancelyn Green, Westport, CT, Greenwood Press, 1971. 2 vols.

———. *The Nursery Alice*. New York, Dover Publications, Inc., 1966.

Cassell's Book of In-Door Amusements: Card Games and Fireside Fun, 2nd ed., London, Cassell, Petter, Galpin, & Co., circa 1882.

Cassell's Complete Book of Sports and Pastimes: Being a Compendium of Outdoor and In-door Amusements. London, Cassell & Co., Ltd., 1892.

Champlin, John D. and Arthur E. Bostwick, editors. *The Young Folks' Cyclopaedia of Games and Sports*. New York, Henry Holt and Company, 1890.

Chan, Winnie. "'The Eaters of Everything': Etiquettes of Empire in Kipling's Narratives of Imperial Boys." *Critical Approaches to Food in Children's Literature*, edited by Kara K. Keeling and Scott T. Pollard, New York, Routledge, 2009, pp. 125–135.

Chilton, Tony. *Adventure Playgrounds: A Brief History*. Fair Play for Children, 2013. Fairplayforchildren.org.

Clark, Edgar O. *Postal Delivery Boys*. New York, circa 1890.

Clarke, William. *The Boy's Own Book: A Complete Encyclopedia of All the Diversions, Athletic, Scientific, and Recreative of Boyhood and Youth*. London, Lockwood and Co., 1861.

C.L.B. *Tyche: The Fireside Oracle*. Chicago, J.S. Goodman, 1876.

Clemens, S.L. *Mark Twain's Memory Builder*, 1891 (Patented 1885).

Cockburn, Tom. *Rethinking Children's Citizenship*. Houndsmills, Basingstoke, Hampshire, UK, Palgrave Macmillan, 2013.

Cohen, Elizabeth F. "Neither Seen Nor Heard: Children's Citizenship in Contemporary Democracies." *Citizenship Studies*, vol. 9, no. 2, May 2005, pp. 221–240.

Cohen, Lara Langer and Meredith L. McGill. "The Perils of Authorship and Nineteenth-Century American Fiction." *The Oxford History of the Novel in English*, vol. 5: "The American Novel to 1870," edited by J. Gerald Kennedy and LeLand S. Person, Oxford, Oxford University Press, 2014, pp. 195–212.

Cohoon, Lorinda B. "'A Highly Satisfactory Chinaman': Orientalism and American Girlhood in Louisa May Alcott's *Eight Cousins*." *Children's Literature*, vol. 36, 2008, pp. 49–71.

———. *Serialized Citizenships: Periodicals, Books, and American Boys, 1840–1911*. Lanham, MD, The Scarecrow Press, Inc., 2006.

Coleridge, Christabel. *Charlotte Mary Yonge: Her Life and Letters*. London, Macmillan, 1903.

Coleridge, Samuel Taylor. *The Rime of the Ancient Mariner. Samuel Taylor Coleridge: A Critical Edition of the Major Works*. Oxford, Oxford University Press, 1985, pp. 46–65.

Collingwood, Stuart Dodgson. *The Life and Letters of Lewis Carroll*. New York, The Century Company, 1899.

Colwell, F.A. *The Race for the Pole*. Woonsocket, RI, 1896.

Cozy Classics. "About." www.mycozyclassics.com/about/.

The Crawley Community Association Adventure Playground Committee. *Crawley Adventure Playground*. Crawley, Sussex, Oliver Burridge & Co., Ltd., 1956.

Daggett, C.J. *Chi Rho*. Buffalo, NY, Peter Paul & Bro., 1892.

Davis, Norma S. *A Lark Ascends: Florence Kate Upton, Artist and Illustrator*. Metuchen, NJ, Scarecrow, 1992.

Decker, F.G. and O.F. *A Game of Characters: American*. Ottawa, 1889.

———. *A Game of Characters: Foreign*. Buffalo, 1889.

Defoe, Daniel. *Robinson Crusoe*. 1719. New York, Barnes and Noble Classics, 2003.

Dixon, Bob. *Catching Them Young: 1. Sex, Race, and Class in Children's Fiction*. London, Pluto Press, 1977.

Dodge, Mary Mapes. *The Protean Cards*. New York, Scribner & Co., 1880.

Druce, Robert. *This Day Our Daily Fictions: An Enquiry into the Multi-Million Bestseller Status of Enid Blyton and Ian Fleming*. Amsterdam, Rodopi, 1992.

E.G. Selchow & Co. *Carnival of Characters from Dickens*. New York, 1876.

Elliott, Alfred. *The Playground and the Parlour: A Handbook of Boy's Games, Sports, and Amusements*. London, T. Nelson and Sons, 1868.

Fellion, Matthew. "Knowing Kim, Knowing in *Kim*." *SEL: Studies in English Literature, 1500–1900*, vol. 53, no. 4, Autumn 2013, pp. 897–912.

Fisher, A.J. *The Game of a Fashionable Boarding House*. New York, 1874.

Flynn, Richard. "Kipling and Scouting, or 'Akela, We'll Do Our Best.'" *Children's Literature Association Quarterly*, vol. 16, no. 2, Summer 1991, pp. 55–58.

"The Game of Croquet and Its Rules." *The Field*, vol. 30, 2 Nov. 1867, p. 349.

Game of Croquêt, its Laws and Regulations: With the New Laws of Croquêt as Agreed by the Conference of Croquet Players, at the Charing Cross Hotel. Jan. 1870.

The Games Book for Boys and Girls: A Volume of Old and New Pastimes. London, Ernest Nister, 1897.

Gardner, Martin. "Introduction." *The Nursery Alice.* New York, Dover Publications, Inc., 1966, pp. v–xi.

Garland, Carina. "Curious Appetites: Food, Desire, Gender and Subjectivity in Lewis Carroll's *Alice* Texts." *The Lion and the Unicorn*, vol. 32, no. 1, Jan. 2008, pp. 22–39.

Gaskell, Charles A. *Gaskell's Popular Historical Game or History Made Interesting to Young and Old.* Chicago, U.S. Publishing House, 1884.

Geer, Jennifer. "'All Sorts of Pitfalls and Surprises': Competing Views of Idealized Girlhood in Lewis Carroll's *Alice* Books." *Children's Literature*, vol. 31, 2003, pp. 1–24.

George S. Parker & Co. *The Dickens Game.* Salem, 1886.

———. *The Good Old Game of Oliver Twist.* Salem, circa 1880.

———. *Ivanhoe: A Social Game.* Salem, 1886.

Gerzina, Gretchen Holbrook. *Frances Hodgson Burnett: The Unexpected Life of the Author of the Secret Garden.* New Brunswick, NJ, Rutgers University Press, 2004.

Gillis, John R. "Epilogue: The Islanding of Children—Reshaping the Mythical Landscapes of Childhood." *Designing Modern Childhoods: History, Space, and the Material Culture of Children*, edited by Marta Gutman and Ning de Coninck-Smith, New Brunswick, NJ, Rutgers University Press, 2008, pp. 316–330.

Goggin, Joyce. "The Playing Card's Progress: A Brief History of Cards and Card Games." *Reconstruction: Studies in Contemporary Culture*, vol. 6, no. 1, Winter 2006.

Goodspeed, S.B. *The Game of American Patriots.* Dwight, IL, 1892.

Goodwin, Mary. "The Garden and the Jungle: Burnett, Kipling and the Nature of Imperial Childhood." *Children's Literature in Education*, vol. 42, 2011, pp. 105–117.

Gordon, Lord Granville. *Sporting Reminiscences*, edited by F.A. Aflalo, London, Grant Richards, 1902.

Gosewinkel, Dieter. "Citizenship, Subjecthood, Nationality: Concepts of Belonging in the Age of Modern Nation States." *European Citizenship: National Legacies and Transnational Projects*, edited by Klaus Eder and Bernhard Giesen, Oxford, Oxford University Press, 2001, pp. 17–35.

Griswold, Jerry. *Audacious Kids: The Classic American Children's Story.* 1992. Revised ed., Baltimore, MD, Johns Hopkins University Press, 2014.

Gubar, Marah. *Artful Dodgers: Reconceiving the Golden Age of Children's Literature.* Oxford, Oxford University Press, 2009.

———. "Risky Business: Talking about Children in Children's Literature Criticism." *Children's Literature Association Quarterly*, vol., 38, no. 4, Winter 2013, pp. 450–457.

Guerra, Douglas. "Forcibly Impressed: Reform Games and the Avatar Figure in Milton Bradley and Walt Whitman." *American Literature*, vol. 83, no. 1, March 2011, pp. 1–27.

Gurney, S.G. *Jungle Plays for Wolf Cubs*. London, Macmillan and Co., Ltd., 1928.

Hagiioannu, Andrew. *The Man Who Would Be Kipling: The Colonial Fiction and the Frontiers of Exile*. Houndmills, Basingstoke, UK, Palgrave Macmillan, 2003.

Hargreaves, Jennifer A. "Victorian Familism and the Formative Years of Female Sport." *From "Fair Sex" to Feminism: Sport and the Socialization of Women in the Industrial and Post-industrial Eras*, edited by J.A. Mangan and Roberta J. Park, London, Frank Cass, 1987, pp. 130–144.

Harte, Francis Bret (F.B.H.). "An Arctic Vision." San Francisco, *Daily Evening Bulletin*, 8 April 1867, pp. 3–4.

"Henrietta." "Correspondence." *The Monthly Packet*, vol. 24, Sept. 1862, pp. 332–335.

———. "Correspondence." *The Monthly Packet*, vol. 25, Jan. 1863, pp. 109–111.

Herrick, Clay. *The Game of Quotations*. Cleveland, OH, 1878.

Hill, Albert A. *Right and Wrong, or the Princess Belinda*. 1876.

"Historic Game of the Life of Washington." *The World*, Sunday, 6 March 1898, p. 16.

"Historical Game of the Life of Abraham Lincoln." *The World*, Sunday, 13 March 1898, p. 16.

Hofer, Margaret K. *The Games We Played: The Golden Age of Board and Table Games*. New York, Princeton Architectural Press, 2003.

Holsinger, M. Paul. "A Bully Bunch of Books: Boy Scout Series Books in American Youth Fiction, 1910–1930." *Children's Literature Association Quarterly*, vol. 14, no. 4, Winter 1989, pp. 178–182.

Holt, Richard. *Sport and the British: A Modern History*. Oxford, Clarendon Press, 1989.

Homans, Margaret. *Royal Representations: Queen Victoria and British Culture*. Chicago, The University of Chicago Press, 1998.

The Home Book for Young Ladies, edited by Laura Valentine, London, Frederick Warne and Co., circa 1876.

Honeyman, Susan. "Manufactured Agency and the Playthings Who Dream It for Us." *Children's Literature Association Quarterly*, vol. 31, no 2, Summer 2006, pp. 109–31.

H.P. Gibson & Sons, Ltd. *The New Artistic and Amusing Game: Peter Pan*. London, circa 1910.

Hubel, Teresa. "In Search of the British Indian in British India: White Orphans, Kipling's *Kim*, and Class in Colonial India." *Modern Asian Studies*, vol. 38, no. 1, Feb. 2004, pp. 227–251.

Huggins, Mike. *The Victorians and Sport*. Hambledon, Cambridge University Press, 2004.

Huizinga, Johan. *Homo Ludens: A Study of the Play-Element in Culture*. London, Routledge & Kegan Paul, 1949.

"imp, n. 5." *OED* [*Oxford English Dictionary*], Oxford University Press, Sept. 2016.

Jacobson, Lisa. "Revitalizing the American Home: Children's Leisure and The Revaluation of Play, 1920–1940." *Journal of Social History*, vol. 30, no. 3, Spring 1997, pp. 581–596.

James, Allison and Adrian L. *Constructing Childhood: Theory, Policy and Social Practice*. Houndsmills, Basingstoke, Hampshire, UK, Palgrave Macmillan, 2004.

James, Henry. *What Maisie Knew*. Chicago, Herbert S. Stone & Co., 1897.

John Jaques & Son, Ltd. *Happy Families*. London, circa 1850.

Johnson, Christine. *Sexism on the Adventure Playground: Making Sense of Practice*. London, Polytechnic of East London, Centre for Institutional Studies, 1990.

Johnson, Elmer E. *A Trip through the United States*. Brooklyn, OH, Educational Game Company of America, 1895.

Jones, Anna Maria. "The Victorian Childhood of Manga: Toward a Queer Theory of the Child in Toboso Yana's *Kuroshitsuji*." *Criticism*, vol. 55, no. 1, Winter 2013, pp. 1–41.

Jones, Raymond E., editor. *E. Nesbit's Psammead Trilogy: A Children's Classic at 100*. Lanham, MD, The Scarecrow Press, Inc., 2006.

J. Ottmann Lithography Co. *The Game of Success*. New York, circa 1910.

J.W. Spear & Sons. *Merry Families*. Nuremberg, Germany, circa 1905.

Jylkka, Katja. "How Little Girls Are Like Serpents, or, Food and Power in Lewis Carroll's *Alice* books." *Carrollian: The Lewis Carroll Journal*, vol. 26, Autumn 2010, pp. 3–19.

Kaiser, Matthew. "The World in Play: A Portrait of a Victorian Concept." *New Literary History*, vol. 40, no. 1, Winter 2009, pp. 105–129.

Keyser, Elizabeth Lennox. "'Quite Contrary': Frances Hodgson Burnett's *The Secret Garden*." *Children's Literature*, vol. 11, 1983, pp. 1–13.

Kidd, Kenneth. "Queer Theory's Child and Children's Literature Studies." *PMLA*, vol. 126, no. 1, 2011, pp. 182–188.

Kimball, Miles A. "Pan, Aestheticism, and Edwardian Children's Literature." *The CEA Critic*, vol. 65, no. 1, 2002, pp. 50–62.

Kincaid, James. *Child-Loving: The Erotic Child and Victorian Culture*. New York, Routledge, 1992.

Kipling, Rudyard. "In the Rukh." [Appendix A]. *The Jungle Books*, edited by W.W. Robson, Oxford, Oxford University Press, 1992, pp. 326–349.

———. *The Jungle Books*, edited by W.W. Robson. Oxford, Oxford University Press, 1992.

———. *Kim*, edited by Harish Trivedi. London, Penguin Books, 2011.

———. "The White Man's Burden." *The Five Nations*. New York, Charles Scribner's Sons, 1903, pp. 78–80.

Knoepflmacher, U.C. "Introduction." *A Little Princess*, by Frances Hodgson Burnett, New York, Penguin, 2002, vii–xxiii.

———. "Kipling's 'Mixy' Creatures." *SEL: Studies in English Literature, 1500–1900*, vol. 48, no. 4, Autumn 2008, pp. 923–933.

———. "Oscar Wilde at Toad Hall: Kenneth Grahame's Drainings and Draggings." *The Lion and the Unicorn*, vol. 34, no. 1, Jan. 2010, pp. 1–16.

Kozlovsky, Roy. "Adventure Playgrounds and Postwar Reconstruction." *Designing Modern Childhoods: History, Space, and the Material Culture of Children*, edited by Marta Gutman and Ning de Coninck-Smith, New Brunswick, NJ, Rutgers University Press, 2008, pp. 171–190.

Kutzer, M. Daphne. *Empire's Children: Empire and Imperialism in Classic British Children's Books*. New York, Garland Publishing, Inc., 2000.

Kuznets, Lois Rostow. *When Toys Come Alive: Narratives of Animation, Metamorphosis, and Development*. New Haven, CT, Yale University Press, 1994.

Lawson, Kate. "Indian Mutiny/English Mutiny: National Governance in Charlotte Yonge's *The Clever Woman of the Family*." *Victorian Literature and Culture*, vol. 42, no. 3, Sept. 2014, pp. 439–455.

Lee, Michael Parrish. "Eating Things: Food, Animals, and Other Life Forms in Lewis Carroll's *Alice* Books." *Nineteenth-Century Literature*, vol. 68, no. 4, March 2014, pp. 484–512.

Levine, Caroline. "From Network to Nation." *Victorian Studies*, vol. 55, no. 4, Summer 2013, pp. 647–666.

Lister, Ruth. "Unpacking Children's Citizenship." *Children and Citizenship*, edited by Antonella Invernizzi and Jane Williams, Los Angeles, CA, Sage Publications, Ltd., 2008.

Livesey, Ruth. *Socialism, Sex, and the Culture of Aestheticism in Britain, 1880–1914*. Oxford, Oxford University Press for the British Academy, 2007.

Love, Brian. *Great Board Games*. New York, Macmillan Publishing Co., Ltd, 1979.

———. *Play the Game*. Los Angeles, CA, Reed Books, 1978.

MacLeod, Anne Scott. *American Childhood: Essays on Children's Literature of the Nineteenth and Twentieth Centuries*. Athens, University of Georgia Press, 1994.

Magyarody, Katherine. "Odd Woman, Odd Girls: Reconsidering *How Girls Can Help to Build Up the Empire: The Handbook for Girl Guides* and Early Guiding Practices, 1909–1918." *Children's Literature Association Quarterly*, vol. 41, no. 3, Fall 2016, pp. 238–262.

Maitland, Robert (Major). *The Boy Scouts with King George, or Harry Fleming's Ordeal*. Chicago, The Saalfield Publishing Company, 1915.

Maltz, Diana. *British Aestheticism and the Urban Working Classes, 1870–1900: Beauty for the People*. Houndmills, Basingstoke, UK, Palgrave Macmillan, 2006.

Mangan, J.A. *Athleticism in the Victorian and Edwardian Public School*. Cambridge, Cambridge University Press, 1981.

Mao, Douglas. *Fateful Beauty: Aesthetic Environments, Juvenile Development, and Literature: 1860–1960*. Princeton, NJ, Princeton University Press, 2008.

"Mary." "Correspondence: Too Much of Everything." *The Monthly Packet*, vol. 25, May 1863, pp. 555–559.

Maxfield, A.C. *Popular Games for Evening Parties*. London, Gaskill & Marriott, 1901.

McCrone, Kathleen E. *Playing the Game: Sport and the Physical Emancipation of English Women, 1870–1914*. Lexington, KY, The University Press of Kentucky, 1988.

———. "Play up! Play up! And Play the Game! Sport at the Late Victorian Girls' Public Schools." *From "Fair Sex" to Feminism: Sport and the Socialization of Women in the Industrial and Post-industrial Eras*, edited by J.A. Mangan and Roberta J. Park, London, Frank Cass, 1987, pp. 98–129.

McLoughlin Brothers. *Battle Game with Boy Scouts*. New York, circa 1910.

———. *The Bugle Horn, or Robin Hood and His Merry Men: A Mirthful Game*. New York, circa 1890.

———. *Cinderella, or Hunt the Slipper*. New York, 1887.

———. *The Errand Boy*. New York, 1891.

———. *Game of the Bewildered Travelers*. New York, circa 1875.

———. *Game of City Life*. New York, 1889.

———. *Game of District Messenger Boy*. New York, 1886.

———. *Game of the Mariner's Compass*. New York, circa 1890.

———. *Game of Nations*. New York, circa 1890.

———. *Game of Nations*. New York, 1898.

——. *Game of Pilgrim's Progress*. New York, circa 1875.

——. *Game of the Telegraph Boy*. New York, 1888.

——. *Improved Authors: The Queens of Literature*. New York, 1889.

——. *Improved Star Authors*. New York, 1887.

——. *The Merry Christmas Games*. New York, 1890.

——. *Mother Goose and Her Friends*. New York, 1892.

——. *The Philosopher's Travels, or the Game of Nations*. New York, circa 1900.

——. *Queens of Literature*. New York, 1886.

——. *Robinson Crusoe Game*. New York, circa 1890.

Metcalf, Chester. *One Hundred Events of U.S. Colonial History*. Momence, IL, 1876.

Michals, Teresa. "Rewriting *Robinson Crusoe*: Age and the Island." *Books for Children, Books for Adults: Age and the Novel from Defoe to James*. Cambridge, Cambridge University Press, 2014, pp. 19–61.

Milton Bradley Company. *The Game of American Politics*. Springfield, MA, 1888.

——. *Game of Nations*. Springfield, MA, circa 1900.

——. *The North Pole Game*. Springfield, MA, 1907.

Mitchell, Sally. *The New Girl: Girls' Culture in England, 1880–1915*. New York, Columbia University Press, 1995.

Modern Out-Door Amusements. London, Frederick Warne and Co., 1871.

Mohanty, Satya P. "Drawing the Color Line: Kipling and the Culture of Colonial Rule." *The Bounds of Race: Perspectives on Hegemony and Resistance*, edited by Dominick LaCapra, Ithaca, NY, Cornell University Press, 1991, pp. 311–343.

"Mona." "Correspondence: Too Much of Everything." *The Monthly Packet*, vol. 26, Aug. 1863, pp. 217–220.

Montgomery, L.M. *Anne of Green Gables*, edited by Mary Henley Rubio and Elizabeth Waterston, New York, W.W. Norton, 2007.

Moruzi, Kristine. *Constructing Girlhood through the Periodical Press, 1850–1915*. Farnham Surrey, UK, Ashgate, 2012.

Mullin, Janet E. "'We Had Carding': Hospitable Card Play and Polite Domestic Sociability among the Middling Sort in Eighteenth-Century England." *Journal of Social History*, vol. 42, no. 4, Summer 2009, pp. 989–1008.

Nakata, Sana. *Childhood Citizenship, Governance and Policy: The Politics of Becoming Adult*. London, Routledge, 2015.

Nelson, Claudia. *Precocious Children and Childish Adults: Age Inversion in Victorian Literature*. Baltimore, MD, Johns Hopkins University Press, 2012.

Nelson, Claudia and Lynne Vallone, editors. *The Girl's Own: Cultural Histories of the Anglo-American Girl, 1830-1915*. Athens, GA, The University of Georgia Press, 1994.

Nesbit, Edith. "Fortunatus Rex & Co." *Forbidden Journeys: Fairy Tales and Fantasies by Victorian Women Writers*, edited by Nina Auerbach and U.C. Knoepflmacher, Chicago, The University of Chicago Press, 1992, pp. 192–205.

——. *The Magic City*. 1910. Radford, VA, SMK Books, Wilder Publications, LLC, 2010.

——. "The Magic World." *The Daily News and Leader*. 6 Jan. 1913, p. 5.

——. *The Phoenix and the Carpet*. 1904. London, Penguin Puffin, 1994.

——. *The Story of the Amulet*. 1906. London, Penguin Puffin, 1996.

———. "The Town in the Library in the Town in the Library." *Nine Unlikely Tales for Children*. London, T. Fisher Unwin, 1901, pp. 245–266.

———. *Wings and the Child*. New York, Hodder and Stoughton, 1913.

Norcia, Megan A. "Playing Empire: Children's Parlor Games, Home Theatricals, and Improvisational Play." *Children's Literature Association Quarterly*, vol., 29, no. 4, Winter 2004, pp. 294–314.

———. "Puzzling Empire: Early Puzzles and Dissected Maps as Imperial Heuristics." *Children's Literature*, vol. 37, June 2009, pp. 1–32.

Nyman, Jopi. "Re-Reading Rudyard Kipling's 'English' Heroism: Narrating Nation in *The Jungle Book*." *Orbis Litterarum*, vol. 56, 2001, pp. 205–220.

Oak Taylor, Jesse. "Kipling's Imperial Aestheticism: Epistemologies of Art and Empire in *Kim*." *ELT: English Literature in Transition, 1880–1920*, vol. 52, no. 1, 2009, pp. 49–69.

Ohi, Kevin. *Innocence and Rapture: The Erotic Child in Pater, Wilde, James, and Nabokov*. New York, Palgrave Macmillan, 2005.

Olson, Marilynn. "Turn-of-the-Century Grotesque: The Uptons' Golliwogg and Dolls in Context." *Children's Literature*, vol. 28, 2000, pp. 73–94.

Pardon, George Frederick [Captain Rawdon Crawley]. *The Handy Book of Games for Gentlemen*. London, Charles H. Clarke, 1860.

Parker Brothers, Inc. *The Amusing Game of Innocence Abroad*. Salem, 1888.

———. *The Game of Authors*. New Edition. Salem, 1897.

———. *The Game of Boy Scouts*. Salem, MA, 1912.

———. *The Game of Robin Hood*. Salem, 1893.

———. *Game of Robinson Crusoe*. Salem, 1895.

———. *Jack and the Beanstalk*. Salem, circa 1895.

———. *Little Mother Goose*. Salem, circa 1890.

———. *The News Boy Game*. Salem, 1895.

———. *The Office Boy*. Salem, 1889.

———. *Pollyanna: The Glad Game*. Salem, 1916.

———. *Sherlock Holmes*. Salem, 1904.

———. *The Wonderful Game of Oz*. Salem, 1921.

Parlett, David. *The Oxford History of Board Games*. Oxford, Oxford University Press, 1999.

"The Philadelphia Grand Jury and Judge Staake Endorse the Playground Movement." *The Playground*, vol. 23, Feb. 1909, pp. 3–5.

Phillips, Jerry. "The Mem Sahib, the Worthy, the Rajah and His Minions: Some Reflections on the Class Politics of *The Secret Garden*." *The Lion and the Unicorn*, vol. 17, no. 2, Dec. 1993, pp. 168–194.

Pingauklt, Emile. *Patriotic Game*. Concord, NH, 1887.

Plotz, Judith. "The Empire of Youth: Crossing and Double-Crossing Cultural Barriers in Kipling's *Kim*." *Children's Literature*, vol. 20, 1992, pp. 111–131.

———. "Whose is *Kim*? Postcolonial India Rewrites Kipling's Imperial Boy." *South Asian Review*, vol. 25, no. 2, 2004, pp. 3–22.

Porter, Eleanor H. *Pollyanna: The Glad Book*. New York, Grosset and Dunlap, 1946.

Powici, Christopher. "'Who are the Bandar-Log?' Questioning Animals in Rudyard Kipling's Mowgli Stories and Ursula Le Guin's 'Buffalo Gals, Won't You Come Out Tonight.'" *Figuring Animals: Essays on Animal Image in Art, Literature, Philosophy, And Popular Culture*, edited by Mary Sanders

Pollock and Catherine Rainwater, Houndmills, Basingstoke, UK, Palgrave Macmillan, 2005, pp. 177–194.

Pratchett, Terry. *Nation*. New York, HarperCollins, 2008.

Puleo, Regina. "Rebecca's Revision: Expectation of the Girls' Novel and Kate Douglas Wiggin's *Rebecca of Sunnybrook Farm* and *New Chronicles of Rebecca*." *Children's Literature Association Quarterly*, vol. 34, no. 4, Winter 2009, pp. 353–378.

Randall, Don. *Kipling's Imperial Boy: Adolescence and Cultural Hybridity*. Houndmills, Basingstoke, UK, Palgrave, 2000.

R. Bliss Manufacturing Company. *Robinson Crusoe*. Pawtucket, RI, 1898.

———. *Stanley Africa Game*. Pawtucket, RI, 1891.

Reimer, Mavis. "Making Princesses, Re-making *A Little Princess*." *Voices of the Other: Children's Literature and the Postcolonial Context*, edited by Roderick McGillis, New York, Routledge, 2000, pp. 111–134.

"R.E.J.A." "Croquet." *The Monthly Packet*, vol. 27, May 1864, pp. 550–554.

Remley, Mary L. "Bancroft, Jessie Hubbell." *Notable American Women: The Modern Period*, edited by Barbara Sicherman and Carol Hurd Green, et al., Cambridge, MA, Radcliffe College, Harvard University Press, 1980, pp. 46–47.

Richards & Kibbe. *Signers of American Independence Game*. Toledo, OH, 1877.

Rose, Jacqueline. *The Case of Peter Pan, or the Impossibility of Children's Fiction*. 1984. Philadelphia, PA, University of Pennsylvania Press, 1993.

Rudd, David. *Enid Blyton and the Mystery of Children's Literature*. Houndmills, UK, Macmillan Press, Ltd., 2000.

———. "From Froebel Teacher to English Disney: The Phenomenal Success of Enid Blyton." *Popular Children's Literature in Britain*, edited by Julia Briggs, Dennis Butts, and M.O. Grenby, Aldershot, UK, Ashgate, 2008, pp. 251–269.

Ruskin, John. "Of Queens' Gardens." *Sesame and Lilies*, edited by Deborah Epstein Nord, New Haven, CT, Yale University Press, 2002.

The Russell and Morgan Printing Company. *Fauntleroy Playing Cards*. Cincinnati, OH, circa 1890.

Russell, Thomas H., editor. *Stories of Boy Life*. Chicago, The Homewood Press, 1914.

Said, Edward. *Culture and Imperialism*. New York, Vintage Books, 1993.

Sambourne, Linley. *Mr. Punch's Book of Sports*, edited by J.A. Hammerton, London, The Educational Book Co., Ltd., 1910.

Sánchez-Eppler, Karen. "Playing at Class." *ELH*, vol. 67, 2000, pp. 819–842.

Sands-O'Connor, Karen. "Why Jo Didn't Marry Laurie: Louisa May Alcott and *The Heir of Redclyffe*." *American Transcendental Quarterly*, vol. 15, no. 1, March 2001, pp. 23–41.

Sattaur, Jennifer. *Perceptions of Childhood in the Victorian* Fin-de-Siècle. Newcastle upon Tyne, UK, Cambridge Scholars Publishing, 2011.

Schaffer, Talia and Kathy Alexis Psomiades, editors. *Women and British Aestheticism*. Charlottesville, VA, University of Virginia Press, 1999.

Schoonover, James S. *Battles of the Civil War*. Indianapolis, IN, 1888.

Selchow and Righter. *The Game of Alice in Wonderland*. New York, 1882.

Sellers, Kelli M. "Tossing the Pink Parasol: *Rebecca of Sunnybrook Farm*, the New Woman, and Progressive Era Reform." *Children's Literature*, vol. 40, 2012, pp. 108–130.

Simmons, Clare A. "Introduction." *The Clever Woman of the Family.* Peterborough, Canada, Broadview Literary Texts, 2001, pp. 7–26.

Singer, J.H. *Game of Ali Baba or the Forty Thieves.* New York, circa 1900.

———. *The Shop Boy.* New York, circa 1890.

Singh, Rashna B. *Goodly is Our Heritage: Children's Literature, Empire, and the Certitude of Character.* Lanham, MD, The Scarecrow Press, Inc., 2004.

Slater, Katharine. "Putting Down Routes: Translocal Place in *The Secret Garden.*" *Children's Literature Association Quarterly*, vol. 40, no. 1, Spring 2015, pp. 3–23.

Smith, W.C. *Centennial, Seventy-Six.* Warsaw, MO, 1876.

Snow, E.H. *The Lion and the Eagle, or the Days of '76.*, 1883.

Sterngass, Jon. "Cheating, Gender Roles, and the Nineteenth-Century Croquet Craze." *Journal of Sport History*, vol. 25, no. 3, Fall 1998, pp. 398–418.

Stevenson, Robert Louis. "Child's Play." *Virginibus Puerisque: And Other Papers.* 1881. New York, Charles Scribner's Sons, 1899.

Stoll and Edwards. *Adventures of Tom Sawyer and Huck Finn.* New York, 1928.

Stover, Deanna. "Alternative Family and Textual Citizenship in Frances Hodgson Burnett's *Little Lord Fauntleroy: A Drama in Three Acts.*" *Children's Literature Association Quarterly*, vol. 40, no. 4, Winter 2015, pp. 339–354.

Sturrock, Jane. "Something to Do: Charlotte Yonge, Tractarianism and the Question of Women's Work." *Victorian Review*, vol. 18, no. 2, Winter 1992, pp. 28–48.

Suleri, Sara. *The Rhetoric of English India.* Chicago, University of Chicago Press, 1992.

Sundmark, Björn. "Citizenship and Children's Identity in *The Wonderful Adventures of Nils* and *Scouting for Boys.*" *Children's Literature in Education*, vol. 40, no. 2, 2009, pp. 109–119.

Sutton-Smith, Brian. *The Ambiguity of Play.* Cambridge, Harvard University Press, 1997.

Swingle, L.J. "Introduction." *Robinson Crusoe.* New York, Barnes and Noble Classics, 2003.

Tazudeen, Rasheed. "Immanent Metaphor, Branching Form(s), and the Unmaking of the Human in *Alice* and *The Origin of Species.*" *Victorian Literature and Culture*, vol. 43, no. 3, Sept. 2015, pp. 533–558.

Tedesco, Laureen. "Progressive Era Girl Scouts and the Immigrant: *Scouting for Girls* (1920) as a Handbook for American Girlhood." *Children's Literature Association Quarterly*, vol. 31, no. 4, Winter 2006, pp. 346–368.

Tilley, Roger. *A History of Playing Cards.* London, Studio Vista, 1973.

Thomas de la Rue & Co., Ltd. *Cheery Families.* London, circa 1893.

———. *Golliwogg—A Round Game.* London, circa 1900.

———. *The New & Diverting Game of Alice in Wonderland.* London, circa 1899.

Thomson, Frank G. *National Game of Presidents.* Chicago, 1881.

Treat, E.B. *Races to the White House.* New York, 1881.

Tuttle, L.A. *The National Game of '76*, 1881.

Upton, Florence and Bertha. *The Adventures of Two Dutch Dolls—and a Golliwogg.* London, Longmans, Green, & Co., 1895.

———. *The Golliwogg at the Sea-Side.* London, Longmans, Green, & Co., 1898.

——. *Golliwogg in the African Jungle*. London, Longmans, Green, & Co., 1909.

——. *The Golliwogg in Holland*. London, Longmans, Green, & Co., 1904.

——. *The Golliwogg in War!* London, Longmans, Green, & Co., 1899.

——. *The Golliwogg's "Auto-Go-Cart."* London, Longmans, Green, & Co., 1901.

——. *The Golliwogg's Bicycle Club*. London, Longmans, Green, & Co., 1896.

——. *The Golliwogg's Desert Island*. London, Longmans, Green, & Co., 1906.

——. *The Golliwogg's Fox-Hunt*. London, Longmans, Green, & Co., 1905.

——. *The Golliwogg's Polar Adventures*. London, Longmans, Green, & Co., 1900.

Valint, Alexandra. "'Wheel Me Over There!': Disability and Colin's Wheelchair in *The Secret Garden*." *Children's Literature Association Quarterly*, vol. 41, no. 3, Fall 2016, pp. 263–280.

Van Wormer, John R. *Political Bluff*. Toledo, OH, 1892.

"Velocipede." "Correspondence: A Few Words From A 'Fast' Young Lady." *The Monthly Packet*, vol. 26, Oct. 1863, pp. 444–447.

V.S.W. Parkhurst. *Uncle Tom and Little Eva*. Providence, RI, 1852.

Walsh, Sue. *Kipling's Children's Literature: Language, Identity, and Constructions of Childhood*. Farnham, Surrey, Ashgate, 2010.

Ward, Mary A. (Mrs. Humphry), "Evening Play Centres: A Better Playground than the Streets." *The Times*, February 6, 1914, p. 10.

Weikle-Mills, Courtney. *Imaginary Citizens: Child Readers and the Limits of American Independence, 1640–1868*. Baltimore, MD, Johns Hopkins University Press, 2013.

Whitley, Mary. *Every Girl's Book of Sport, Occupation, and Pastime*. London, Routledge and Sons, 1897.

Wiggin, Kate Douglas. *Rebecca of Sunnybrook Farm*. Boston, MA, Houghton Mifflin Company, 1903.

Wilhelm, N.O. *Literary Whist, or Games of Great Men*. Chicago, A. Flanagan, 1887.

Wilson, Anna. "Little Lord Fauntleroy: The Darling of Mothers and the Abomination of a Generation." *American Literary History*, vol. 8, no. 2, Summer 1996, pp. 232–258.

Wilson, Penny. *The Playwork Primer*. College Park, MD, Alliance for Childhood, 2010.

Wood, John George, editor. *The Boy's Modern Playmate: A Book of Sports, Games, and Pastimes*. London, Frederick Warne and Co., 1891.

Yarbrough, Wynn. *Masculinity in Children's Animals Stories, 1888–1928*. Jefferson, NC, McFarland and Company, Inc., 2011.

——. "'Raging Beast': Performative Gender in *The Jungle Book*." *Of Mice and Men: Animals in Human Culture*, edited by Nandita Batra and Vartan Messier, Newcastle upon Tyne, UK, Cambridge Scholars Publishing, 2009, pp. 218–228.

Yonge, Charlotte. *The Clever Woman of the Family*, edited by Clare A. Simmons, Peterborough, Canada, Broadview Literary Texts, 2001.

——. *The Daisy Chain*. New York, Garland Publishing, Inc., 1977.

——. *The Pillars of the House*, vol. II. London, Macmillan, 1873.

——. *The Trial*, vol. II. London, Macmillan, 1864.

——. *Womankind*. London, Mozley and Smith, 1877.

Zelizer, Viviana A. *Pricing the Priceless Child*. New York, Basic Books, Inc., 1985.

Index

www.ingramcontent.com/pod-product-compliance
Ingram Content Group UK Ltd.
Pitfield, Milton Keynes, MK11 3LW, UK
UKHW020430010325
455677UK00029B/1086